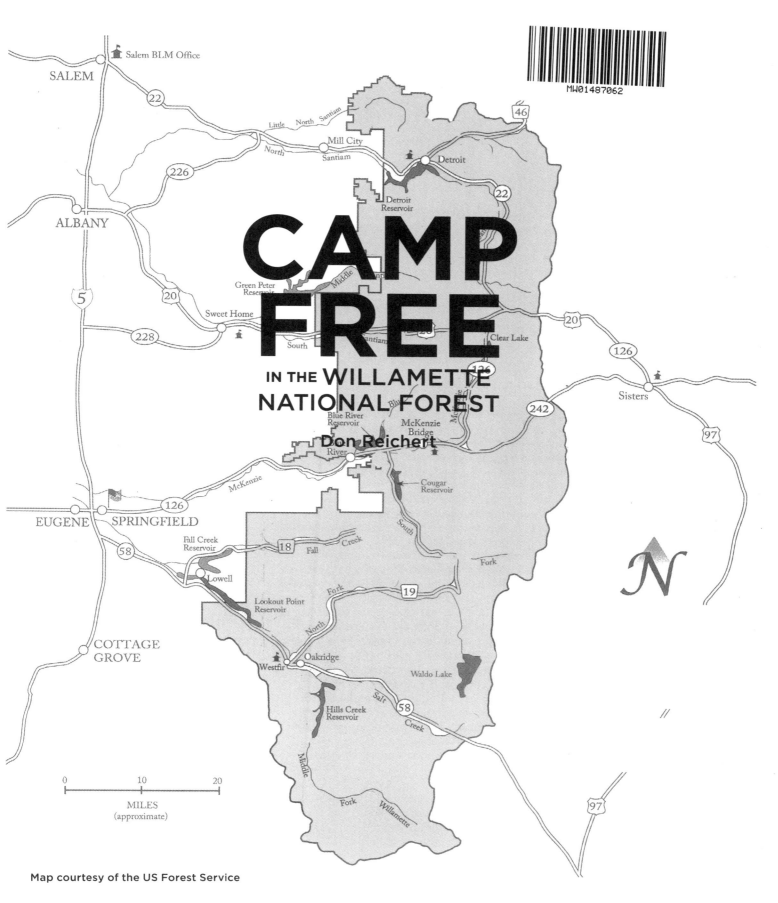

CAMP FREE

IN THE WILLAMETTE NATIONAL FOREST

Don Reichert

Map courtesy of the US Forest Service

A GUIDE TO FREE CAR CAMPING AWAY FROM THE HERD IN THE WILLAMETTE NATIONAL FOREST

Other books by Don Reichert
Camp Free in the Mount Hood National Forest

Copyright 2016 by Don Reichert
Revised edition
Cover photo from Shutterstock.com
Pictures and text by author, except as noted
Maps by permission of National Geographic Society, Inc. and US Forest Service
Original cover and book design by Elena Cronin
Production design by Michelle Leigh

Published by Lonesomeburger Press
PO Box 83814
Portland, OR 97283
lonesomeburger@gmail.com

ISBN: 978-0-9889070-3-4

DISCLAIMER: Almost without exception, the sites included in this book are those that appeared to have been used as campsites by others in the past, as evidenced by the presence of a fire ring and a bare patch of ground where a tent can be erected. This book cannot be relied upon as an authoritative guide to the ever-changing landscape of laws, policies, rules, regulations and guidelines promulgated by the US Forest Service. Because a site is listed in this book does not mean that you are free to drive your vehicle into or onto the site. Virtually all of the campsites listed in this book were in use prior to the inception of the new MVUM guidelines, and the main roads leading to them were, to the best of my knowledge, open to highway-legal vehicles at the time of discovery, with the possible exception of those sites discovered from the saddle of a non-motorized mountain bike. Though I have made a diligent effort to exclude and delete any campsites located along roads that are closed to motor vehicles and where dispersed camping is prohibited and have tried to indicate which campsites are not accessible to motor vehicle traffic, I cannot guarantee that I have been one hundred percent successful in doing so. Because of missing or damaged road signs and, sometimes, discrepancies between what I saw on the ground and on the map, it was sometimes difficult to identify a location or road precisely from cues on the ground. Any errors will have been inadvertent. Therefore, to the reader falls the responsibility to be informed of all current county, state and federal laws, regulations and restrictions and guidelines that apply and are in force in the Willamette National Forest, including, but not limited to those pertaining to dispersed camping, fishing, hunting, the use of fire, firearms, the operation of motor vehicles and the cutting, digging or harvesting of plant or animal life of any kind. Especially, it is the reader's responsibility to carry and consult the proper Motor Vehicle Use Map before driving in any part of the Willamette National Forest.

Furthermore, the information provided in this and other chapters is based on the author's opinions, insights, research, knowledge and practical experience, and is not presented as either definitive or authoritative. The book is intended only as a guide and is not a substitute for the reader's knowledge or judgment.

TABLE OF CONTENTS

PART I: THE "HOW TO"

Chapter 1: Using this book and getting started

Chapter 2: Safety and Security (risk assessment)

PART II: THE "WHERE TO..."

ACKNOWLEDGEMENTS

To Nancy for having my back in all things.

To Jane Pullman for her ability to think outside the box.

To Elena Cronin for generously allowing the use her design ideas.

To Michelle Leigh, my gratitude for stepping in and bringing the game home in the ninth inning.

To Louise Craft for the nimbleness of her pen as well as her marketing savvy.

To Nena Rawdah of St. Johns Book Sellers, whose advice and knowledge about the book business has helped guide me through the production of two books.

To the people of the U.S. Forest Service who helped me keep to the higher ground throughout the production of this book.

To Dave, Shane, Sarrah and the rest of the crew at Copy Pilot on Lombard Street for being able to solve almost any problem almost any time.

And to the many others who gave of their time and talent to make this book possible.

INTRODUCTION
PRIVACY, SOLITUDE, FREEDOM AT NO COST TO YOU

This well-organized and easy-to-use book is a field guide to some of the Willamette National Forest's best kept secrets. If you are accustomed to camping in one of the for-profit campgrounds that dot the Forest, it will pay for itself the first night you use it. And no matter how late you leave home on a Friday afternoon, it will give you the confidence and knowledge to enjoy a camping experience on your own terms. It lights the way to almost 2,000 places where you can pitch your tent *for free* and let your spirit soar among the rugged mountains, narrow canyons, crystal-clear rivers, and magnificent tree-covered slopes of this nearly 1.7 million acre car campers' paradise.

Extending 110 miles along the spine of the Cascades, the Willamette National Forest is easily accessible from almost anywhere along the I-5 corridor, from Portland to Eugene. It is two-thirds larger than the Mount Hood National Forest, the subject of the first book in this series on car camping in our national forests.

Once you've discovered the joys of camping away from the herd, you'll become a convert for life.

Let's go camping!

Looking NW from the Park Creek Bridge in the Sweet Home District

Willamette National Forest after a rain

FOREWORD: WHY SUCH A BOOK?

Camping in the summertime is a rite of passage for many Oregonians. Each spring, as the snow starts to melt off in the lower elevations of the Cascades, we begin to feel the need to reconnect with Oregon's wild places. As the summer progresses, we often find ourselves making multiple weekend pilgrimages to the mountains to throw off the dreck of civilization for as long as time will allow. Whether we are native Oregonians or emigrated here from Kansas or Tijuana, once we experience the Cascade Mountains up close and personal, we imprint like goslings on their beauty and solitude. They become another realm of fulfillment and self-actualization that make the Pacific Northwest a part of our identity for the rest of our lives.

Making the mountains our residence in a tent or RV, even for a weekend, allows us to reconnect with our pre-historic roots in ways we can't in the city. The sounds of nature bring a peace to our hearts that changes the quality of time for us and nourishes our dreams. Some of us prefer to strike out on the trails, carrying all we'll need to see us through the duration of our stay on our backs. Others simply seek solitude and a place near a stream where they can stake a limited land claim for a weekend or a week. This book is about finding that place

I discovered most of the campsites listed in this book over the handlebars of a mountain bike that I carried on the back of my car for two summers spent documenting campsites throughout the Willamette National Forest. What kept me going most days was the feeling that Shangri-La could be just around the next bend in the road. And often it was. Gliding silently into the cathedral-like serenity of many of these sites on a mountain bike often evoked feelings of the mystical and the magical that were reward enough. If such a spot happened to overlook a crystalline mountain river or creek, the magic was escalated to approximately the third power. Many Oregonians have learned that camping on their own, at large in the Forest, has rewards and compensations that can't be found in a public campground. This book is about that, too.

Camping outside of a designated Forest Service campground is called *dispersed* camping. While many people don't realize that it's legal to camp outside of developed campgrounds in our National Forests, we do have the right to do so. No right comes without responsibility, however, and it is incumbent upon those of us who camp in this fashion to do so respectfully and in accordance with the rules and guidelines laid down by the U.S Forest Service. Here are several good reasons for taking advantage of your right to camp in this fashion:

1. Freedom from the many rules and regulations necessary in public campgrounds where many people are camped closely together.
2. A superior camping experience
3. A better night's sleep.
4. Money saved.

During the summertime camping season, most of the corporate-managed, for-profit campgrounds along the main roads into the Forest fill up fast and become small tent towns on the weekend. Visit one on almost any Friday evening during the summer and you'll see what I mean. There are people strolling, dogs barking, radios playing, diesel pickups driving around and around, generators 'genning,' and kids yelling — "the whole catastrophe," to quote Zorba the Greek. Anyone who has stayed in an official campground on a busy Fourth-of-July weekend knows that getting a good night's sleep will depend on what time your neighbors decide to stop partying and go to bed. This goes double for campgrounds that don't have resident camp hosts (and several of the more remote ones don't). If you have ever set up camp in a public campground with the expectation of enjoying a weekend of peace and tranquility, only to have a group of summertime revelers arrive with multiple ice chests full of beer to set up camp right next to you in preparation for partying into the night, you already know what I'm talking about.

Consider this: when camping on your own, away from other people, only you and those in your party will be driven nuts when your dog barks incessantly into the night. You and you alone get to decide when to run your generator and your radio. When you're on your own and alone in the woods, you can pretty much do what you want, within reason. Heck, you can walk around camp in the nude if you're so inclined. The squirrels and jays in the trees aren't going to complain.

Camping in a public campground might seem cheap when compared to the cost of taking the family to Disneyland for a week, but the fees for campsites, extra vehicles, and firewood mount up, especially if you happen to be one of the many Oregonians still suffering from the financial debacle of 2008. What you get for your hard-earned money in the majority of public campgrounds is a patch of bare ground for your tent, the use of a pit toilet and toilet paper, a serviceable fire ring with a grate, and a picnic table. Sometimes even the picnic table part of the deal is questionable if the company with the contract to manage the campground for the Forest Service fails to replace them when they rot away. Likewise, potable water is also not always offered. In about twenty percent of the campgrounds in the Willamette National Forest, you will have to either bring your water or fetch it from nearby streams and rivers.

When you throw in the fees for parking an extra car and the cost of buying firewood, the monthly cost of camping in a public campground for a family of six would roughly equal the rental cost of a small apartment in the city. And, because there is usually a limit on the number of people allowed per campsite, you can probably almost double that for a larger family.

This book is intended both as a plan "A" for those who have had enough of public campgrounds and as a plan "B" for those who still prefer the public option.

The plain truth is that some campers who use our National Forests do not do so responsibly. In the course of my travels through two National Forests, I found many an otherwise beautiful campsite to have been left abused and littered by a careless and disrespectful public. This caused me to wonder whether the publication of a book about dispersed camping would result in providing the feckless and irresponsible a few hundred more places in which to party down. What gave me the resolve to continue was the appreciation and respect for the legacy of our National Forests that I had observed in so many of the campers I had met. It is my hope that you, the user of this book, are a kindred spirit of these good people and will proactively pay our

legacy forward by leaving your campsites in better condition than you found them, if only a bit. That said, and if you are still with me, do read on....

Say it's a hot Friday afternoon in July in the Willamette Valley. The temperature hasn't been under ninety for the last week, and you begin to fantasize about how good it would feel to escape to the mountains. Overcome by that old, familiar urge for summertime adventure, you think about loading your camping gear, some food, the kids and your dog Barney into your trusty vehicle and taking off for the cool, tree-covered valleys of your favorite nearby national forest. But just as suddenly, you realize with a stab of disappointment that you should have thought about this a month ago. At this time of the year, everybody wants to head for the mountains for the weekend, and all the non-reservable campsites within reasonable driving distance are probably already claimed. Driving around aimlessly, looking for a campsite when you and yours are tired and hungry has a way of melting morale faster than butter in a microwave. Sadly, you put the idea of your spontaneous summertime camping trip back in the box, close the lid and resign yourself to spending the weekend in the city with the A/C turned up.

But, hold it! With this book in your hand as "Plan B", you'll still be able to go camping. It won't cost you a dime. You'll probably find more of the solitude and solace you seek than if you'd stuck with "Plan A". And with the money you'll have saved on camping and parking fees, not to mention firewood, your investment in this book will be back in your pocket by breakfast time the next morning.

About those who practice dispersed camping: Most people who practice dispersed camping have one thing in common. Once they have discovered the freedom that they enjoy when doing so, they refuse to consider the alternative of public campgrounds. Most of them express a respect for the beauty of the Forest that borders on reverence as well as a strong commitment to maintaining it for future generations. Several of the Forest Service people I talked to while writing these books admitted off the record that they, also, clearly preferred dispersed camping to camping in a public campground.

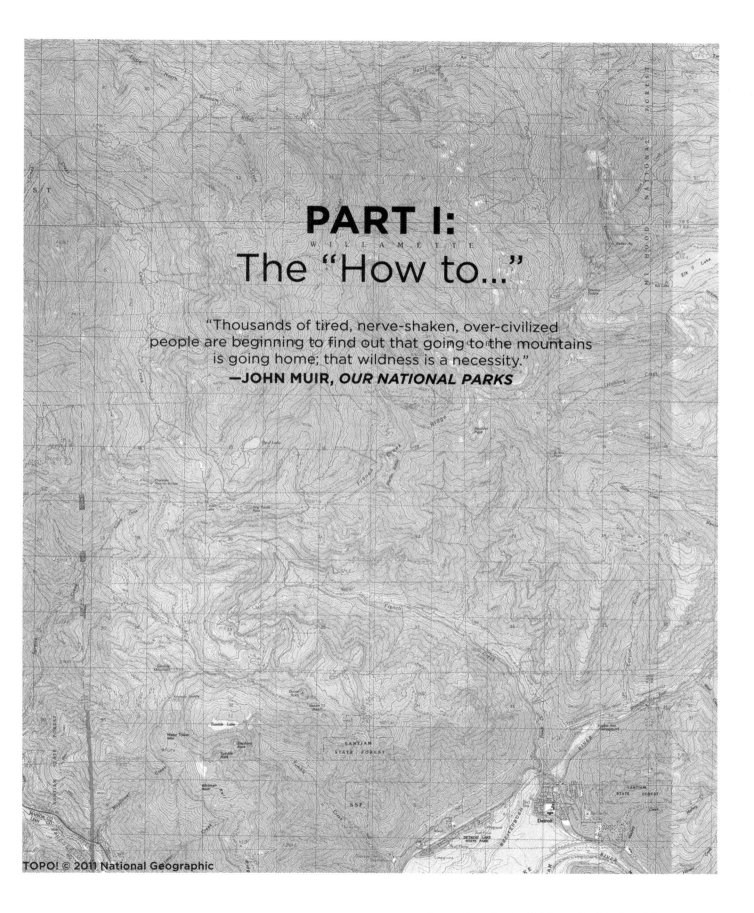

PART I:
The "How to..."

"Thousands of tired, nerve-shaken, over-civilized people are beginning to find out that going to the mountains is going home; that wildness is a necessity."
—JOHN MUIR, *OUR NATIONAL PARKS*

TOPO! © 2011 National Geographic

Chapter 1
Using This Book and Getting Started

Congratulations on having made the decision to camp away from the herd. Chapter 1 of this book will give you much of the basic information you'll need to know in order to have the confidence to strike out and start camping on your own. Chapter 2 will give you information that will help you assess the risks involved in doing so. Part II will help you find your campsite (See "How to Use Part II" on page 22).

Note: throughout this book, the Willamette National Forest will be referred to simply as "the Forest".

Off-season camping

That this book was written primarily for the summertime recreational camper does not mean that it won't be useful to those who wish to camp in the spring and fall, when there is less competition for campsites. The standard information included in every campsite in Part II, such as the altitude, information about the road on which the site is located, the location of nearby sources of water for camp use, and even where to find a cell phone hot spot, will also be useful to the off-season camper.

Don't expose yourself to unnecessary risk when camping at higher altitudes in cold weather. Be aware that the Forest Service doesn't plow the majority of its roads during the winter, even the major ones. If you get caught out in the Forest by the first serious snowstorm of the year, you could be in deep, white trouble. Carry a weather radio and make sure you can get to a place where it will receive a strong signal. Alternatively, FM radio reception seems to be strong in many places throughout the Forest.

Rules and restrictions

Dispersed camping is allowed throughout most of the Forest. The US Department of Agriculture "Be a Good Camper" guide to dispersed camping for the Willamette National Forest states that dispersed camping "is generally allowed anywhere except in the vicinity of developed recreation sites or in areas posted as closed." The guidelines for dispersed camping posted on the Willamette National Forest website at the time of the writing of this book are as follows:

Many people enjoy the solitude and primitive experience of camping away from developed campgrounds and other campers. "Dispersed camping" is the term used for camping anywhere in the National Forest OUTSIDE of a designated campground, and is generally allowed anywhere except within 100 feet of a lake, trail, or stream or where posted as closed. Please see the section on choosing a campsite (below) for more guidelines.

Dispersed camping may mean that no toilet facilities, treated water or fire grates are provided. Typically, dispersed camping is not allowed in the vicinity of developed recreation areas such as campgrounds, picnic areas or trailheads. Many people drive out on Forest Service roads into the woods and find a clearing or a spot near a stream or with a view of the mountains.

There are extra responsibilities and skills that are necessary for dispersed camping. By applying "Leave No Trace" practices, you will ensure a safe, clean and positive experience for your family and the environment.

Choosing a Campsite

If you are going to an area where others have camped before, pick an established "hardened" site. Many existing "campsites" – areas where others have camped before you – are located near water on riverbanks and lakeshores. Whether you are using an existing site or camping in an area where camping use is not evident, it is important to follow these steps:

- Camp on bare or compacted soil when possible to avoid damaging or killing plants and grass.
- Keep activity on durable ground to prevent site expansion.
- Park Vehicles on roads and barren ground to avoid disturbing vegetation.
- Where no campsites exist, camp at least 100 feet away from a water source, as plants and wildlife near water are especially fragile.

- When camping at existing sites near water, be prepared to wash dishes and to bathe well away from your campsite to avoid polluting streams and lakes.
- Select a campsite with good natural drainage to eliminate the need to trench or level tent sites.
- Avoid creating new "roads" to access your campsite.
- Refrain from cutting or damaging vegetation, including standing dead trees. Use removable ropes instead of nails to hang things from trees.

Campfires

Many wildfires are caused by human activity, including escaped campfires from dispersed campsites. Campfires are generally allowed when you are dispersed camping UNLESS there are fire restrictions in effect due to high fire danger conditions. It is YOUR responsibility to know if fire restrictions are in effect before you go camping.

Campfire tips:

- Use camp stoves for cooking to minimize the use of downed wood for fuel. Animals, insects and micro-organisms need downed, rotting wood to survive.
- Use existing fire rings whenever possible. This minimizes the scarring of new rocks, soil, and plants and prevents campsite expansion.
- Bring plenty of garbage bags to pack out all of your garbage, including food scraps. Burning garbage is unacceptable.
- Select an area for your campfire that is AT LEAST 100 feet from any water sources as well as meadows and trees with low, overhanging branches.
- Use a fire pan, or learn how to build a "Leave No Trace" mound-fire. If you don't bring your own firewood, collect only dead and downed wood that is on the ground, wrist size or smaller. Branches on live trees should be left intact. If a popular camping area does not have dead and downed wood, bring your own firewood and use a camp stove. Burn the wood completely to ash.
- NEVER LEAVE A FIRE UNATTENDED.
- You should have a bucket, shovel and ax available to control or extinguish an escaped fire.

- BEFORE YOU LEAVE YOUR CAMPFIRE, MAKE SURE IT IS DEAD OUT. Put your whole hand into the ashes – it should be cool to the touch.

Properly Dispose of Waste

Improper disposal of human waste, wastewater, or garbage will contaminate water and attract unwanted animals to campsites.

Human Waste

Dispersed camping often means no toilet facilities. Extra care must be taken to properly dispose of human waste.

- To dispose of feces, dig a hole 6 to 8 inches deep, at least 100 feet from any water source, campsite or trail.
- When you're done, fill the hole with the dirt you dug up and place your toilet paper in a sealed Ziploc baggie for disposal in a proper waste container.
- Empty built-in or portable toilets at sanitary dump stations.

Waste Water and Washing

- Do all washing and dispose of waste water at least 100 feet from any source of water. Dig a small hole to act as a sump for dishwater.
- Use small amounts of biodegradable soap.

Treating your water

Increased visitation to our National Forests has led to the contamination of water sources by invisible, micro-organisms such as Giardia and Cryptosporidium. These organisms can lead to serious illness when consumed by humans. No untreated water source can be considered safe for consumption. **Be prepared to treat undeveloped water sources or bring your own water.** Heat water to a rolling boil. Using purification tablets or a filter is also effective for treating water. Water from faucets in developed recreation areas has been tested and treated and is safe to use.

Camp Waste: Pack it in, Pack it out.

This mantra applies to your camp waste as well as waste left behind by previous campers. Be prepared to pack out all garbage, including tin, glass, plastic, paper, and food scraps such as peels and bones.

Remember, your fire ring is not a garbage receptacle. Well-intended campers often consolidate their garbage in a fire ring expecting the following campers to dispose of it properly. **Garbage that is left behind is typically dispersed by animals**, making the cleanup job much more difficult and creating unwanted behavior in birds and animals. Yellow jackets are attracted to meat juices and sugars and can render a campsite unpleasant and unsafe for future use.

Respect Your Neighbors

Keep noise levels down to avoid disturbing other campers and recreationists in the area. If you bring pets, keep them in control at all times. Also, respect private landowners and refrain from camping or trespassing on private lands.

Have Fun!

If you follow the tips above, you can have a safe, low impact, primitive camping experience. Thank you for helping care for YOUR National Forest!

Length of stay

Forest Service regulations and guidelines are subject to continual change and are kept current on its website. The Forest Service currently allows camping in dispersed sites "for a period no longer than 14 consecutive days", after which the site must be vacated.

Though areas where camping is prohibited are generally posted on the ground, there are certain trailheads and areas next to campgrounds where dispersed camping is prohibited and you won't find a sign. If in doubt, contact the district ranger station.

Forest Service contact information

It is always a good idea to inform yourself about current conditions in the Forest before you leave home. The Forest Service may close certain sensitive areas to protect wildlife habitat or watersheds, or when there is a danger to public safety posed by fire or other natural disaster. You can find out by calling or visiting the Forest Service District offices or checking their websites. You will find a wealth of information in the District offices in the form of pamphlets and maps that you will need to help you stay in compliance with Forest Service driving and camping guidelines and

restrictions. Here are the telephone numbers:

Springfield Interagency Office	541 225 6300
Salem Office	503 375 5646
Detroit District	541 854 3366
Sweet Home District	541 367 5168
McKenzie District	541 822 3381
Middle Fork District	541 782 2283

*Keep in mind that you might also be able to call these numbers from any one of the cell phone hot spots, many of which are noted in this book.

More toilet options

Many of the popular dispersed camping sites listed in this book have been in use for years, if not decades. Sometimes there is not enough shrubbery left in the surrounding forest understory to provide the privacy desired when answering the call of nature. This is especially true in some of the more popular campsites along the major rivers that drain the Forest. Broadly speaking, too many sites close to streams and rivers have suffered the problem of too many people digging catholes too close to running water for too many years. Another problem with burying human feces in a shallow grave is the possibility that animals will dig it up. The Forest Service does not seem to recognize this, but most dog owners will not find it so hard to imagine.

For the above reasons, many campers are turning to the use of inexpensive portable *privacy shelters* in combination with some form of portable toilet. This arrangement not only allows the privacy needed for toilet functions, but makes it possible to dispose of the resultant poop by removing it from the scene and dumping it somewhere else. I have heard more than one Forest Service employee admit off the record that this is what they would prefer that campers do, so long as the "somewhere else" in question is not one of the nearby Forest Service campground vault toilets. Dumping your sewage in Forest Service toilets may be an effective solution to the problem of reducing fecal run-off along rivers and streams, but it is not fair to the corporations that run these campgrounds and have to pay to keep toilets pumped out throughout the summer camping season. And it would be doubly egregious to do so if you use one of the portable toilet

A double-tank toilet that works well for camp use and is fairly odor free

systems that collect human waste in a plastic bag of any kind. **THE PLASTIC BAG WILL PLUG UP THE PUMPING EQUIPMENT USED TO EMPTY THE FOREST SERVICE VAULT TOILETS!** For this reason, you should think twice about buying a portable toilet system that collects waste in a plastic bag.

If you can't stand the idea of having to haul a container of sewage in your vehicle one more mile than you absolutely have to, you will find a list of RV dump stations in the area by googling for "RV dump stations around (your city), OR". Some dump stations charge a nominal fee of around five dollars, but a few are free. Don't drive too far in search of a free one.

A preferable, though somewhat more expensive toilet system is one that has two tanks that allow it to be flushed like an ordinary household toilet. The upper tank holds clean water used for flushing and the lower tank (usually around 3.5 to 5 gallons) collects and holds the waste. These gravity flushing devices are quite effective and odor-free. The only problem with them is that the small volume of water released from the upper tank doesn't always remove every bit of fecal deposit from the inside of the bowl. One solution to this problem is a *cheap garden weed sprayer*, which will send out a jet of water strong enough to wash down anything that doesn't disappear with the first flush.

Privacy Shelters

Privacy shelters are free-standing tents about the size and shape of a traditional one-seat outhouse. They are available at most sporting goods stores for as little as $40 and are ideal for housing your portable toilet. The great thing about them is that you can also use them for changing clothes or taking a bath. Many of them are designed to support a plastic camp shower bag, which normally holds about five gallons of water and is designed to use passive solar heat to warm your shower water. Water is heavy, so if you intend to use your privacy shelter as a shower stall, make sure that it has a frame sturdy enough to support the weight of about five gallons of water, or about 42 pounds. For most people, merely hoisting and securing a forty-pound bag of water high enough overhead to function as a shower will present a challenge. If money is tight and you have an extra tent, spend your money on the portable toilet system and use your spare tent as your privacy shelter

A portable toilet and a privacy shelter like this will add greatly to your peace of mind when camping in some parts of the Forest.

as well as multi-purpose room. I have used tents for storage rooms, kitchens, rain shelters, nap rooms, conference rooms, changing rooms, bathrooms and offices, among other things. For exasperated parents, they might also make a good time-out room.

Fire season camping

During extremely dry periods, the Forest Service may

prohibit open fires entirely in the forest at large. Those for whom a campfire is the defining experience of a camping trip are going to find their options drastically limited during these times, and may be advised to either stay home or head for one of the official public campgrounds, which are the only places where the no-fire rule does not normally apply during periods of forest fire danger.

Maps and Roads

There are over 6,000 miles of roads in the Willamette National Forest. Most are "low-standard, one-lane roads with turnouts for meeting oncoming traffic". In fact, looked at from the air, the Forest is a veritable maze of roads. Anyone driving in that maze should carry a Forest Service map, preferably a district map, which shows contour lines and elevations as well as much greater detail than the map of the entire Forest.

MVUM

Motor vehicle use is restricted to designated roads, trails and areas throughout the National Forest. Motor Vehicle Use Maps or MVUMs, are available free from Forest Service District offices. The MVUM displays roads that are open seasonally or year-round. Roads not on the MVUM are not open to motorized vehicles. Because it comes in black and white and shows only a few reference points and landmarks, your MVUM is an adjunct, not a replacement for a Forest Service district map. It is also important to add that the MVUM tells you where you can drive your car in the National Forest, not where you can camp. **It is, however, a legal document that gives the Forest Service the right to issue a citation to you if you are found not to be in compliance with it.** And ignorance of the law is, once again, not an excuse. Do not assume that you can drive directly into a campsite just because it is listed in this book. It is your responsibility to carry and consult the MVUM before driving in any part of the Willamette National Forest.

Four-wheelers

This book was not written for four-wheelers. The majority of sites described in it are on established Forest Service roads below 3200 feet elevation. Most of my exploration was done in a Toyota Corolla. When the

quality of a road I was driving on deteriorated beyond what I judged to be the ability of the average driver, my practice was to turn around and find another road to explore. That said, many of the sites listed in this book were discovered by mountain bike along spur roads that may not be suitable for the average 2WD vehicle.

Before driving any road in the Forest, it is your responsibility to check the MVUM to determine whether driving a motorized vehicle is permitted there. Road conditions in the Forest are subject to constant change, especially during the winter. A road that is easy to drive one year may become an impassible quagmire the next. Always check with the Forest Service for road closures before your trip into the woods. Drive all Forest roads, even the paved ones, as if there might be a tree across the road around the next bend, because that is entirely possible, even in the summertime. Make it a practice to walk spur roads leading to campsites before you drive them, especially if you can't see the terrain ahead of you well, such as at night. If you are driving a four-wheel-drive vehicle, avoid damaging an already damaged road, even at the cost of having to park and carry your gear a little farther. Do not disturb the ground or damage the vegetation beside a road by trying to drive around a bad spot.

Motorhome set up for boondock camping

Recreational vehicle camping

Most of the campsites listed in Part II will accommodate some form of recreational vehicle. The decision about whether a particular campsite was suitable for a motorhome, but not a travel trailer, was based on the

MVUM, the terrain, the nature of the road and the placement of the trees. In short, it was fairly subjective. Most of the campsites in the book are away from the road and under the shelter of the trees, where it can be difficult to maneuver with a travel trailer. It was usually my opinion that, where the MVUM allows motor vehicle access to a campsite, a smaller motorhome was the better choice.

GPS devices
(Or: You can use technology in the woods, but you should never depend on it entirely)

There are so many intersecting and diverging roads in the Forest that the casual or distracted driver without a map and compass is likely to become quickly confused. In addition, there is often a lack of signage on the ground that identifies intersecting Forest Service roads. Getting around in the Forest is easier if your car is equipped with a GPS. I found my little Garmin Nuvi to be very helpful during my two summers of field work in the Forest. On the main Forest Service roads with at least a four-digit designation, such as FS1928, it provided a constant read-out of the name or number of the road on which I was driving. It also indicated the direction I was driving and provided a fairly accurate depiction of the twists, turns, intersections, and forks in the road ahead of me, not to mention the names or numbers of intersecting roads. It also helped me identify nearby bodies of water and landmarks. Still, I never felt confident enough to leave my maps and compass behind. Nor should you. When in the woods, don't ask more of your GPS than whether you have gone the right distance on the right road and whether you have arrived at the correct coordinates. *Use the directions given in Part II of this book,* **along with a Forest Service district map**, *to find your campsite.*

I found that programming a desired set of coordinates into my Nuvi by following the Garmin menu was very easy. Here's how: Touching the "Where To?" icon brings you to a screen that gives various choices of places to go. Tapping the "down" arrow in the bottom right of the screen brings you to a second screen where one of the choices is "Coordinates". The "Coordinates" screen allows you to enter the coordinates you seek,

but only after formatting the device to accept the kind of coordinates you prefer to use. There are three formatting options:

"ddd .ddddd": Measures the coordinates in degrees to the hundred-thousandth degree,

"ddd mm.mmm": Expresses coordinates in degrees, minutes and thousandths of a minute and is the format I prefer.

"ddd mm' ss.s": Gives the coordinates in degrees, minutes, seconds and tenths of a second.

For more on using your GPS in the Forest, refer to Chapter 2.

Cell phones

Contrary to what many believe, there are a few places in the Forest where one can place a cell phone call. I discovered many of them by checking for bars on my cell phone as I drove through the Forest. In the campsite data tables in Part II of this book, I have indicated the closest location to each campsite where I have been able to find cell phone receptivity, along with the other information pertinent to the site. This does not mean that your cell phone will reliably receive a signal at that location, however. Places where cell phone reception has been noted are indicated by the symbol: 🔊 on the area maps in Part II of the book. By monitoring your cell phone, especially while driving on higher elevation Forest Service roads, you may discover other cell phone hot spots.

You can find a wealth of information on using cell phones in the backcountry on the Don F. Jones, Jr., website: www.highcountryexplorations.com.

Gear

There is an extensive discussion of gear for dispersed camping in Chapter 2 of my book, *Camp Free in the Mount Hood National Forest – A Guide to Free Car Camping Away From the Herd.*

Before you set up camp

Inspect your site for hazards: The author's inspections of campsites were limited to checking for the essentials necessary for camping, as well as any obvious safety concerns in the immediate area. Some of the sites in this book, though beautiful and otherwise desirable, are not suitable for children. Examples are

Camping at Scott Lake, one of the crown jewels of the McKenzie District

those located on the banks of fast-moving rivers and streams that could sweep a distracted child downstream. Others might be too close to a precipice, dead tree or another potential hazard. I cannot claim to have covered every possible risk factor and must leave it to you to make a more thorough inspection of the site and its environs when you arrive on the spot. If you have children or someone with special needs in your party or are planning on indulging in any mind-altering substance during the course of your stay, taking the time to do this before you set up camp is critical. There will be more on safety and security issues in Chapter 2.

Helpful camping hints

- Fir cones and moss make good pot scrubbers.
- A round river stone works as well as steel wool for removing burnt-on material from the bottom of a pot or pan.
- Use tree moss as emergency TP.

- A dark-colored 4' × 6' plastic tarp, draped over four small logs arranged on the ground in a rectangle will make an excellent wilderness bathtub when filled with water. Cover it with clear plastic and let it heat all day under the sun for a warm bath in the evening. Remove one of the supporting logs to drain the water.
- WD-40 is handy for dissolving sticky pitch.
- If you don't have waterproof boots, a couple of sturdy plastic grocery bags inside your shoes will keep your feet dry in the rain until the sun comes out again.
- One of those wheeled, folding carriers used for jogging with tiny children is also a great tool for ferrying gear from car to camp and back again when you are camping at one of the "Park and Carry" campsites listed in this book
- The little, reflective apple on the back of your iPhone can be used for inspecting for zits and nose hairs when the phone won't work for anything else.

Why you should bring some rope

Always bring a chunk of good, sturdy rope when you go camping at large in the woods. You never know when you're going to need it to help you descend a steep trail to a campsite or to fetch water from a creek or river.

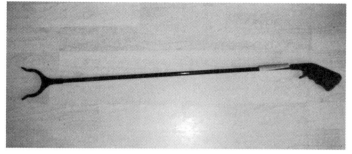

Garbage Glomper

Cleaning up your site—the "trash plus ten percent" plan

The Willamette National Forest's proximity to the I-5 corridor, though a blessing to those who live and work in the Valley, has brought to it the twin curses of litter and pollution. *The plain truth is that if this book contributes to the Forest's further degradation it might as well not have been written.* You and I both know that some people who use our National Forests do not feel that the world loves them and act accordingly. And just as the Biblical declaration, "The poor we shall always have with us" is true, so it is true that there will always be those among us who are immature, ignorant, disaffected and disrespectful. But, thankfully, they are in the minority. From time to time, you'll have the experience of arriving at a beautiful and otherwise pristine and desirable campsite, only to realize that the previous users did not treat the place with the respect and reverence that is its due. When this happens it is my hope that, instead of throwing up your hands in disgust, going into a tirade about "some people's kids", and driving on, you will choose to stay and *pay it forward* by cleaning the place up.

Cleaning up a campsite doesn't have to be an all-or-nothing proposition. What is important is to leave it better than you found it. As a matter of fact, with the proper equipment, it is surprising how quickly a campsite can be cleaned up. Some of the sites in this book are popular enough to be occupied during almost every one of the twelve official weekends of summer. If

enough of us commit to hauling out our own trash plus another rough ten percent, by the end of the summer most of even the most heavily used campsites will be ready for the next camping season. Call it the "trash plus ten percent" plan: a true bootstrap, grass roots, "Yes we can!" approach to making our corner of the world a better place to live that doesn't require bi-partisan Congressional approval.

To police your camp in a quick and sanitary fashion, you'll need several sturdy 30-gallon plastic bags, some disposable gloves or sturdy rubber ones, a bucket or two, and a couple of "garbage glompers" (the kind of grabbing tool used for picking up litter in parks). These devices can be purchased inexpensively at many stores. Harbor Freight Tools always seems to have them on hand. Give the devices a few test squeezes in the store before buying them, to make sure they operate smoothly. A side benefit of these useful tools is that they are good for developing hand-eye coordination. I got so good with mine by the end of a summer of using it as part of my duties as a camp host that I could pick up a cigarette butt at a fast walk without breaking stride. Setting your children about the task of picking up litter while you are busy setting up camp is a win-win-win situation. It simultaneously improves your camping experience while keeping them from wandering off into the forest alone before you know what's out there. It also gives them a sense of having made an valuable contribution to the quality of your family's camping experience as well as to the Forest itself. If you don't have any children, borrow some. If that doesn't work, do that game with your friends where everyone has to draw a chore out of a hat.

Whatever you do, don't leave plastic bags full of garbage behind when you go home! Crows, raccoons, and squirrels will smell the food odors through the plastic and get to work scattering the contents as soon as your car is out of sight. Once it's in a plastic bag, take it home with you.

Toilet paper gardens

As the summer wears on, it is not uncommon to see gardens of toilet paper beginning to sprout in the woods around many of the more popular campsites in the Forest. Curiously, the campsites along FSR 19 and south of Oakridge in the Middle Fork District seemed to be mostly free of this. That the majority of these campsites are located along roads that loop out of the college town of Eugene and back suggests that there might be a correlation between their relative cleanliness and the level of education of the members of the public who use them. We are all part of the web of life. The livelihoods of many people living in the small towns in and around the Forest depend on the flow of tourists, fisher people, campers and other recreationists flooding into and out of the mountains throughout the year. In that sense they, too, are a part of the Forest ecosystem. Imagine the disgust of an out-of-state camper who comes here to experience the legendary beauty of an Oregon Forest when, right after unloading the car and setting up camp, he or she stumbles into a field of discarded toilet paper just beyond the perimeter of camp. If there are no Forest Service fire restrictions in force at the time, one way to deal with the problem is to use your garbage glompers to collect the offensive clumps of paper in large, brown paper shopping bags, and then burn them in your fire pit.

Disclaimer

Almost without exception, the sites included in this book are those that appeared to have been used as campsites by others in the past, as evidenced by the presence of a fire ring and a bare patch of ground where a tent can be erected. This book cannot be relied upon as an authoritative guide to the ever-changing landscape of laws, policies, rules, regulations and guidelines promulgated by the US Forest Service. Because a site is listed in this book does not mean that you are free to drive your vehicle into or onto the site. Virtually all of the campsites listed in this book were in use prior to the inception of the new MVUM guidelines, and the main roads leading to them were, to the best of my knowledge, open to highway-legal vehicles at the time of discovery, with the possible exception of those sites discovered from the saddle of a non-motorized mountain bike. *Though I have made a diligent effort to exclude and delete any campsites located along roads that are closed to motor vehicles and where dispersed camping is prohibited and have tried to indicate which campsites are not accessible to motor vehicle traffic, I cannot guarantee that I have been one hundred percent successful in doing so.* Because of missing or

damaged road signs and, sometimes, discrepancies between what I saw on the ground and on the map, it was sometimes difficult to identify a location or road precisely from cues on the ground. Any errors will have been inadvertent. *Therefore, to the reader falls the responsibility to be informed of all current county, state and federal laws, regulations and restrictions and guidelines that apply and are in force in the Willamette National Forest, including, but not limited to those pertaining to dispersed camping, fishing, hunting, the use of fire, firearms, the operation of motor vehicles and the cutting, digging or harvesting of plant or animal life of any kind. Especially, it is the reader's responsibility to carry and consult the proper Motor Vehicle Use Map before driving in any part of the Willamette National Forest.*

Furthermore, the information provided in this and other chapters is based on the author's opinions, insights, research, knowledge and practical experience, and is not presented as either definitive or authoritative. *The book is intended only as a guide and is not a substitute for the reader's knowledge or judgment.*

Chapter 2
Safety and Security (risk assessment)

Are you really safer in a public campground?

Many people feel that camping in an official public campground is safe because there's a camp host present to deal with situations that arise and summon the police and emergency help, if necessary. Unfortunately, this is not always true. For one, landline phone service is not available in the majority of the campgrounds and may be miles away from the campground in question. And the same is true of cell phone reception.

Only about 50 percent of the campgrounds in the Willamette National Forest have a resident camp host who is on-site 24 hours a day. A nonresident camp host often services smaller and more remote campgrounds, typically residing in one and shuttling back and forth to clean, collect fees, and sell wood in the others.

Camp hosts are not cops. They don't carry badges or guns, do not have the authority to arrest people, and are not required to be medically trained. A camp host's life isn't easy, especially during the prime camping weekends of the summer. For good or bad, many people choose to avoid paying their legitimate campground fees, often forcing the conscientious camp host to make multiple trips to their campsite to collect them. Meanwhile, he is also busy selling firewood, cleaning toilets, and talking to people who come in off the road looking for a place to camp. When conflicts between campers arise, he is expected to resolve them. And with so many people crowding into our campgrounds on summer weekends with dogs, music, alcohol, and sometimes drugs, there is a high potential for conflict to develop.

Buy any seasoned camp host a beer in a bar in Oakridge, and you are sure to hear stories about disagreeable camper behavior that ranges from the merely rude and disrespectful to the outright criminal. In remote campgrounds with no phone service or law enforcement nearby, camp hosts may have to drive miles to summon help in those few instances when campground disturbances get out of hand. When someone is on the ground bleeding or suffering a heart attack, the time lost trying to get to a phone could well mean the difference between life and death.

In this chapter, we'll try to take a realistic look at some of the hazards that could await us when we choose to go off the beaten path and camp away from the herd. Here is a list of some of them:
- Fire
- Wild animals and insects
- Waterborne illness
- Weather, including hypothermia and lightning strikes
- Random violent crime
- Organized crime (marijuana grows)
- Exposure to toxic chemicals, such as from a meth lab operation
- Carelessness and lack of vigilance
- Alcohol and drug use
- Drowning
- Blue-green algae
- Dead Trees
- Getting lost

Fire

The Forest Service goes into a state of hyper-vigilance during the dry months of July and August when the danger of a forest fire goes up. It may impose restrictions or bans on certain kinds of activity or, in extreme cases, close off access to an entire section of the Forest. Here are some of the restrictions on camping activities that you might encounter when the woods are excessively dry:
- Campfires are banned throughout the Forest, except in Forest Service campgrounds.
- Cooking must be done with a stove that can be turned off, as with a valve or button.
- No barbecue grills or coal or fuel-fired fires are allowed.
- Cigarette smoking may only be allowed in an enclosed building or car.

If you can't abide the thought of going camping without a campfire, even in 90 degree heat, this may be the one time of the year when it would be better to camp in a designated campground. The problem is that there is typically more campsite demand than campsite supply in campgrounds at this time of year. On the other hand, there are benefits to being able to shift perspective and do without a fire during the hot months of summer. The spectacular Perseid meteor showers occur from late July to September when clear skies and warmer nights are a practical guarantee of stunning views of the night sky.

Bottom line, when the Forest Service is hyper-vigilant, so should you be. Forest Service rules and restrictions can change rapidly during fire season, and it is your responsibility to be informed about them before you enter the Forest.

Bear scat on road near Breitenbush

Wild animals

Camp in the Forest long enough and you are going to run into the creatures that live in it and take over the night while you are sleeping. Observe wildlife from a distance. Do not attempt to approach or feed them, no matter how cute they are. The lesson that an animal takes away from being fed by a human is that humans are a source of food. Habituating wild animals to charity is likely to have the undesirable effect of disrupting their natural life cycles by contributing to overpopulation and interfering with their hibernation patterns and food-gathering activities. Your National Forest is not a city park; it is a wild ecosystem in which you have visiting privileges.

BEARS: When gathered around the campfire at night the imaginations of most people seem to embrace the scary prospect of being attacked by a large carnivore, such as a bear or a cougar. While I have seen some large bear scat in my travels through the Forest, I have the assurance of the Forest Service that these are from black bears (Ursus americanus), and not their much more frightening cousins, grizzly bears (Ursus arctos horribilis). It is true that black bears have attacked humans, but such attacks are rare to the point of being highly unlikely. Black bears that are unaccustomed to seeing humans tend to be shy around them. Throughout the summer, the prime directive of normal black bears in the Forest is to build up enough fat reserves to survive through the winter hibernation period. During this time, they are perennially hungry scavengers that are relentless, clever, opportunistic, and fully capable of killing or maiming a human being.

Be especially vigilant if there are bears in the vicinity that don't appear to be afraid of humans. When black bears both lose their fear of humans and come to see us as a source of food, they are going to develop a laser-like focus on the food. Anyone standing in the way could easily become collateral damage. If you should happen to come upon an unattended bear cub, remember that mom is likely to be nearby. And she probably won't be able to grasp the concept that you just think her kid is cute.

Bears have an unusually keen sense of smell and can easily detect food through layers of plastic and around the lid of your cooler. Keeping food in the trunk of your car can be risky. A large, hungry bear can peel off the lid of a car's trunk with the same ease you might rip off the lid of a sardine can. Armed with that knowledge, you have to ask yourself whether it is worth the price of a huge bill at an automotive body shop to protect your fried chicken. You can buy bear-proof food canisters from REI or another outdoor store. They are supposed to be effective, but they are expensive. When camping in bear country, hang your food at least ten feet in the air and four feet away from the nearest tree trunk, especially at night, when bears are likely to be actively scavenging. Try to store your food at least one hundred yards from camp, if possible. Likewise, cooking and food odors will be a beacon to any animal downwind of you, so cooking should be done well away from where you are sleeping. Don't dump waste grease from cooking on the ground. Collect it in airtight containers and store it with your food to take home and dispose of later.

When traveling on foot in the woods, always be alert for any signs that there may be bears in the vicinity and announce your presence by making plenty of noise as you hike. As much as you love your dog, keep it on a leash when hiking in the woods. A dog that wanders off into the woods, especially a larger dog, is liable to end up being chased right back to its owner by an enraged black bear. The author of this book once found himself face-to-face with a large, angry black bear for exactly this reason.

COUGARS are another matter of concern. I'm beginning to think that there are far more of them in the Forest than most people think. In the summer of 2009 while working as a camp host, several campers who had been coming to the same campground for years told me of having seen them in the campground in prior years. One family reported finding a young cougar on their picnic table around dusk just after I'd come to collect their camp fees the night before. I saw two of them while out exploring the Forest during the summer of 2010. Both were fleeting sightings from a distance on hot summer days when the cougars' quick movements alerted me to their presence.

Cougars are silent and cunning hunters. They have been known to stalk children and small household pets even in urban environments that are contiguous to forested habitat. It is never a good idea to relax vigilance too much while in the forest, no matter the circumstances or the location. A camp host once told me that he was standing at the door of his RV talking to a camper, when a large cougar ambled nonchalantly past on the way to the river. Make sure that children are instructed not to wander too far from camp without the presence of an adult. Be sure to keep dogs tethered so they won't be able to run off into the woods after a tempting scent. Small dogs are attractive prey to a hungry predator.

RACCOONS can be persistent, determined and clever little problem solvers, especially in areas where campsite larceny has paid big dividends in the past. Their very cuteness often earns them an invitation to approach people. Working in groups under the cover of darkness, these masked and opportunistic little bandits will zero in on your food supplies with all the efficiency, silence, and cunning of black-ops "Team Alpha". However, the concern about raccoons goes beyond merely protecting the sanctity of your corn chips. Raccoons also can carry rabies. Estimates are that up to a third of the population carry the disease in some years. This fact should give any sensible person pause before he or she extends a hand or a tidbit to one of these appealing little guys.

When it comes to rabies, any wild animal with canine teeth should be suspect, but bats and foxes are the next most likely carriers of the disease. Bats are the good guys of the Forest because they pay their ecological freight by eating thousands of mosquitoes. They rarely bite people, but it can happen when humans frighten them by suddenly entering an area used by bats for resting during the day.

Anyone bitten by a wild animal should receive immediate medical attention.

MICE are everywhere in the forest during the summer and will be out foraging in and around your food as soon as you settle in for the night. Their lives are governed by biological imperatives no less demanding for the minuscule scale of their bodies than those of their larger mammal cousins. Leave a bag of crackers or nuts out overnight and they will inevitably find it and make it their own with their tiny, pellet-sized calling cards.

WEST NILE VIRUS: The fast-moving waters of the Forest's valleys aren't ideal for the development of mosquito larvae into adults. Nevertheless, they do manage to reproduce there. For the last several years, scientists and public health officials have been concerned about the inexorable northward and westward march of the West Nile virus, which is primarily carried by mosquitoes. The first cases in birds and animals began occurring in Malheur County in southeast Oregon in 2004. Of the 53 species of mosquitoes known to inhabit this part of the world, only a few are known to carry the virus. The good news is that the disease has only managed to gain a relatively small foothold in Oregon. According to the Oregon Department of Fisheries and Wildlife website, there were only 8 cases of human infection in 2014, with six of those being in far eastern Oregon. In the two cases reported in western Oregon, the infections occurred were contracted out of state.

Quoting the Oregon Department of Fish and Wildlife website again, "Approximately 80% of people (about 4 out of five) who are infected with WNV will not show any symptoms. Up to 20% of those infected will have mild symptoms such as fever, headache, body aches, nausea, vomiting, and sometimes a skin rash on the chest, stomach, and back. Symptoms can last for a few days to several weeks. People typically develop symptoms 3 to 14 days after they are bitten by an infected mosquito. Approximately one in 150 people infected with WNV will develop severe illness. The severe symptoms can include high fever, headache, neck stiffness, stupor, disorientation, coma, tremors, convulsions, muscle weakness, vision loss, numbness, and paralysis. These symptoms may last several weeks, and neurological effects may be permanent. If you experience these types of symptoms, you should contact your healthcare provider. People over 50, those with high blood pressure or those who are immunosuppressed are more likely to develop serious symptoms of WNV. Follow the guidelines below to decrease the risk of becoming the victim of any mosquito-borne illness when camping in Oregon's National Forests:

- Mosquitoes tend to be most active at dawn and dusk, especially from April through October. Wearing long pants and sleeves during these times when outdoors is highly recommended during these times.
- Use an insect repellent containing an EPA-registered active ingredient on exposed skin according the instructions on the package.
- Place mosquito netting over infant carriers when outdoors."

TICKS are of concern because of the threat of Lyme disease. According to the CDC website, the total number of cases of Lyme disease in the United States ranged from a low of 19,804 in 2004 to a high of 29,959 in 2009. Of the 27,203 cases occurring nationwide in 2013, more than of 90% were in the thirteen northeastern and upper Midwestern states of Connecticut, Delaware, Maine, Maryland, Massachusetts, Minnesota, New Hampshire, New Jersey, New York, Pennsylvania, Vermont, Virginia, and Wisconsin. The list below compares the number of cases of Lyme disease reported per 100,000 inhabitants in Oregon and several other states in 2013:

Virginia	107.6
New Hampshire	100.0
Maryland	84.8
Connecticut	58.7
Rhode Island	42.2
Pennsylvania	39
Oregon	0.3
California	0.2

According to the OSU Extension Service, of the twenty species of tick found in the state, the western black-legged tick is the only tick known to carry the disease. Phillippe Rossignol, professor in the fisheries and wildlife department at OSU says that both adult and immature ticks can transmit the disease to humans, but they must be attached to a host for 24 to 48 hours to do so.

If you discover a tick on yourself or anyone in your party, follow the instructions below from the Oregon State University website:

- If possible, have someone else remove the tick from your body.
- Use tweezers or forceps rather than fingers.
- Grasp the mouth parts or head end of the tick as close to the skin as possible.
- Gently pull the tick straight out, steadily and firmly.
- The mouth parts are barbed like a harpoon and might break off in the skin. If so, don't be concerned. They do not carry the bacterium and are no more harmful than a sliver.
- Wash hands and the bite area with soap and water; apply an antiseptic to the bite area.
- Keep the tick for identification if disease symptoms occur later. Place the tick in a small container of alcohol labeled with the date removed and the place it was picked up.
- Use the same procedures and precautions when removing ticks from pets.

BEE STINGS are a threat because some people's bodies are allergic enough to be sent into a state of anaphylactic shock by them. If anyone in your party is allergic, make sure that you are carrying a dose of epinephrine and a good magnifying glass to help in removing stingers before you go into the woods.

If a bee sting occurs, carefully remove the stinger, because it can release even more venom into the body if improperly removed. If visible to the naked eye or with a magnifying glass, carefully try to flick it out with a fingernail. If allergy symptoms are suspected, administer the epinephrine and a dose of an antihistamine such as Benadryl, which may prevent or reduce some allergic reactions, as well. Use your discretion and get the victim to a doctor or medical facility to be checked out and treated as soon as possible. If you choose to do none of these things, keep the victim under close observation for signs of a reaction.

Other risk factors

"In wine there is wisdom, in beer there is Freedom, in water there is bacteria."
— **Benjamin Franklin**

WATERBORNE ILLNESS: Cryptosporidium and Giardia are just two of the protozoan, viral and microbial parasites in the cold mountain streams and lakes of the Willamette National Forest that are undetectable to the naked eye. Drink straight from the streams and they will take up residence in your gut and make you sick. Depend on it. To avoid this, you must first decontaminate water from streams or rivers before drinking it. Do this either by treating it with iodine or by filtering or boiling it. Iodine leaves an unpleasant aftertaste. Filters are fine for a small party, but when a larger quantity of water is needed, boiling is usually the most practical method. I bring my drinking water from home or fetch it from one of the few sources of potable water along the way, and then supplement as needed with boiled water from a stream or river. For drinking purposes, boil a full five minutes.

BLUE-GREEN ALGAE blooms contain toxins that can present a danger to humans and animals. Signs alerting the public to their danger have been posted in parts of the Forest where they are likely to occur, and at least one health advisory was issued when algae blooms were discovered in the Blue River Reservoir in 2014.

Blue-green algae blooms are most likely to occur in ponds, lakes, and slow-moving streams. Avoid contact with water that is foamy, scummy, thick like paint, pea green, or brownish red in color. Likewise, avoid any water topped with a thick coat of algae or which has an unpleasant odor. Toxins cannot be removed from the water by boiling. Remove all fat, skin and organs from

fish caught in the vicinity of a HAB (Harmful Algae Bloom) before cooking, since this is where the toxins will tend to concentrate.

HABs can cause the following respiratory symptoms in people: sore throat, congestion, coughing, wheezing, or difficulty breathing. Skin contact can result in itchy, reddish skin, hives, blistering, or other kinds of rash. Other symptoms are earaches, agitation, headache, abdominal pain, diarrhea, vomiting, or eye irritation. Animals exposed to a toxic bloom may exhibit vomiting, lethargy, diarrhea, convulsions, difficulty breathing, or general weakness.

To report a case of exposure, call 971-673-0400.

Sign near Fay Lake warning about blue-green algae

SANITATION IN CAMP requires planning and some forethought. From food handling and preparation to personal hygiene practices, whatever you do at home you should also do in camp, and this is especially true in the case of a group or family. Bring a spray bottle of bleach to use for sanitizing cutting boards. Take along a water container equipped with a spigot and dedicate it to hand washing. Keep a few bottles of hand sanitizer in strategic locations and encourage people to use them, especially after answering the call of nature.

DROWNING: Many of the campsites listed in this book are located near fast-moving streams or rivers that are easily capable of sweeping someone downstream. Children at play are especially vulnerable here, but so are people whose senses are dulled by either alcohol or drugs. Even a fisherperson who is intent on trying to land a fly on just the right section of a river is liable to lose his or her balance and fall into the river. Disaster can materialize very quickly on the banks of a swift, powerful stream.

GETTING LOST in the Forest is always a possibility, though it's much more likely to happen to those traveling on foot than to someone in a car. Many of the roads in the Forest are poorly marked, and it is all too easy to become confused, especially without a map or GPS. While exploring the Forest, I met many people who had become quickly confused after driving into its labyrinth of intersecting and branching roads without a proper map. The good news is that, unless you're running low on gas or your car breaks down, getting lost on a Forest Service road in the summertime is probably more likely to result in being late to dinner than it is to end in disaster. Most Forest Service roads branch off from one of the main Forest Service roads in a river valley and go relentlessly upward, which means that, when one is completely lost, salvation more than likely lies downhill. The Forest is large, but not immense. One is seldom more than 15 or 20 miles from a main road or a major landmark in any direction. Your map and compass are a cheap and low-tech form of insurance. Don't go into the Forest without them.

Getting lost while hiking in wild country is a serious matter, however. According to George Kleinbaum, State Search and Rescue Coordinator for the Oregon Office of Emergency Management, an astounding 207 men and 53 women remain listed as officially missing in Oregon's forests since 1997. Kleinbaum said, "It only takes a mile before you get totally turned around and don't know which way to go." There were over 800 search and rescue missions conducted in Oregon in 2013.

Whether you plan to hike or not, you should **file a flight plan** before going into the woods. Tell a friend, family member, boss or co-worker where you're going and approximately when you plan to return. If hiking, try to call home from one of the cell phone hot spots before you start your hike. And be sure to fill out one of the Forest Service hiking forms and deposit it in the box at the trailhead as you set out on your hike.

CARELESSNESS AND LACK OF VIGILANCE: The importance of vigilance and awareness of one's surroundings in the woods cannot be overstressed. Neither police protection nor ambulances with EMTs

are just a phone call away from most places in the Forest. Because of this, an extra measure of caution and forethought is required when venturing into the woods. Carry a first-aid kit and always know where it is. Make sure that children are properly instructed and supervised when using any tool or device that could hurt them. Use common sense and don't operate power equipment of any kind when drinking. If you choose to keep a gun around for security purposes, make sure that children don't have access to it. Always try to anticipate safety issues before they can arise.

THE USE OF ALCOHOL AND DRUGS increases the amount of risk involved in almost any activity. The fact many campers of sound mind feel that the use of one or the other adds value to their experience of nature puts this question entirely into the realm of personal judgment. With regard to the use and possession of illegal substances, it is critical to remember that State laws do not necessarily apply on federally managed lands. Specifically, the production and use of marijuana remain illegal in our National Forests, despite the recent passage of Measure 91, legalizing the possession and growth of marijuana in the State of Oregon.

RANDOM VIOLENT CRIME is one of the first things that come to mind when most people think about dispersed camping. Unfortunately, I was unable to interview the law enforcement officer for the Willamette National Forest about current trends in crime in that Forest. Forest Service policy about granting interviews with its law enforcement officers has changed since I first started writing about the subject in 2010. To paraphrase Jude McHugh, Public Affairs Officer for the Willamette National Forest, "For (the purpose of) drawing conclusions and making summary statements, (National Forest) law enforcement officers are now required to rely almost exclusively on data obtained through actual write-up of contacts made in the field. Those data are stored in a centralized database and the process of accessing that through the Freedom of Information Act can take weeks to months." In short, law enforcement officers can no longer speak their mind about Forest Service business. However, an interview I did in 2010 with Andrew Coreill, Patrol Captain for the northern Oregon Law Enforcement and Investigation Section of the U.S.

Forest Service yielded some valuable information on the subject of crime in Oregon's National Forests in general, and we shall have to rely on that.

Coreill said that conflicts between campers at dispersed camping sites usually started out when a camper was behaving in a way that was inconsiderate of other campers, such as making an undue amount of noise or shooting guns. He added that, though police had on occasion been called in to resolve them, these disputes usually stayed at the argument level.

Campers in dispersed sites need to apply the rules of common sense and notify the Forest Service if they see anyone or anything suspicious. Cars left unattended anywhere in the Forest become a target for thieves. Remove your valuables from them and take them with you when leaving camp for any extended period. Broken car glass on the ground is an indication that you are in an area where cars have been broken into in the past.

Throughout the summers of 2013 and 2014 as I was doing the fieldwork for this book, I took every opportunity to talk to campers in the Willamette National Forest. Most, but not all, were weekend campers who had been doing dispersed camping for years, often returning to the same spot year after year. None reported having had any serious confrontations with other campers.

An effective strategy for minimizing the possibility of ending up with unpleasant neighbors is to choose a campsite just large enough to accommodate the number of people in your party. Sometimes it is possible to block the entrance to a campsite with a vehicle or vehicles, if it can be done without blocking access to a through road, violating Forest Service rules or depriving someone else of legitimate access to a campsite. Also, there is safety in numbers, so a party of four (adults) is more secure than a party of two, and so on. **TO CARRY A GUN OR NOT TO CARRY A GUN** is the question. And it's an entirely personal one. Many city dwellers disapprove of guns. But when law enforcement isn't just a 911 call and a few minutes away, it is hard to deny that the advantage shifts dramatically to the side of a would-be malefactor. For this reason, many serious and sober people do carry firearms when camping in the woods.

Exposure to toxic chemicals from a meth lab operation

It is safe to say that methamphetamine production is now a lesser concern in Oregon National Forests than it was several years ago. State efforts to control access to the cough and cold medicines made with ephedrine that are used in the illegal manufacture of methamphetamines have led to something like a seventy-percent reduction of the number of meth labs discovered in the Mount Hood National Forest, according to one Forest Service employee. These medications were formerly sold freely over the counter in most pharmacies and drug stores, but now require a prescription in Oregon. In Washington, a signature and ID are needed to purchase a limited quantity of them over the counter, and each sale is documented in a statewide database.

Meth manufacturers do not typically want to locate their operations near a road, where they would be more easily detected. Even though most of the campsites listed in this book are within sight of a road, the possibility stumbling upon a meth lab still exists.

Meth lab operations are not confined to apartments and houses, but can be set up in campgrounds, rest areas, abandoned cars, storage sheds, barns, vacant buildings or even a suitcase.

Many substances besides ephedrine are used in the production of meth, including some toxic ones, like red phosphorous, iodine crystals and lithium battery acid. Usually, meth labs are a collection of chemical bottles, hoses and pressurized cylinders, which can take the form of modified propane tanks (sometimes spray-painted or burned, with bent or altered valves or blued fittings), fire extinguishers, scuba tanks and soda dispensers. The tanks contain anhydrous ammonia or hydrochloric acid, both of which are very poisonous and corrosive. Labs are frequently abandoned, leaving explosive and toxic chemicals behind and hanging taxpayers and the Forest Service with the expense of clean-up.

Some of the supplies used in a meth lab operation are plastic tubing, ammonia, funnels, rock salt, iodine, lithium batteries, camp stove fuel, glass containers, hydrogen peroxide, ephedrine or pseudoephedrine tablets and starter fluid, to name a few.

• Below is a list of other things that might help you

identify a possible meth site:
- Strong odors that don't belong in the woods, such as cat urine, acetone, ammonia, ether or other chemical odor are all indicators that you should consider vacating the area. The absence of any odor is not an indication that a site has not been used for meth production.
- Soft drink bottles with tubes coming out of them, plastic "Heet" bottles, Red Devil lye bottles, empty pill bottles or pill blister packs, evidence of cold medications containing ephedrine or pseudo-ephedrine, glass containers (jars or cookware) with a white residue, other evidence of white crystal residue, red chemically stained coffee filters, empty pill bottles, empty cans of toluene, alcohol or paint thinner, and/or iodine-stained fixtures of any kind, large numbers of antifreeze containers, lantern fuel cans, and drain cleaner containers, excessive amounts of duct tape, numerous plastic "Baggies", coffee filters, matchbook covers with the striker plates removed or torn lithium battery casings.

If you happen to stumble upon a suspicious site, you should immediately vacate the area and report the finding as quickly as possible. If the site is currently in use, you may be in danger from those who put it there. It is dangerous to breathe the fumes or handle the substances and materials you may find there. Some of the chemicals may explode if exposed to air or water. Only trained hazmat people should enter the site.

Marijuana grow operations

Again, because of the problem of getting current and anecdotal information about crime in the Willamette National Forest, the author is reduced to extrapolating from the previous 2010 interview with Andrew Coreill about crime in that forest. Coreill told me that Marijuana grow operations were at the time on the increase in the Mount Hood National Forest, but that there had not been any conflicts between growers and recreational users of the Forest. Coreill went on to say that these operations were commonly located in sites that are away from roads and well hidden from the eyes of the public.

Growers need a water source and have been known to pipe water through the forest from a creek or spring to the grow site. Hunters tramping about the woods during hunting season are the ones most likely to stumble upon a marijuana grow operation. Coreill indicated that car campers accessing the Mount Hood National Forest via official Forest Service roads ran little risk of encountering a marijuana grow operation. He advised against following any road or track leading off into the woods that is not an official Forest Service road.

Reason dictates that Coreill's advice would apply equally to the Willamette National Forest. Anyone who happens to come upon a trail in the Forest that looks suspicious, especially one near a source of water, should report the information to the Forest Service.

Again, my own experience bears out Coreill's words. During two summers of driving and mountain biking over thousands of miles of Willamette National Forest roads, I encountered no evidence of illegal drug activity of any kind. Many of these roads were far off the beaten path, and not all of them were marked as official Forest Service roads..

It is interesting to speculate on the effect that the recent passage of Measure 91, legalizing the cultivation and recreational use of marijuana in Oregon, will have on illegal marijuana grow operations in our National Forests. Marijuana grown in Oregon's National Forests may be destined for sale in another state, after all.

WEATHER HAZARDS can range from dehydration to heat stroke, hypothermia and lightning strikes.
LIGHTNING: Lightning strikes can kill and maim. The electrical charge of a lightning bolt can exceed 100,000 volts. Lightning storms in mountainous areas are more likely to occur in the afternoon during the summer. Ridges and mountain tops are the worst places to be during a lightning storm. The thirty-second rule says if the thunder occurs less than thirty seconds after the lightning it's time to seek shelter because the lightning is close enough to reach out and touch you. The safest shelter is a structure of some kind. A car is less safe, but still better than a tent, especially a tent with a metal frame, since the tent's metal frame can act as a conductor. If your hair wants to stand on end, you feel a tingling sensation on your skin or hear crackling sounds, a lightning strike in

the area is imminent. If you're outside with a group of people and there is no other shelter possible, seek a low spot. Don't huddle together and give the current several bodies to run through, but separate yourself and assume a crouching position on the ground with your feet touching. The ground will carry the current to you from any nearby lightning strike, but with the feet touching each other, it will run up one foot and down the other instead of harming vital organs. Something else to remember is that lightning can reach up to ten miles from the edge of the storm as it retreats. You cannot assume you are safe from it until a full half-hour after the last lightning strike.

HYPOTHERMIA The Encarta Dictionary defines "hypothermia" as a "dangerously low body temperature caused by prolonged exposure to cold." There are three levels of hypothermia, from mild to severe. In this book intended for the summertime camper, I am going to limit myself to addressing just the first stage, mild hypothermia, which, if properly treated, usually ends with a complete recovery. As the body's core temperature drops below 98.6 degrees F., symptoms are numbness in the hands, slurring of the speech and shivering. In addition, the victim's judgment may be impaired to the point that he or she may not be capable of making rational decisions. Treatment: Move the victim to a warm, dry environment out of the wind – a car with the heater going full blast would work. Any wet clothes should be removed and replaced with dry, warm ones. If a building or car is not available, get the victim into warm, dry, windproof, waterproof gear and build a fire. Or place the victim into a pre-warmed sleeping bag that is insulated from the ground by pine boughs, moss, clothes, or an insulated mattress (not an air mattress). Ply the victim with hot drinks, followed by candy or another high-sugar food. If this protocol is followed, the victim's core temperature should return to normal, though it may take some time.

In the summer of 2009, while working as a camp host, I had a personal experience with hypothermia. After a vigorous bike ride early one hot August afternoon, nothing seemed more appealing than a good long soak in the cold, mountain river running near my camp. I had been doing this routinely for fifteen or twenty minutes at a time all summer with no ill effects, but this time it felt so good that I lengthened my stay to

a full half-hour. It wasn't until I finally got out of the water and retreated to the inside of my motorhome, where the temperature was around eighty degrees Fahrenheit, that I even realized I had become hypothermic. I felt cold and weak for about an hour and a half, even after putting on long johns, drinking a couple of cups of hot, instant soup and getting into the heaviest sleeping bag I had aboard. After that, I limited my cold water soaks to a maximum of twenty minutes.

Learn to recognize the symptoms of hypothermia and take action to reverse it early. If it is allowed to progress to the second stage of severity, the victim's life can be in danger.

DEAD TREES pose a silent menace to the unsuspecting camper. Inspect the area where you intend to set up your temporary living quarters in the woods. Don't camp near or under any tree that shows signs of insect damage or appears to be questionable. And make sure that children do not play on or around them. Old rotted stumps left after some ancient logging operation can pose a danger to children playing on them by suddenly crumbling under their weight.

Summing up

There is no doubt that camping away from the herd brings some measure of added risk, but probably not as much as most people might think. And most of it is the kind of risk that is manageable. The amount of risk in any adventure is almost always inversely proportional to the amount of common sense and planning involved.

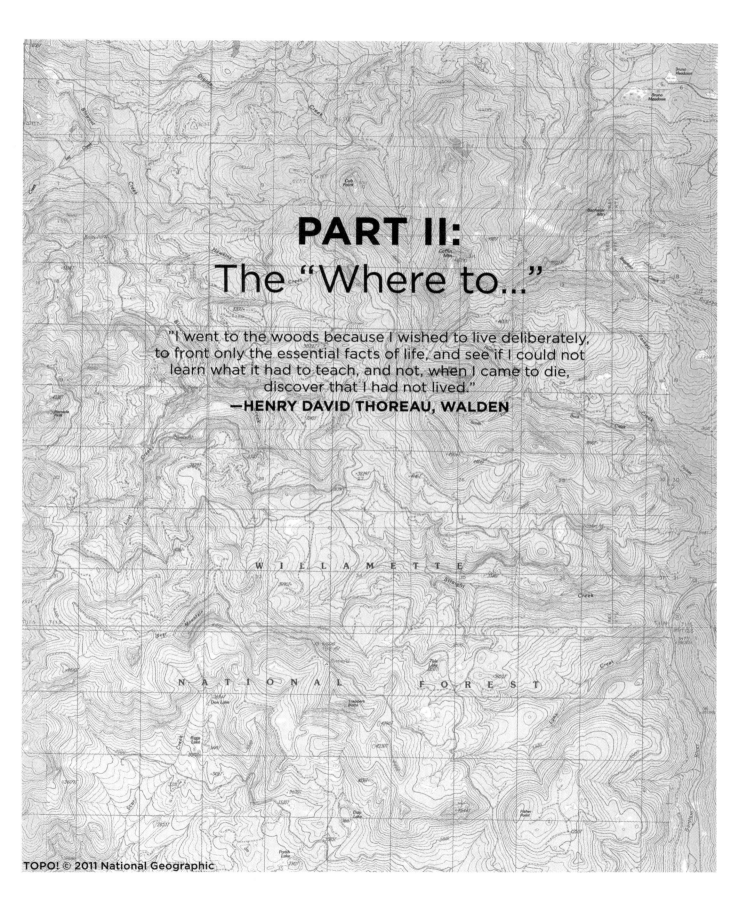

PART II:
The "Where to..."

"I went to the woods because I wished to live deliberately,
to front only the essential facts of life, and see if I could not
learn what it had to teach, and not, when I came to die,
discover that I had not lived."
—HENRY DAVID THOREAU, WALDEN

HOW TO USE PART II

The Willamette National Forest is a huge place, and I do not claim to have found all its campsites. This book will guide you to some 300 locations, which, combined, provide close to 2000 places to put your tent along roughly 5000 miles of Forest Service roads in the four districts of the Forest. Campsites are numbered consecutively within each Forest Service district. Users of this book should use the individual Forest Service District maps to locate campsites, rather than the overall map showing the entire Forest.

You will find campsites in each of the Forest Service Districts on the following pages:

1. DETROIT
Pages 26–72

2. SWEET HOME
Pages 73–92

3. MCKENZIE
Pages 93–119

4. MIDDLE FORK
Pages 120–165

To find a campsite in any section of a Forest Service district, first go to the map key for that district. Then refer you to the map page showing the approximate locations and numbers of the individual campsites and the roads on which they are located in the section of the district where you wish to camp. Choose the number of the campsite you'd like to explore (white number in a black circle), and then go directly to that number in the campsite description pages following the map section for that Forest Service district. Most, but not all, campsites are near a source of running water or a lake. Campsites that are not close to a source of water are described as either "dry" or "waterless". It is important to remember that the locations of the campsites on the maps are not precise because of the scale of the maps. Also, due to the scale of the maps showing the campsites, not all roads are identified.

You will find detailed descriptions of each campsite in the campsite description section which follows each district's map pages. Each campsite description uses the same format: Essential data for the campsite is given in a table format, followed by a general description, as well as directions to the site.

Below is a sample of a typical campsite description found in this book:

Loc: FS4685, 3.6 miles from FS46	**Road:** Primitive
L/L: N44 45 366/W121 54 380	**Access:** P&C, Check MVUM
Cell: Detroit	**Tents:** 4–5
Nearest H2O: In camp	**El:** 2950
Lndmk: Breitenbush Gorge Trail #3366, 1.2 miles NW	**RV:** No

Description: A site that is wonderful for its proximity to a beautiful section of the river. There is ample shelter from the trees, and the river forms a pool here that is easily deep enough for a summertime soak. High marks for solitude and scenic view!

Getting there: Follow FSR46 out of Detroit or approach from the direction of Estacada. About halfway between mileposts 11 and 12, turn south on FS4685 and go 3.6 miles to a rough dirt road heading steeply downhill to the river, 0.2 miles away. Park and carry gear to site.

Here's what the campsite data table will tell you:

Loc: Located on Forest Service Road 4685, 3.6 miles from Forest Service Road 46

L/L: The GPS coordinates of the site.

Cell: The nearest place where you might find cell phone reception (in this case, the nearby town of Detroit).

Look for this symbol 🔊 *on maps to indicate where cell reception can be found in the Forest at large. And remember that cell reception may depend on the carrier used or other factors.*

H2O: The nearest source of water for camp use (in this case, in camp)

Lndmk: A nearby identifiable landmark: (Breitenbush Gorge Trail #3366, 1.2 miles NW)

Road: This campsite is located on a primitive road (as opposed to gravel or dirt). Sometimes there will be other comments in this section concerning the quality of the road, such as "Paved, then dirt", which usually indicates that the campsite is a short distance off a paved road on a dirt track.

Access: Whether it is possible to drive directly to the campsite or whether you will have to park some distance away and carry your gear. Here are the two most common designations to be found in this field and what they mean:

DTC, UOP: You can drive your car all the way to your campsite, Unless Otherwise Prohibited.

Park and carry or P&C: You will need to park some distance away and carry your gear to your campsite. If the distance is over a hundred yards, it will usually be noted.

Check MVUM: A special caution to consult your "Motor Vehicle Use Map" before driving off the road to access a given campsite.

Tents: How many family-size tent sites are to be found at this site (admittedly, this is somewhat subjective).

El: The elevation above sea level, in feet.

RV: An RV won't work at this site. Other possibilities would be: "Small MH okay", meaning that the site and the road into it would work with a small motorhome, or "Road too rough".

Following each campsite description data table you will also find the following information:

Description: A short physical description of the site

as per the example above.

Getting there: Turn-by-turn directions from one of the main access points in the Forest to the campsite

ADDITIONAL ABBREVIATIONS:

Cg.: Campground

Cr.: Creek

D.T.: Dirt Track

Fk.: Fork, as in fork of a river, road, creek, etc.

FS or **FSR:** Forest Service road, such as FS46, FSR46

Grp.: Group, as in "Group Camp"

MP: Milepost

N, S, E, W, and **M:** North, South, East, West, and Middle, as in Middle Fork

OR: Oregon Route, as in OR 126. Sometimes used interchangeably with SR (State Route), as in SR 126

PCT: Pacific Crest Trail

POYP: Pack out your (own) poop

Rd.: Road

SR: State Route. Sometimes used interchangeably with OR

TH or **T.H.:** Trailhead

W/in, w/in: within

WNF: Willamette National Forest

Mileages between points may have been derived from any one of three different sources: an automobile GPS, an automobile odometer, or by computer, using a recreational mapping program, none of which may exactly match the mileage of your car's odometer, especially over longer distances. For this reason, I have tried to include a local landmark to help locate each campsite.

In a few instances, you will find a break in the sequence of campsite numbers. This happens when it was discovered too late that a campsite should not have been included in the book for some reason.

Campsites located along the major rivers, such as those along FS46 and OR 20 and 22, are generally easier to get to and very popular, especially during the hotter months of the summer. Many of them are sandwiched between a road and a river, which means that the large numbers of humans drawn to them throughout the summer begin to pose serious risks to the health of the river and the nearby vegetation. In some cases, the Forest Service may choose to prohibit camping at these sites in order to preserve the forest habitat.

The Middle Fork of the Willamette, south of Oakridge

Public disregard for our National Forest is a huge issue that can have an undesirable impact on the Forest and its inhabitants. It also impacts the lives of the people in and around the Forest, including those living in the small communities nearby whose motels, restaurants, grocery and hardware stores and coffee houses depend on the annual tide of summertime visitors flowing through on their way to camp, play, hunt, fish, and forage. Due to the loss of logging revenue, the Forest Service no longer has the resources it had in past decades. It cannot afford to clean up after those who consider the Forest their back yard when it comes to recreation, but somebody else's responsibility when it comes to clean-up.

As previously explained, not all of the campsites listed in the book are located near a river or stream. The dry campsites in the book are included for a particular reason. Often it's because they are located conveniently close to a popular recreation site, such as a lake or hiking trail. A few were included because

of some notable feature about the site itself, such as a commanding view, exposure to a cooling breeze or the capacity to accommodate a large number of tents.

Snagging a prime campsite near water

Not all campsites are created equally. Some are more appealing than others. By Friday evening during the months of July and August there is as much demand for prime dispersed campsites along rivers and streams as there is for the campsites in designated Forest Service campgrounds. Want to snag a great campsite at this time of the year? Be packed and on the road before the rest of the herd charges out of the city at rush hour on Friday afternoon.

Though I have made a diligent effort to ferret out every possible campsite in my two summers of driving the roads of the Forest, there are thousands of campsites still out there, waiting to be discovered. Chances are always good that you will find a campsite near a stream or other body of water, but don't despair if you can't. There is always a shady spot for your tent up the road a ways in our welcoming National Forest. And there is almost always a creek somewhere in the vicinity that will provide water for camp use though some of them are so small and well-hidden that it's easy to drive by without noticing them. Experience will teach you to keep an eye peeled for potential dry campsites as well as streams that would be good sources of water as you drive through the Forest. If you get there too late and end up having to spend the weekend in a dry campsite, don't let your expectations color the experience negative for you. Be open to the possibilities around you. Chances are that by giving up one thing, you will be gaining another. Meadow camping has its charms for someone who approaches it with an open mind, for example. Likewise, camping on a ridge with a view out over the valleys below you is another kind of experience that has to be tried to be appreciated. There's a lot of National Forest out there to be explored. Experience the entire Forest. Don't confine yourself to one kind of ecosystem.

Caveat

Inspect your site for hazards: During the summertime fieldwork phase of this book, the inspections of the sites noted herein were limited to checking for the essentials necessary for camping as well as obvious safety hazards. Some of the sites in this book, though beautiful and otherwise desirable, are not suitable for children. Examples are sites located on the banks of fast-moving rivers and streams that could sweep a distracted child downstream. A few might be located too close to a precipice, dead tree or another potential hazard. I cannot claim to have discovered every possible risk factor and must leave it to you to make a more thorough inspection of the site and its environs when you arrive on the spot, especially if you have children or someone with special needs in your party.

Disclaimer

Almost without exception, the sites included in this book are those that appeared to have been used as campsites by others in the past, as evidenced by the presence of a fire ring and a bare patch of ground where a tent can be erected. This book cannot be relied upon as an authoritative guide to the ever-changing landscape of laws, policies, rules, regulations and guidelines promulgated by the US Forest Service. Because a site is listed in this book does not mean that you are free to drive your vehicle into or onto the site. Virtually all of the campsites listed in this book were in use prior to the inception of the new MVUM guidelines, and the main roads leading to them were, to the best of my knowledge, open to highway-legal vehicles at the time of discovery, with the possible exception of those sites discovered from the saddle of a non-motorized mountain bike. Though I have made a diligent effort to exclude and delete any campsites located along roads that are closed to motor vehicles and where dispersed camping is prohibited and have tried to indicate which campsites are not accessible to motor vehicle traffic, I cannot guarantee that I have been one hundred percent successful in doing so. Because of missing or damaged road signs and, sometimes, discrepancies between what I saw on the ground and on the map, it was sometimes difficult to identify a location or road precisely from cues on the ground. Any errors will have been inadvertent. Therefore, to the reader falls the responsibility to be informed of all current county, state and federal laws, regulations and restrictions and guidelines that apply and are in force in the Willamette National Forest, including, but not limited to those pertaining to dispersed camping, fishing, hunting, the use of fire, firearms, the operation of motor vehicles and the cutting, digging or harvesting of plant or animal life of any kind. Especially, it is the reader's responsibility to carry and consult the proper Motor Vehicle Use Map before driving in any part of the Willamette National Forest.

Furthermore, the information provided in this and other chapters is based on the author's opinions, insights, research, knowledge and practical experience, and is not presented as either definitive or authoritative. The book is intended only as a guide and is not a substitute for the reader's knowledge or judgment.

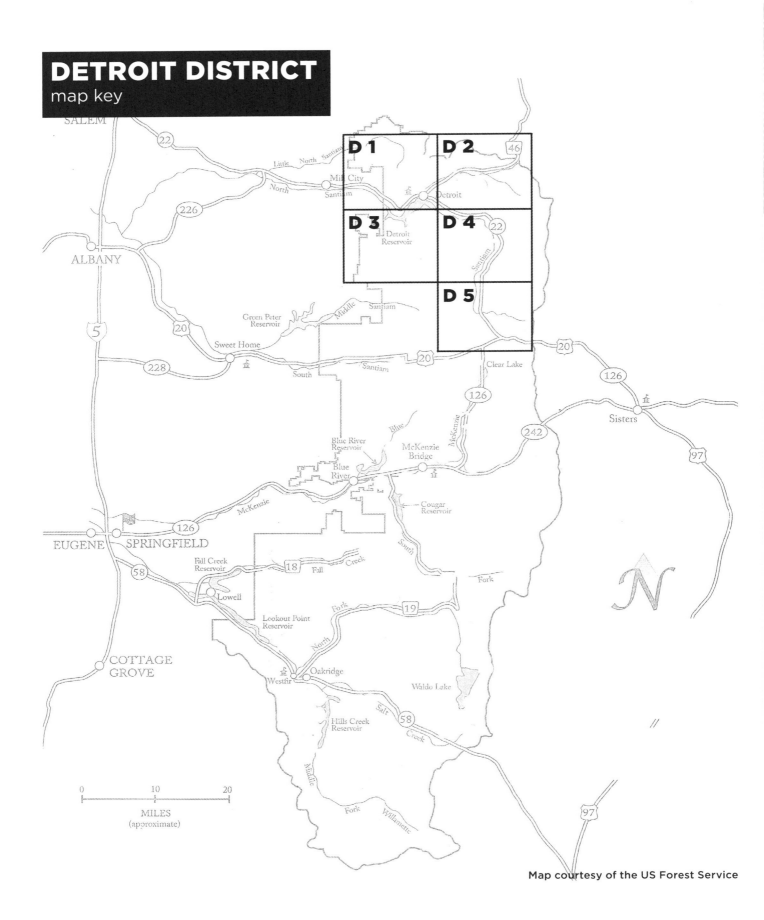

DETROIT DISTRICT
map key

D 1
D 2
D 3
D 4
D 5

SALEM

22
228
226
ALBANY
5
20
EUGENE
SPRINGFIELD
228
58
COTTAGE
GROVE

Little   North   Santiam
Mill City
North   Santiam
Detroit
Detroit
Reservoir
22
46

Green Peter
Reservoir
Middle   Santiam
Sweet Home
South   Santiam
20
Clear Lake
20
126
126
Sisters
97

Blue River
Reservoir
Blue
River
Blue
McKenzie
Bridge
McKenzie
242

McKenzie
Cougar
Reservoir
South
Fork
Fall Creek
Reservoir
18
Fall   Creek
Lowell
Fork
19
Lookout Point
Reservoir
North
Fork
Oakridge
Westfir
Waldo Lake
Hills Creek
Reservoir
58
Salt
Creek
97
Middle
Fork   Willamette

N

0   10   20
MILES
(approximate)

Map courtesy of the US Forest Service

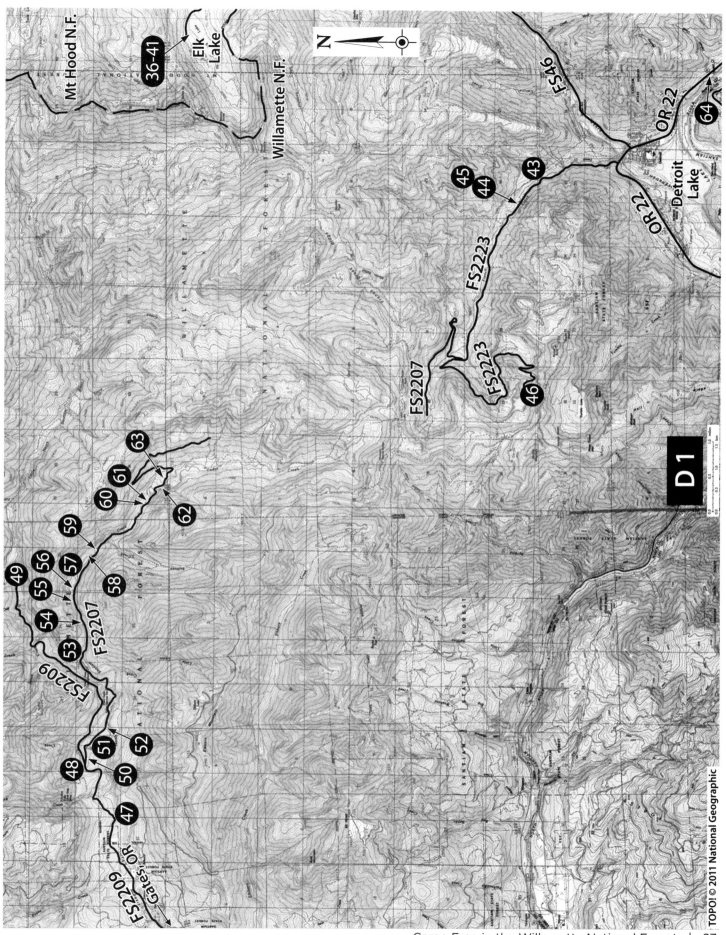

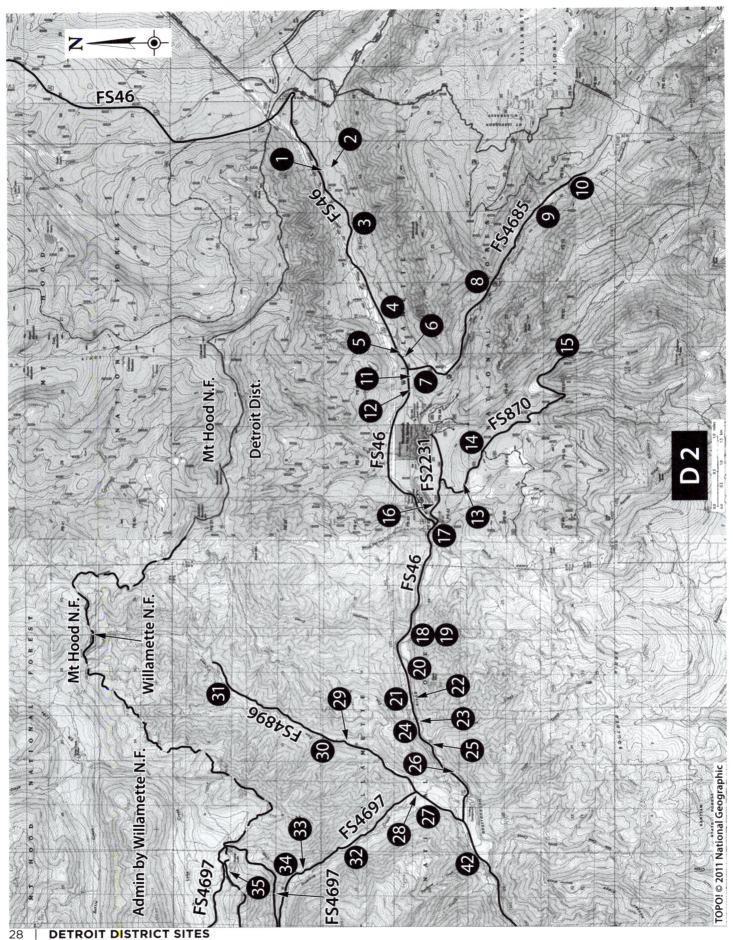

TOPO! © 2011 National Geographic

D 2

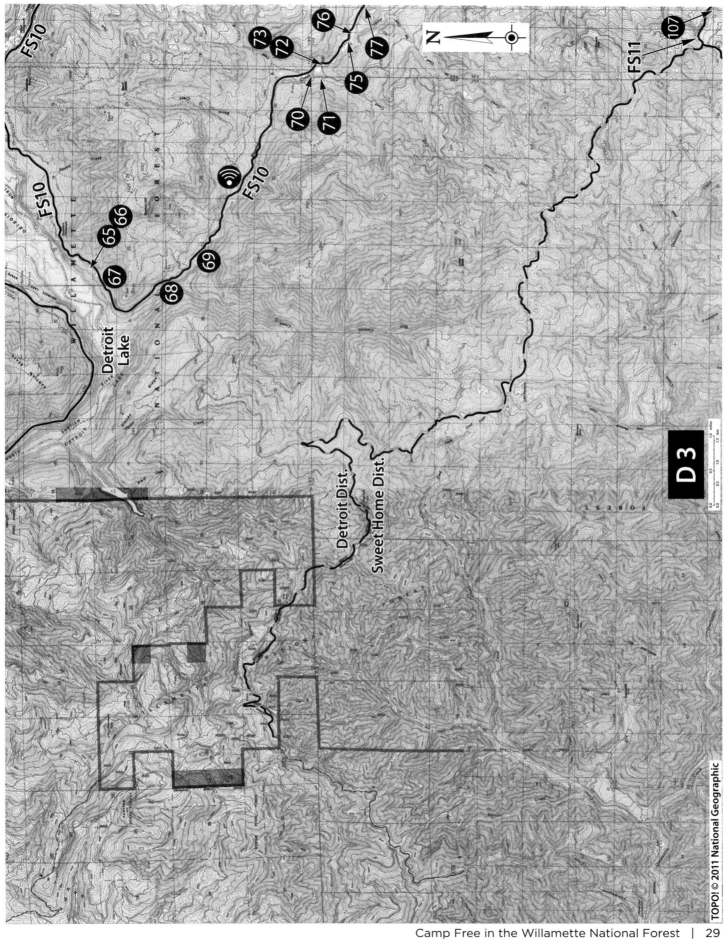

TOPO! © 2011 National Geographic

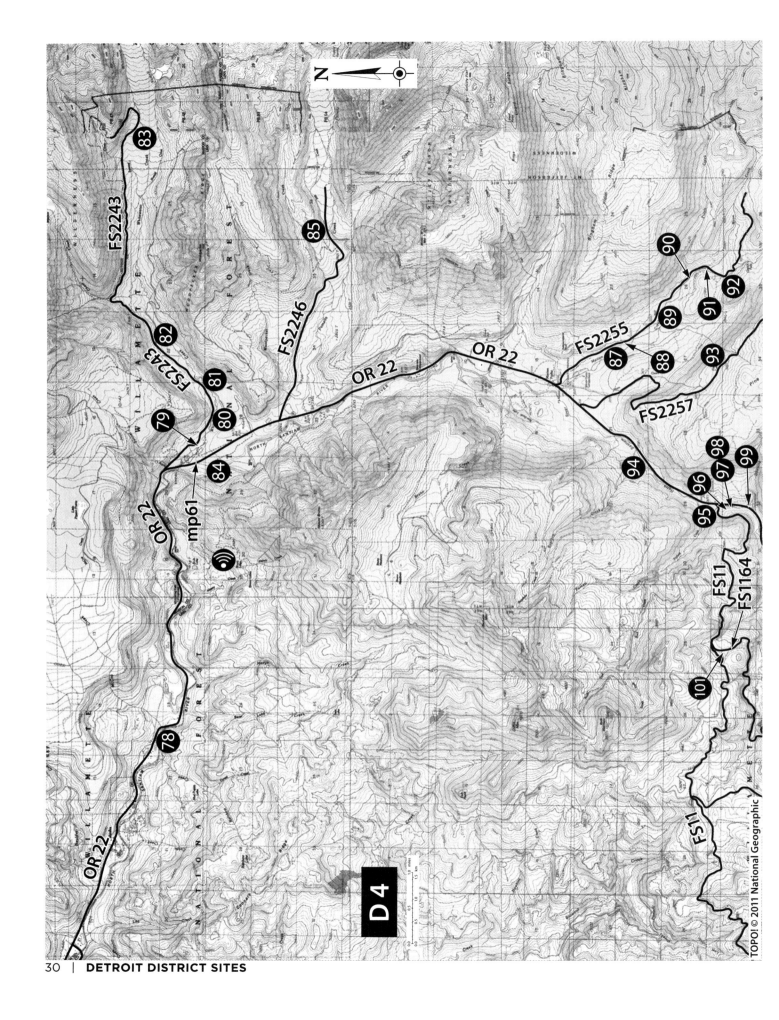

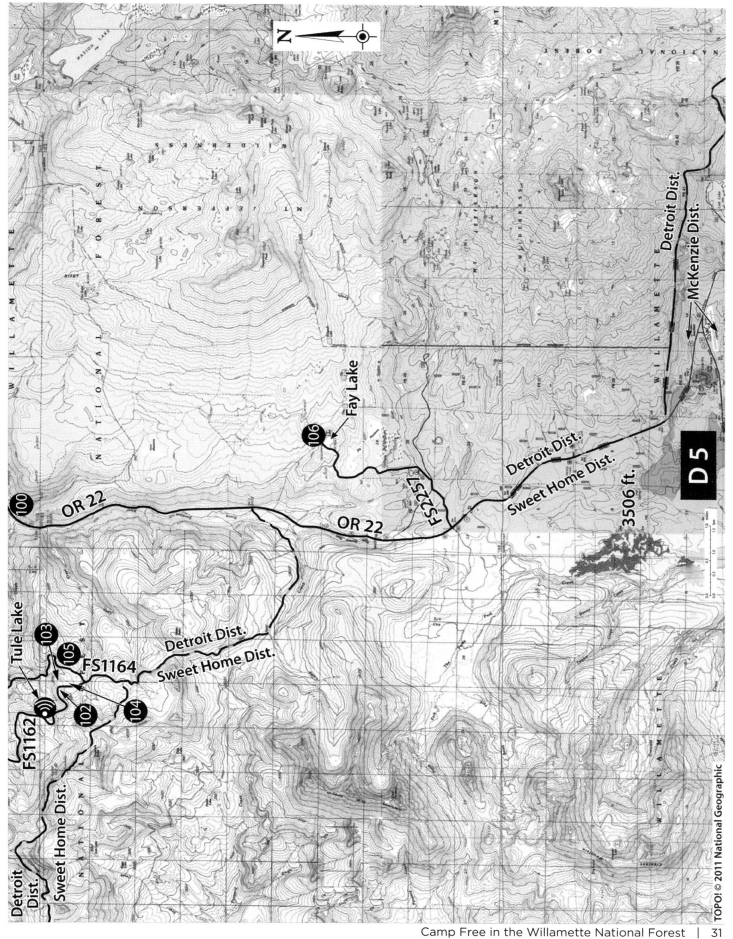

N

Fay Lake
106

100 OR 22

FS2257

OR 22

Detroit Dist.
Sweet Home Dist.

Detroit Dist.

McKenzie Dist.

D 5

3506 ft.

Tule Lake
103
105
102   104
FS1164
Detroit Dist.
Sweet Home Dist.

FS1162

Sweet Home Dist.

Detroit Dist.

DETROIT DISTRICT SITES

"The clearest way into the Universe is through a forest wilderness."
—John Muir

Loc: On FS46-013, 1.8 miles south of the Mt. Hood N.F.	**Road:** Paved, then dirt
L/L: N44 47 981/W121 53 894	**Access:** Park and carry, 2–300 yards
Cell: Detroit	**Tents:** 3–9
Nearest H2O: N.Fk. of the Breitenbush River	**El:** 2900
Lndmk: Mount Hood N.F., 1.8 miles north on FS46	**RV:** On dirt road only

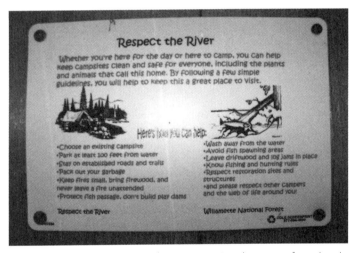

The Forest Service asks campers to observe a few simple rules to preserve this site.

Description: (a twofer) Two of the nicest camp-sites you are liable to find along the North Fork of the Breitenbush River. Both are far enough from FS46 to provide privacy and solitude and shield you from the sound of motorcycles roaring by on FS46 on warm, summer days. The first site is 0.3 miles from FS46 on Spur 013, on the right, next to a fast section of the river. It is well shaded, with several flat tent sites. If you choose this site, be respectful of the fact that the Forest Service is trying to restore the habitat near this camp. The second site is located on a slow section of the river about 0.6 mile from FS46 on the other side of a creek that flows across the road. After you cross the creek, look for pull-out where a trail leads through the trees toward the river. This site features a rocky bar that would serve as a shaded beach overlooking the river. Be prepared to schlep your gear a few hundred yards over a fairly even trail.

Getting there: *(See map pg. 28)* Coming From Detroit on FS46, look for a dirt road at or near MP 15 that leads down to the river. From Estacada, go about 1.8 miles past the southern boundary of the Mount Hood N.F. Turn downhill on Spur 013, which is very near MP 15. Both sites require campers to park and carry gear from Spur 013.

Loc: FS46-015, 0.7 mile from FS46 on the N.Fk., Breitenbush River	**Road:** Paved, then dirt
	Access: Check MVUM
L/L: N44 47 846/W121 53 753	**Tents:** Up to 15
Cell: Detroit	**El:** 2680
Nearest H2O: N.F of the Breitenbush River	**RV:** Use judgment with small MH
Lndmk: MP 14, 0.2 miles west	

Description: (a "threefer") Two nice sites and one spectacular one, located along Spur 015:
1. Two to three tent sites located a hundred yards, or so, from the river. In the summer of 2013 this site was in

Views of Breitenbush River and campsite

need of clean-up. A path leads from camp to the river, where water is easily accessible.

2. Though heavily littered when discovered in 2013, this site will have much potential when cleaned up.

3. A large, prime campsite in an open area under a canopy of mixed fir and cedar trees! This site was relatively clean in 2013. It has everything you will want for an extended stay: view, shade, privacy, easy access to water. There is a comfortable log bench near the fire pit and a cooling pool on the opposite side of the river. You will also find A-frame fencing near camp, signifying that the Forest Service is trying to protect nearby habitat. Be respectful.

Getting there: *(See map pg. 28)* Coming from Detroit on FS46, turn onto dirt Spur 015 about 0.2 miles east of MP 14. Coming From Estacada, go 2.3 miles beyond the boundary of the Mount Hood N.F., then turn left on Spur 015. Site #1 is 0.1 mile from FS46 and about 100 feet toward river. Site #2 is about 0.6 mile from FS46, to the right. Site #3 is about a hundred yards beyond Site #2. Be sure to check MVUM regarding driving on Spur 015.

(3)	**Loc:** FS46-115, 2.8 miles from the Mount Hood N.F. , 0.2 miles from FS46	**Road:** Paved, then dirt
		Access: Park and carry, 100'
	L/L: N44 47 574/W121 54 723	**Tents:** 3–5
	Cell: Detroit	**El:** 2714
	Nearest H2O: Breitenbush River, 50'	**RV:** No
	Lndmk: MP 14, 0.3 M. east	

Description: *(a twofer)* There are two campsites at the end of Spur 115, both near the river. Both were occupied when discovered, and no close inspection was possible. The first is immediately to the right of the end of the road and very near the river. The second and larger site is about a hundred or so feet further on and more isolated. Both camps are well protected from the elements, but the first is the shadier of the two. The shore is brushy, and there is no open beach nearby, but access to the river for camp water is possible.

Getting there: *(See map pg. 28)* Coming from Detroit on FS46, turn right onto Spur 115 about 0.7 miles past MP 13. From Estacada, turn onto Spur 115 2.8 miles after leaving the Mount Hood N.F and 0.3 miles past MP 14. Both camps are near the end of a dirt road, which dips steeply for about a hundred feet at about 0.2 mile from FS46, just before reaching the first campsite. Caution is advised for those driving low-clearance vehicles.

Loc: FS46-014	Road: Paved, then dirt
L/L: N44 47 282/W121 56 144	Access: DTC, UOP
Cell: Detroit	Tents: 2–3
Nearest H2O: Breitenbush River	El: 2495
Lndmk: MP 13	RV: Small MH, Use judgment

Description: *(a twofer)* Here are two wooded sites on a bench about fifteen feet above the river, where the road ends. The site on the left is the larger of the two. The site on the right will probably only comfortably accommodate one tent. Spur 014 crosses a small but rambunctious little creek on the way that would be an easier source of water for camp use than trying to negotiate the steep river bank below camp.

Getting there: *(See map pg. 28)* From Detroit on FS46, turn right onto Spur 014 at 1.6 miles east of the FS46/4685 junction, just past MP 13.

Loc: FS46, 0.1 mile east of FS4685	Road: Paved, then dirt
L/L: N44 47 065/W121 56 861	Access: DTC, UOP
Cell: Detroit	Tents: 4–6
Nearest H2O: Breitenbush River	El: 2450
Lndmk: FS4685, 0.1 mile SW	RV: No

Description: *(a twofer)* There are two campsites on elevated flat areas above the river that would be prime destination sites were it not for the trash left by previous revelers. The larger of the two sites sits under a grove of sheltering cedar trees and would be an excellent choice for the cool, rainy weather that sometimes lingers through June in the mountains. The river here is fast-moving and about a hundred yards away across an overgrown rock-strewn shelf.

Getting there: *(See map pg. 28)* Headed west on FS46, turn left onto a primitive dirt track (Spur 111) about 0.1 mile east of FS4685. About a hundred yards from FS46, take the fork to the left and proceed another 100 yards to campsites.

Loc: FS46, 0.1 mile east of FS4685	Road: Paved, then dirt
L/L: N44 46 996/W121 57 002	Access: Check MVUM
Cell: Detroit	Tents: 1–2
Nearest H2O: Breitenbush River	El: 2310
Lndmk: Spur 111	RV: Use judgment with small MH

Description: This is smaller but cleaner than Site #5 in 2013, but with fewer level tent sites. Getting to the Breitenbush involves walking through or over a small stream that has split off from the river, and may be a bit tricky.

Getting there: *(See map pg. 28)* Headed west on FS46, turn left onto a primitive dirt track (Spur 111) leading toward the river about 0.1 mile east of FS4685, then drive 0.2 mile downhill. Follow the road as it forks right past an open field, then flattens to parallel the river to site.
This site was considerably trashed when discovered.

Loc: FS4685-301, 0.1 mile south of FS46, just past the bridge over the N. Fork of the Breitenbush River	Road: Gravel and Primitive
	Access: Check MVUM
L/L: N44 46 848/W121 57 204	Tents: 10–15
Cell: Detroit	El: 2400
Nearest H2O: 200 yards	RV: MH and TT
Lndmk: Bridge over the N. Fork of the Breitenbush	

Description: Here you will find five nice, private campsites well spread out along Spur road 301, which loosely parallels the river and dead ends at about 0.3 miles from FS4685. Each campsite will accommodate at least two tents. One site is walk-in only and is about 150 yards from the road, near the river. For the three campsites on the side of the road opposite the river, access to the river is via two trails near the bridge, both of which descend rather steeply. The campsite at the end of the road is pleasant and might also have easier access to the river. There someone has flattened a six-foot log to make a comfortable bench in front of the fire pit. In the summer of 2013 the site across the road from the walk-in site had been left littered by previous campers.
The Breitenbush Gorge Trail, #3366, is about 2 miles southeast on FS4685.

Getting there: *(See map pg. 28)* Follow FS46 out of Detroit or approach from the direction of Estacada. About halfway between mileposts 11 and 12, turn south on FS 4685 and go 0.3 miles to Spur 301 and campsites, on right, just after crossing the North Fork of the Breitenbush River. Spur 301 is overgrown, and there is a steep downhill stretch approximately 100 feet long that starts just past the second or third campsite on the left. Check MVUM.

Loc: FS4585, 2.3 M. south of FS46, on Roaring Creek	Road: Gravel
L/L: N44 45 982/W121 55 676	Access: DTC, UOP
Cell: Detroit	Tents: 2–3
Nearest H2O: In camp	El: 2750
Lndmk: Breitenbush Gorge T.H., 0.1 mile SE	RV: MH and TT

Description: A unique site about a hundred feet off FS4685 where Roaring Creek Falls tumbles over rock and downed logs to form a clear, calm pool conveniently situated for collecting water for camp use. A steep canyon lined with cedar and other conifer trees yawns away upstream. Find level campsites closer to the road or near the fire pit. A small motor home would work near the fire pit. Downside: the Creek lives up to its name as it flows through camp to join the South Fork of the Breitenbush River.

Getting there: *(See map pg. 28)* Follow FS46 out of Detroit or approach the direction of Estacada. About halfway between mileposts 11 and 12, turn south and go 2.3 miles on FS4685. Site is on left. If you pass the Breitenbush Gorge Trailhead, you have gone too far.

Loc: FS 4685, 3.6 miles from FS46	Road: Primitive
L/L: N44 45 366/W121 54 380	Access: P&C, Check MVUM
Cell: Detroit	Tents: 4–5
Nearest H2O: In camp	El: 2950
Lndmk: Breitenbush Gorge Trail #3366, 1.2 miles NW	RV: No

Description: A site that is wonderful for its proximity to a beautiful section of the river. There is ample shelter from the trees, and the river forms a pool here that is easily deep enough for a summertime soak. High marks for its solitude and scenic view!

Getting there: *(See map pg. 28)* Follow FS46 out of Detroit or approach from the direction of Estacada. About halfway between mileposts 11 and 12, turn south on FS4685 and go 3.6 miles to a rough dirt road heading steeply downhill to the river, 0.2 miles away. Park and carry gear to site.

Loc: 0.1 mile from FS4685 and 4.3 miles from FS46		**Road:** Primitive
L/L: N44 44 958/W121 53 900		**Access:** Park and carry
Cell: Detroit		**Tents:** 4–5
Nearest H2O: 100'		**El:** 2950
Lndmk: FS4685-200, 0.1 mile		**RV:** No

Description: Located in a thick stand of tall conifer trees along the Breitenbush River Gorge, this site would be a prime choice for those looking for dense shade and scenic beauty during the hot months of summer.

Getting there: *(See map pg. 28)* Follow FS46 out of Detroit or approach from the direction of Estacada. About halfway between mileposts 11 and 12, turn south and go 4.3 miles on FS4685. At this point, camp and the river are located at the end of an unmarked primitive road leading downhill to the right. Parking and carrying gear is recommended. There was a convenient spot nearby that provided concealed parking in the summer of 2013.

* Campsites overlooking the Breitenbush River though strikingly scenic, are often perched on bluffs or cliffs near precipitous drops to the river. The steep walls of the canyon along this stretch of the river can make access to the water difficult and sometimes dangerous. In addition, because of their location along a paved road, many of the sites are overused and left in need of cleanup.

Loc: FS46, 0.1 M. west of FS4685		**Road:** Paved
L/L: N44 46 978/W121 57 298		**Access:** Park and carry
Cell: Detroit		**Tents:** 3–4
Nearest H2O: Breitenbush R.		**El:** 2230
Lndmk: Junction FS46/4685, 0.1 M. E		**RV:** No

Description: A pleasant site on a rise between a small, unnamed creek and the Breitenbush River, with easy access to both. Due to dense foliage and vegetation, this site offers a surprising amount of privacy and solitude for being so near to FS46. The creek and the river provide pleasant water noise from two sides. Nice!

Getting there: *(See map pg. 28)* From Estacada on FS46, drive 5.3 miles south of the border with the Mount Hood National Forest. Site is on left, 0.1 mile past FS4685. From OR 22 at Detroit, drive 11 miles to site, on right. If you pass FS4685 on your right, turn around and drive 0.1 mile west to site. Park just off the road and carry gear over a short, rock causeway across the unnamed creek. Camp is another 50' beyond.

Loc: South side of FS46, between MP 11 and 12	Road: Paved, then dirt
L/L: N44 46 956/W121 57 536	Access: DTC, UOP
Cell: Detroit and possibly Breitenbush H.S.	Tents: 2–3
Nearest H2O: Breitenbush R.	El: 2410
Lndmk: FS46/050, 0.1 mile west	RV: Small MH only

Description: This site, located on a sloping bench dropping steeply to the river in a grove of tall fir trees on the south side of FS46 midway between FS050 and FS4685, may be considered less than optimal by some. Access to the river is restricted by the steepness of the bank here though it can be heard quite clearly through the trees.

Getting there: *(See map pg. 28)* On FS46, Look for a dirt road to the south between MP 11 and 12 and about 0.2 mile east of Spur 050 and 0.3 mile west of FS4685. Camp is about 200 feet south of FS46.

Loc: FS2231, 1.2 miles from FS46	Road: Gravel, then dirt
L/L: N44 46 356/W121 59 143	Access: DTC, UOP
Cell: Detroit	Tents: 5–7
Nearest H2O: Breitenbush R., about 1.5 mi N	El: 2570
Lndmk: Breitenbush Hot Springs, 1.3 miles NW	RV: No

Description: *(Overnight/emergency)* A large, flat, dry, and very private campsite about 100' off the east side of FS2231.

Getting there: *(See map pg. 28)* On FS46, take FS2231 very close to Cleator Bend Group Camp and MP 9. Drive 1.2 miles to site, which is identifiable by a faint primitive road leading off through the trees to the left. Camp is about 100 feet off the road. Check MVUM before driving.

Loc: At FS2231/870 junction	Road: Gravel
L/L: N44 46 112/W121 58 605	Access: DTC, UOP
Cell: Detroit, or possibly Breitenbush Hot Springs	Tents: 2–3
Nearest H2O: Probably Skunk Cr., 1.8 miles SE on spur 870	El: 2650
	RV: MH and TT
Lndmk: FS2231/870 junction	

Description: *(A last resort)* This misused disrespected, and waterless site is a last resort campsite only. It is much less appealing than #13, but when you're desperate, it may look good to you. There was broken glass in the fire pit in 2013, so use care.

Getting there: *(See map pg. 28)* On FS46, turn onto FS2231 very close to Cleator Bend Group Camp and MP 9. Campsite is on the left at 1.8 miles, where Spur 870 joins FS2231.

Loc: FS2231-870, 2.8 miles from FS2231	**Road:** Gravel, fair
L/L: N44 45 099/W121 56 993	**Access:** DTC, UOP
Cell: Detroit, or possibly Breitenbush Hot Springs	**Tents:** 2-3
Nearest H2O: Cascade Creek, 20'	**El:** 2921
Lndmk: Cascade Creek	**RV:** Use judgment w/small MH, No TT

Description: *(Diamond in the rough)* This little-used, though somewhat small campsite on Cascade Creek less than 2 miles from the Mount Jefferson Wilderness offers more than the eye can immediately see. It is private and protected and features easy access to Cascade Creek, which drops energetically through willow, maple and alder to meet Devil's Creek, 0.2 mile below. Visitors who wander across the road will discover a beautiful grotto-like pool about 30' across and several feet deep that will make the trip worthwhile all by itself. The camp gets some sun in the afternoon, but its location in the trough between a high ridge and Devil's Peak to the east provides shade when it counts. Spur 870 is the road less traveled. It deteriorates badly about a half-mile beyond camp.

Getting there: *(See map pg. 28)* On FS46, turn onto FS2231 very close to Cleator Bend Group Camp and MP 9. At 1.8 miles, go left on Spur 870 and practice defensive driving for the remaining 2.8 miles to camp, where a short, unmarked road takes off to the right. In the summer of 2013, alder trees were beginning to overgrow the road along the last quarter mile to camp and might make it difficult for a wider vehicle such as a motorhome to pass. Check MVUM before driving.

Loc: FS2231-869, 0.3 miles from FS46	**Road:** Gravel, then primitive dirt
L/L: N44 46 705/W121 59 551	**Access:** DTC, UOP
Cell: Detroit, or possibly Breitenbush Hot Springs	**Tents:** 4-6
Nearest H2O: Breitenbush R., 0.3 mile	**El:** 2255
Lndmk: Cleator Bend Group Camp	**RV:** MH and TT

Description: This waterless site, hidden from the road by tall conifers is wonderfully pleasant and shady and far enough from the river to provide almost complete privacy for the lucky party who gets to it first. Spur 869 is easy to drive. A faint trail leads from camp down toward the river, but peters out about a hundred feet above the river due to the steepness of the canyon.

Getting there: *(See map pg. 28)* On FS46, take FS2231 very close to Cleator Bend Group Camp and MP 9. Drive 0.3 miles and follow Spur 869 to camp, on left, about 200 yards. Check MVUM before driving.

Loc: FS2231 on the south shore of the Breitenbush R.	**Road:** Gravel
L/L: N44 46 638/W121 59 829	**Access:** Park and carry, short distance
Cell: Detroit or possibly Breitenbush H.S.	**Tents:** 8-10
Nearest H2O: Hill Creek and Breitenbush R.	**El:** 2200
Lndmk: FS4693/2231 junction	**RV:** On road nearby only

Description: These two sites at the end of the bridge across the Breitenbush are on opposite sides of FS2231. Both offer easy access to the Breitenbush River for recreation and camp water. Hill Creek runs through the smaller site on the west side of the road to join the Breitenbush just a hundred feet or so further on. The larger site on the east side of the road, set in a grove of second-growth fir trees, is the more inviting and has more level tent sites. *These sites are easy to reach from FS46 and are liable to be crowded on summer weekends.*

Getting there: (See map pg. 28) On FS46, turn onto FS2231 very close to Cleator Bend Group Camp and MP 9. Find campsites on the south side of the bridge across the river, about 0.1 mile from FS46.

Loc: FS46, 1.5 miles west of Cleator Bend Grp Camp.	Road: Paved, then dirt, primitive
L/L: N44 46 938/W122 01 712	Access: DTC, UOP
Cell: Detroit	Tents: 10–12
Nearest H20: Breitenbush River, 200 yards	El: 2250
Lndmk: Scorpion Cr.	RV: Small MH

Description: This large site on a bluff high above the Breitenbush River features two nice campsites. The higher of the two offers more level tent sites. Nevertheless, parties with children should think twice before camping here because of the precipitous drop to the river below, even though picturesque wooden barricades are in place to keep campers away from the edge. Water for camp use is easily available from Scorpion Creek, near site #19, a few hundred yards down the road.

Getting there: (See map pg. 28) Follow FS46 out of Detroit or approach from the direction of Estacada. About halfway between mileposts 7 and 8 and about 200 yards west of Scorpion Creek look for a primitive dirt road heading downhill about 100 yards to the upper campsite. Follow a narrow, rocky, road a few hundred yards to reach the lower site.

Loc: FS46, 1.4 miles west of Cleator Bend Grp. Camp	Road: Paved, then dirt
L/L: N44 47 021/W122 01 611	Access: DTC, UOP
Cell: Detroit	Tents: 6–7
Nearest H20: 100 feet	El: 2300
Lndmk: Scorpion Creek	RV: MH and TT

Description: (a twofer) Two nice campsites on Scorpion Creek and the north side of FS46. The first site has one level tent site and may be visible from cars passing by on FS46. The second campsite is about 0.1 mile further on the dirt road and has more level tent sites as well as a pool of cold, clear water that appears to be deep enough for soaking in hot weather. Both sites offer good shade as well as easy access to the creek for water for camp use.

Getting there: (See map pg. 28) Follow FS46 out of Detroit or approach from the direction of Estacada. About halfway between mileposts 7 and 8 look for Scorpion Creek and take the primitive dirt road leading northward to campsites.

Loc: 0.1 off FS46, between MP 6 and 7	Road: Paved, then primitive
L/L: N44 47 026/W122 02 306	Access: DTC, UOP
Cell: Detroit	Tents: 3–4
Nearest H20: Scorpion Creek, 0.7 mile east on FS46	El: 1920
Lndmk: Cleator Bend Group Camp, 2.1 miles, east	RV: MH and TT

Description: This otherwise pleasant campsite had been left littered by some previous user or users early in the summer of 2013. There is a firepit here and ample shade, but getting to the river for water is problematic and potentially dangerous due to the steepness and depth of the river canyon. The best bet for water is to drive the 0.6 M. east to Scorpion Creek.

Getting there: *(See map pg. 28)* Follow FS46 out of Detroit or approach from the direction of Estacada. About halfway between mileposts 6 and 7 and 0.7 mile west of Scorpion Creek take a primitive dirt road leading downhill toward river about 0.1 mile to site.

Loc: FS46, 6.4 miles from Detroit	Road: Paved, then a short, primitive dirt road
L/L: N44 47 020/W122 02 821	Access: DTC, UOP
Cell: Detroit	Tents: 5–10
Nearest H2O: Fox Creek, 0.3 miles west	El: 1805
Lndmk: Fox Creek Grp. Cmp., 0.3 miles west	RV: Use judgment due to drop-off from road

Description: Not the most desirable camp in the west, but definitely large enough to accommodate a group, especially when everything else is taken. There is adequate shade, but the nearest water is either from the Breitenbush on the other side of FS46 or from Fox Creek, 0.3 mile to the west. Expect to do some cleanup here.

Getting there: *(See map pg. 28)* Follow FS46 out of Detroit or approach from the direction of Estacada. Somewhere between MP six and seven and about 0.3 mile east of the Fox Creek Group Camp take a short dirt road on the north side of the road for about a hundred yards through the trees to camp. Be careful of the drop-off as you leave FS46.

Loc: FS46, 1.8 miles NE of Humbug Cg. and 0.1 mile from Fox Grp. Site	Road: Paved, then dirt, primitive
	Access: DTC, UOP
L/L: N44 46 942/W122 02 858	Tents: 3–4
Cell: 3 bars noted near camp, otherwise, Detroit	El: 2000
Nearest H2O: Scorpion Creek	RV: MH and TT
Lndmk: Fox Creek Group Camp, 0.1 mile west	

Description: An acceptable overnight campsite on a sheer bluff above a swift section of the Breitenbush. In addition to a fire ring, there are two or three large and relatively flat rocks in camp that provide handy places for stoves and gear. In the summer of 2013 a brushy spot to the immediate northeast bore evidence of having been used as a toilet area. Use your glompers to pick up and burn any toilet paper in evidence (a large brown paper bag is handy for both collecting and burning). The downside to this campsite is a dangerous slope near camp which plunges precipitously to the river with no safeguards in sight. No kids here. No hard drinking, either. No kidding!

Getting there: *(See map pg. 28)* Follow FS46 out of Detroit or approach from the direction of Estacada. Somewhere between MP six and seven and bout 0.1 mile east of the Fox Creek Group Camp, take a short dirt road toward the river. Campsite is partially visible from the road.

Loc: FS46, 1.5 miles east of Humbug Cg., 0.1 mile west of Fox Cr. Grp. Cmp	**Road:** Paved, then dirt
	Access: DTC, UOP
L/L: N44 46 852/N122 03 336	**Tents:** 4–5
Cell: Detroit	**El:** 1935
Nearest H2O: Scorpion or Fox Creeks	**RV:** Small MH only
Lndmk: Fox Creek Group Camp, 0.1 mile east	

Description: Just off the road and with a view of the river immediately below, this pleasant site comes with a picnic table. There is plenty of shade, but there should also be some exposure to the morning sun. Small logs span the distance between triangular supports to provide a barrier between campers and the steep drop-off to the Breitenbush. In dry weather, leave the surrounding area clean and pristine by using your glompers and a large paper bag to collect and burn any toilet paper in evidence.

Getting there: *(See map pg. 28)* Follow FS46 out of Detroit or approach from the direction of Estacada. One-tenth of a mile west of the Fox Creek Group Camp and very close to MP 6, turn south on a primitive dirt road leading about 150 yards downhill to camp.

Loc: FS46, 1.4 miles east of Humbug Cg. and 0.25 mile west of Fox Cr. Group Camp	**Road:** Paved, then dirt
	Access: DTC, 150', UOP
L/L: N44 46 867/W122 03 416	**Tents:** 4–5
Cell: Detroit	**El:** 1985
Nearest H2O: Probably Humbug, Fox or Scorpion Creeks	**RV:** Small MH (use judgment)
Lndmk: Fox Cr. Group Camp, 0.25 miles east	

Description: An otherwise shady and pleasant camp on a bluff above the river that was left badly littered by some previous camper in the summer of 2013.
Caution: There is no safety barricade between the campsite and the steep drop into the nearby river canyon below.

Getting there: *(See map pg. 28)* Follow FS46 out of Detroit or approach from the direction of Estacada. A quarter of a mile west of the Fox Creek Group Camp and very close to MP 6, turn south and drive 200 feet to camp on a primitive dirt road.

Loc: FS46, 0.9 mile east of Humbug Cg. And 0.5 mile west of Fox Cr. Grp. Camp	**Road:** Paved, then 150 yards of primitive dirt road
L/L: N44 46 724/W122 03 609	**Access:** DTC, UOP
Cell: Detroit	**Tents:** 4–5
Nearest H2O: Breitenbush R.	**El:** 1910
Lndmk: Humbug Cg.	**RV:** MH and TT

Description: This site is one of few along this several mile-long section of the river with comparatively easy access to the river. A pool below camp is deep enough for swimming, but judgment should be used, since the water here is still moving along at a good pace, creating obvious currents and eddies. The crystal-clear depths of a pool just below the rock bluff seem to call for a fishing line. The bank near camp is steep for the last six feet. Use care (and maybe a rope) when trying to draw water from the river for camp use. Because the campsite is roomy and open to the sun, heat may be a problem the months of July and August. As with most popular campsites along paved roads, be prepared to do some cleanup.

Getting there: *(See map pg. 28)* Follow FS46 out of Detroit or approach from the direction of Estacada. At 0.9 miles east of Humbug Campground and 0.5 mile west of Fox Cr. Grp. Camp, turn south on an unmarked primitive dirt road. Camp is 150 yards from FS46.

Loc: FS46, 0.6 miles NE of Humbug Cg.	**Road:** Paved, then primitive dirt
L/L: N44 46 504/W122 04 109	**Access:** Park and Carry, 75 yds.
Cell: Detroit	**Tents:** 4-5
Nearest H2O: Breitenbush R., Fox or Scorpion Cr.	**El:** 2090
Lndmk: Humbug Cg., 0.6 mile SW, MP5	**RV:** No

Description: Though the road into this site becomes impassible after the first fifty feet, it would make a wonderful sunny weekend retreat for those willing to schlep their gear the last 75 yards to the campsite. There are two levels that will accommodate roughly two tents each. The rocks overlooking the river provide an arresting view up and down the river gorge and would make a wonderful lounging spot on a warm day. Water for camp use might be drawn here, but access to the river would be a bit of a challenge.

Getting there: *(See map pg. 28)* Follow FS46 out of Detroit or approach from the direction of Estacada. At 0.6 mile east of Humbug Campground, drive 50' downhill. Park and carry gear the rest of the way to campsite.

Loc: FS4696-720	**Road:** Gravel, then dirt
L/L: N44 46 643/W122 04 751	**Access:** DTC, UOP
Cell: Detroit	**Tents:** 1
Nearest H2O: West Humbug Creek, 0.5 mile	**El:** 1870
Lndmk: Junction FS46/4696, 0.3 mile	**RV:** MH and TT

With warnings like this, you would think that FS4697 would be the road less traveled, but it is not.

Description: Located in a grove of tall, straight second growth fir trees and sheltered from the wind by a steep hill to the west, this site will provide eight out of ten campsite essentials. There may not be a drop of water in sight, but you'll appreciate its solitude and privacy. It was also relatively clean, at least when discovered.

Getting there: *(See map pg. 28)* Follow FS46 out of Detroit or approach from the direction of Estacada. About 0.2 mile west of Humbug Campground, turn north on FS4696 and drive 0.3 miles to where Spur 720 forks off to the left. Go another 0.1 mile to site, where another primitive road forks off to the left.

Loc: FS4696/4697 Junction	Road: Gravel
L/L: N44 46 902/W122 04 479	Access: Park and Carry
Cell: Detroit	Tents: 15–20
Nearest H2O: West Fork of Humbug Cr., 50' or less	El: 1850
Lndmk: Junction of FS4696 and 4697	RV: Access road too steep

Description: Meadow camping near the junction of two Forest Service roads that respectively follow the courses of the east and west forks of Humbug Creek. Here campsites are spread out across the somewhat uneven ground of an open meadow a few acres in size with easy access to the limpid water of the Humbug. Seven to ten large rocks block access to the meadow by vehicle. Downsides would be the exposure to the sun in hot weather and lack of privacy from the road though the latter might be dealt with by camping farther from the road. Also, since the ground here tends to be rocky and uneven, cots would be the best bet for a good night's sleep.

Getting there: (*See map pg. 28*) Follow FS46 out of Detroit or approach from the direction of Estacada. About 0.2 mile west of Humbug Campground, turn north on FS4696 and drive 0.8 mile to the junction with FS4697. You will see the meadow and west fork of Humbug Creek on the left. Turn onto FS4697, then park and carry gear down the steep hill to campsites on the meadow.

Loc: FS4696, 2 miles from FS46	Road: Gravel, then dirt
L/L: N44 47 732/W122 03 558	Access: DTC, UOP
Cell: Detroit	Tents: 5–7
Nearest H2O: East Humbug Creek, in camp	El: 2040
Lndmk: Junction FS4696/4698, 0.1 mile	RV: Small MH

Description: Located close to where East Humbug Creek crosses under FS4696, this site is cool and heavily shaded and would be a good choice for hot weather camping. Due to its size and ability to accommodate a fair number of tents, it would also be a great choice for a moderate-sized group. The creek is easily accessible. There are barriers in place to prevent vehicles from getting too near the creek.

Getting there: (*See map pg. 28*) Follow FS46 out of Detroit or approach from the direction of Estacada. About 0.2 mile west of Humbug Campground, turn north on FS4696 and drive 2 miles to site, on right, just past the junction with FS4698.

Loc: FS4696, 0.4 mile north of Site #14	Road: Gravel
L/L: N44 47 990/W122 03 499	Access: DTC, UOP
Cell: Detroit	Tents: 1–2
Nearest H2O: East Humbug Creek	El: 1755
Lndmk: FS4696/4698 Junction, 0.5 miles	RV: MH and TT

Description: *(Overnight/emergency)* Though not the most scenic site in the Forest, this site has most of the essentials and would make a great overnight campsite if nothing else is available. About 50 feet off of the west edge of FS4696, it features good tent sites, and there was abundant firewood in the summer of 2013. A path leads about a hundred yards downhill to East Humbug Creek, which flows swiftly here as it drops to cross the road 0.4 mile below. Campsite faces ESE and should be open to the morning sun.

Getting there: *(See map pg. 28)* Follow FS46 out of Detroit or approach from the direction of Estacada. About 0.2 mile west of Humbug Campground, turn north on FS4696 and drive 2.4 miles to site, on left and about 0.4 miles north of Site #29.

Loc: FS4696, 3.7 miles N of FS46	**Road:** Gravel, then dirt
L/L: N44 49 101/W122 02 669	**Access:** DTC, UOP
Cell: Detroit	**Tents:** 2–3
Nearest H2O: East Humbug Creek	**El:** 2415
Lndmk: Junction FS4696/4698, 1.7 miles south	**RV:** MH and TT, UOP

Description: But for the difficulty of getting to the creek for water, this would be a delightfully shady, cool and private retreat among tall trees. Solution: fetch your water near Site #30.

Getting there: *(See map pg. 28)* Follow FS46 out of Detroit or approach from the direction of Estacada. About 0.2 mile west of Humbug Campground, turn north on FS4696 and drive 3.7 miles. Site is about 200 yards off of FS4696. Watch for a primitive road that Y's off to the left and downhill just north of camp.

Loc: FS4697, 1.2 miles from FS4696, on W. Humbug Cr.	**Road:** Gravel. Use caution
L/L: N44 47 723/W122 05 405	**Access:** DTC, UOP
Cell: Detroit	**Tents:** 2–3
Nearest H2O: West Humbug Creek, in camp	**El:** 2250
Lndmk: Dunlap Creek, 0.8 miles northwest	**RV:** No

Description: You will find this sheltered site, which is directly on the creek in a steep and heavily wooded canyon, much to your liking. Non-fisher people who don't mind a little cold water in hot weather will find a pool or two that are deep enough for summertime soak. Fisher people will be tempted to take the trail that leads upstream in the hope of catching dinner or breakfast. The two best tent sites are both underneath the maple trees near where the road debouches into the campsite. Here the ground slopes slightly but is well drained, if a bit rocky. The Humbug runs from the northwest to the southeast here, and dense foliage to the north and south should block most cold wind from that direction.

Getting there: *(See map pg. 28)* Follow the directions to Site #28. Turn left onto FS4697 and continue 1.2 miles until you come to a steep, dirt track heading downhill. Camp is about 0.1 mile from FS4697, at the end of the dirt track.

Loc: Unnamed spur road off FS4697, 1.9 miles from FS4696	**Road:** Gravel. Use caution
L/L: N44 48 246/W122 05 822	**Access:** DTC, UOP
Cell: Detroit	**Tents:** 4–5
Nearest H2O: 4–500 yards	**El:** 2640
Lndmk: Dunlap Creek, 0.1 mile north	**RV:** Small MH only

Description: Two or three of the tents sites in this shaded and private campsite are not perfectly level. Access to West Humbug Creek is at the end of a path that is a couple of hundred yards long and ends in a bit of a scramble. Water might be best drawn from nearby Dunlap Creek, 0.1 north of camp along FS4697.

Getting there: *(See map pg. 28)* Follow the directions to Site #28. Turn left onto FS4697 and drive 1.9 miles to the entry road leading downhill approximately 0.1 mile to camp. If you pass Dunlap Creek, you have gone too far.

Loc: On Dunlap Cr. And FS4697, 2 miles north of FS4696	**Road:** Gravel
L/L: N44 48 310/W122 05 824	**Access:** DTC, UOP
Cell: Detroit	**Tents:** 2–3
Nearest H20: Dunlap Creek, in camp	**El:** 2525
Lndmk: Junction FS4697/spur350, 0.9 mile NW	**RV:** MH and TT

Description: A site on Dunlap Creek that is probably best used as a waypoint on the way to another destination. Dunlap Creek plunges energetically out of a stand of maple and alder trees to cross under the road and join the West Humbug Creek about an eighth of a mile below. It provides easy water for camp use and that quintessential soothing gurgle of a mountain stream. Start looking for blooming rhododendrons by mid to late June here.

Getting there: *(See map pg. 28)* Follow the directions to Site #28. Turn left onto FS4697 and drive 2 miles north to site, on right. FS4697 changes direction abruptly from northwesterly to easterly about 0.9 miles further on up the road.

Loc: Dunlap Lake, 0.1 mile from FS4697, near Elk Lake	**Road:** Rocky and rutted. Use caution.
L/L: N44 49 125/W122 05 763	**Access:** DTC, UOP
Cell: Detroit	**Tents:** 5–6
Nearest H20: Dunlap Lake	**El:** 3810
Lndmk: Junction FS4697/spur 385	**RV:** No (Road too rough)

Description: This campsite overlooking small, sub-alpine Dunlap Lake (about one-eighth mile across) is good news for those who value solitude and the silence of nature, because it tends to be overlooked in favor of the larger and more scenic Elk Lake nearby. Rhododendrons and bear grass bloom abundantly here in the summer months. The water temperature in late June was already well on its way to being tolerable for a swim. Access to the water is by descending 40 feet via a steep slope or by way of a longer but less steep path leading out of camp and downhill to the southwest. Downsides: It is difficult to find a shady spot in which to pitch a tent, and some cleanup may be required, but the view over the lake, combined with the sound of the wind through the trees nearby makes it worth the trouble.

Getting there: *(See map pg. 28)* Follow the directions to Site #28. Turn left onto FS4697 and drive 5 miles before taking a sharp left turn onto FS4697-385. Find the campsite at the end of very rough 0.1 mile-long Spur 385.

Loc: Off FS4697, on dirt road along Elk Lake Creek	**Road:** Rocky and rutted. Use caution.
L/L: N44 49 446/W122 06 796	**Access:** DTC, UOP
Cell: Detroit	**Tents:** 2–5
Nearest H2O: Elk Lake Creek	**El:** 3720
Lndmk: NE end of Elk Lake	**RV:** No, because of FS4697

Description: This site is definitely not as attractive as the sites on nearby Elk Lake, but it has the basics of privacy, shade, and access to water for cooking. One downside is that it tends to be damp, and it might therefore be more pleasant in the months of July and August, when the woods are dryer. *Be careful of camping here under heavy rain, lest you wake up to find yourself in the middle of a large puddle of water.*

Getting there: *(See map pg. 27)* Follow the directions to Site #28. Turn left onto FS4697 and drive 6.2 miles of rutted, rocky FS4697 to Elk Lake. Follow the unmarked road about 100' to the right, just before Elk Lake Creek crosses under FS4697.

Loc: Elk Lake near its Elk Creek Outlet	**Road:** Rocky and rutted. Use caution.
L/L: N44 49 477/W122 06 823	**Access:** Park and Carry, 200'
Cell: Detroit	**Tents:** 3–4
Nearest H2O: Elk Lake Creek, near camp	**El:** 3710
Lndmk: Elk Lake and Elk Lake Creek	**RV:** No

View of Elk Lake from Campsite #37

Description: If campsites were rated with stars in the same manner that hotels are, then this one, with its stunning view down the lake, would definitely rate four of them. Set up camp here on Friday afternoon and you won't want to go home again come Sunday.

Getting there: *(See map pg. 27)* Follow the directions to Site #28. Turn left onto FS4697 and drive 6.2 miles on rutted, rocky FS4697 to Elk Lake. Watch for Elk Lake Creek, which crosses under FS4697 near this campsite. There is a pullout just right for two cars near the trailhead for Trail #559, which parallels the creek in a northeasterly direction for many miles into the Bull of the Woods Wilderness and the Mount Hood National Forest. Across the road from the trailhead you will find a cobbled-up walkway made of logs and boards to help you cross over about fifteen feet of marshy area dotted with skunk cabbage. Site is about 200' from the road, very near the lake.

Loc: Elk Lake	**Road:** Rocky and rutted. Use caution.
L/L: N44 49 519/W122 06 904	**Access:** Park and Carry
Cell: Detroit	**Tents:** 3–4
Nearest H2O: In camp	**El:** 3710
Lndmk: Elk Lake	**RV:** No

Description: A prime site with a magnificent view of the length of the lake to the southwest. Even though surrounded by closely growing fir trees, this site should get some sun in the evening due to its southwest exposure.

Getting there: *(See map pg. 27)* Follow the directions to Site #28. Turn left onto FS4697 and drive 6.3 miles on rutted, rocky FS4697 to Elk Lake. Park near a small, unnamed rivulet that crosses under the road, about 0.1 mile beyond Elk Lake Creek.

Loc: FS4697, on Elk Lake	**Road:** Rocky and rutted. Use caution!
L/L: N44 49 545/W122 06 993	**Access:** Park and Carry
Cell: Detroit	**Tents:** 1
Nearest H2O: Elk Lake or Elk Lake Creek, in camp	**El:** 3710
Lndmk: Elk Lake	**RV:** Road too rough

Description: One tent site right by the lake about twenty feet below the road that is shady and unbelievably scenic! Access is by a steep bank. Be safe and use a rope.

Getting there: *(See map pg. 27)* Follow the directions to Site #28. Turn left onto FS4697 and drive 6.4 miles on rutted, rocky FS4697 to Elk Lake. Camp is visible from road about 0.2 mile beyond Elk Lake Creek.

Loc: Shore of Elk Lake, off FS4697	**Road:** Rocky and rutted. Use caution.
L/L: N44 49 576/W122 07 071	**Access:** Park and Carry
Cell: Detroit	**Tents:** 2
Nearest H2O: Elk Lake	**El:** 3720
Lndmk: Elk Lake	**RV:** No

Description: The tent sites here may be slightly off level, but the view is unforgettable.

Getting there: *(See map pg. 27)* Follow the directions to Site #28. Turn left onto FS4697 and drive 6.5 miles on rutted, rocky FS4697 to Elk Lake. Park on the lake side of the road about a quarter mile past Elk Lake Creek and carry gear down a walkable grade to site.

Loc: Shore of Elk Lake, off FS4697	**Road:** Rocky and rutted. Use caution.
L/L: N44 49 571/W122 07 118	**Access:** Park and Carry
Cell: Detroit	**Tents:** 2
Nearest H2O: Elk Lake	**El:** 3720
Lndmk: Elk Lake	**RV:** No

Description: This site may not be the best campsite around the lake, but it does have a great view, and that's worth a lot.

Getting there: *(See map pg. 27)* Follow the directions to Site #28. Turn left onto FS4697 and drive a little over 6.5 miles on rutted, rocky FS4697 to Elk Lake. Site is about 0.3 mile beyond Elk Lake Creek.

Loc: FS46, 3.7 miles east of Detroit	**Road:** Paved, then dirt, 30'
L/L: N44 46 165/W122 05 596	**Access:** DTC, UOP
Cell: Detroit	**Tents:** 3–5
Nearest H2O: Breitenbush R., 0.1 mile	**El:** 1855
Lndmk: Bridge over the Breitenbush R., 0.1 mile SW	**RV:** MH and TT

Description: This site near Deadhorse Creek isn't wilderness camping, but it will work fine for those who want to be near the amenities of Detroit Lake.

Getting there: *(See map pg. 28)* From Detroit, drive 3.7 miles on FS46. About 0.1 mile after crossing the bridge over the Breitenbush, look for the campsite, about 30' off the north side of the road.

Loc: FS2223, French Creek, 1.1 mile from FS22	**Road:** Paved
L/L: N44 45 323/W122 09 642	**Access:** Park and Carry, about 20'
Cell: On road near camp, Detroit	**Tents:** Max of 2
Nearest H2O: French Creek, 20'	**El:** 1830
Lndmk: Junction, FS2223/SR22, 1.1 miles SSE	**RV:** No

Description: Besides being able to call home on your cell phone from the road above camp and its proximity to Detroit, this site has many charms for those interested in an actual camping experience. In spite of its nearness to FS2223, the spot is private, shady, cool and picturesque by virtue of its location in a steep-walled canyon directly above a small waterfall on French Creek. There are two disadvantages: First, you will probably need a rope to help you lower your gear down to the campsite, some ten to fifteen feet below the road bed. Secondly, the narrow, steep canyon will restrict exploration up and down the creek. This is one of those sites sandwiched between a road and a beautiful mountain stream. Put a smile on the faces of the next campers to use the place. Leave no trace. And POYP, please.

Getting there: *(See map pg. 27)* Follow OR 22 three-tenths of a mile NW of Detroit across the north arm of Detroit Lake. Turn right on FS2223 and drive 1.1 miles to site, on right. The site is difficult to see from the road, so keep a careful eye as you approach. Get there early. Any site this close to Detroit Lake going to be in demand during the prime camping months of summer.

Loc: On French Creek, 1.6 miles from OR 22 and near the FS2223/2225 junction	**Road:** Paved
	Access: Park and Carry, 50–100'
L/L: N44 45 599/W122 10 082	**Tents:** 3–4
Cell: Detroit or along FS2223	**El:** 1850
Nearest H2O: French Creek, near camp	**RV:** Small MH
Lndmk: FS2225 bridge	

Description: A well-shaded and private site under a canopy of alder trees along sometimes slow, sometimes fast, but always picturesque French Creek. This is another sandwich site, so be on your best and most responsible camping behavior.

Getting there: *(See map pg. 27)* On OR 22, just after crossing the north arm of Detroit Lake, 0.3 mile from the junction of OR 22 and FS46, turn right on FS2223 and drive 1.6 miles to site, on right and near the bridge. Park and carry gear some 50 to 100 feet on a wide, rocky path.

Loc: FS2225, 0.1 mile from FS2223	**Road:** Gravel, then dirt
L/L: N44 45 642/W122 10 039	**Access:** Park and carry, 100 yards, or so
Cell: On road near camp and in Detroit	**Tents:** 2–3
Nearest H2O: French Creek	**El:** 1850
Lndmk: Bridge over French Creek	**RV:** No

Description: Set in a clearing surrounded by tall conifers and densely growing alder trees, this campsite is located at the end of a dirt road that takes off from a low berm at the edge of FS2225. A faint trail out of camp peters out in the foliage long before it can reach French Creek, which is only 0.1 mile away via the road above camp. The site is virtually invisible from the road.

Getting there: *(See map pg. 27)* From FS46 near Detroit, drive 0.3 miles west on OR 22, then go right for 1.6 miles on FS2223 to its junction with FS2225. Cross the bridge and find campsite at 0.1 mile from FS2223 and below berm on the right. Park and carry gear about 100 yards to campsite in the trees below.

Loc: FS610 off FS2223, 7.1 miles from OR 22 and 3.1 miles from the end of paved FS2223.	**Road:** Dirt, primitive near Lake
	Access: Park and carry
L/L: N44 45 481/W122 13 130	**Tents:** 1–2
Cell: Detroit and along FS2223	**El:** 3970
Nearest H2O: Steel Creek on FS2223, 1.9 miles NW	**RV:** Use judgment with small MH
Lndmk: Dome Rock and Tumble Lake to the SE and SW	

View from Site 46 campsite

Description: *(overnight/emergency)* The brightly blooming rhododendrons and the surrounding mountains reflected in the still waters of this tiny unnamed mountain lake will have you groping for your camera before the car rolls to a stop, guaranteed. Whether you will want to linger the night is another question: The mud bottom and shallowness of the lake discourage swimming, while the lake itself, on closer inspection, appears to be stagnant. The short road dropping down to the lake is so steep as to be difficult to climb out of again without risking damage to your vehicle. And most of the ground at the edge of the lake is rocky and uneven, leaving room for but one small, two-person tent. There is scant shade to be found anywhere, so campers will have to find a way to provide their own in hot weather. The good news here is that you will be able to sit outside on warm summer nights and watch the universe wheeling overhead, making it an excellent site for watching the Perseid meteor showers that occur in late summer. There is a space above the lake that might accommodate a motorhome or two. Water? Try nearby creeks.

Getting there: *(See map pg. 27)* From FS46 near Detroit, drive 0.3 miles west on OR 22, then go right 7.1 miles on FS2223, climbing continually to Spur 610, which is 3.1 miles from the junction of FS2223/2207. Campsite is 0.1 mile from FS2223.

Loc: FS2209-310, near entrance to Opal Cr. Scenic Rec. Area	**Road:** Paved, then dirt
L/L: N44 50 328/W122 20 639	**Access:** Park and Carry
Cell: Probably along OR 22	**Tents:** 2–3
Nearest H2O: Local creeks	**El:** 1450
Lndmk: MP 14 and entrance to Opal Cr. Scenic Rec. Area	**RV:** Small MH or camper

Description: A waterless but secluded site that would be a good place to pitch your tent if darkness catches you just as you are entering the national forest. You will find three campsites on one side of the little access road with at least one tent site and fire ring each and another site at the end of the road, about a hundred yards further on. Most of the campsites here will probably be in need of some clean-up. Do your best to be part of the solution, and not part of the problem. The Little North Santiam winds through a deep canyon cut into solid rock here and for all practical purposes is inaccessible to bipeds.

Getting there: *(See map pg. 27)* From OR 22 look for the Gates Hill Road, which takes off to the north about 0.1 mile east of MP 33. Bear right at 3.7 miles, where Gates Hill Road intersects the North Fork Road, somewhere between the North Fork Road's MP 9 and 10. The North Fork Road turns into FS2209. Look for Spur 310, which cuts off to the right about 0.1 mile beyond MP 14, where the pavement ends and FS2209 enters the Opal Creek Recreation Area. Campsites are about 0.1 mile from FS2209.
Note: Sections of FS2209 are steep and washboard and may be difficult for a heavy vehicle or one with poor tires.

Loc: FS2209, near junction with FS2207	**Road:** Gravel, mountain
L/L: N44 50 714/W122 19 750	**Access:** Park and carry
Cell: Along OR 22	**Tents:** ?
Nearest H2O: Little N. Santiam R. or Dry Cr.	**El:** 1350, approximately
Lndmk: Junction FS2207/2209, 0.1 mile east of coordinates	**RV:** No

Description: A tantalizing but very secluded campsite at the end of a rough dirt track that drops steeply from FS2209. Unfortunately, I was unable to inspect the site due to the happy camper voices that told me that it was occupied. It's for you to find out if it's a gem or a lump of coal.

Getting there: *(See map pg. 27)* Follow the directions to Site #47. Continue on FS2209 another 1.2 miles past the entrance to the Opal Creek Recreation Area to a rough dirt track taking off downhill toward the river about 0.1 mile west of where FS2207 forks off to the right. Due to the steepness of the road, park near FS2209 and carry gear the rest of the way to camp.
Be sure to visit the Three Pools Day Use Area while you're in the area!

Loc: FR2209 at Tincup Creek	Road: Graveled. Sections are steep and wash boarded
L/L: N44 51 569/W122 16 540	Access: DTC, UOP
Cell: Along OR 22	Tents: 2 and 4–5
Nearest H2O: Tincup Cr., in camp	El: 1760
Lndmk: Trailhead #3356	RV: MH and TT, south side site only

Descriptions: *(A twofer)* You will find two nice campsites on opposite sides of the road here. The larger site is on the south side of FS2209. Both have easy access to the water of Tincup Creek.

Getting there: *(See map pg. 27)* Follow the directions to Site #47 and continue on FS2209. The site is approximately 4.8 miles past the FS2209/2207 junction, where Tincup Creek crosses the road, somewhere between MP 20 and 21. If you pass the sign announcing Trailhead #3356, you will have gone too far.

There are many fine campsites along FS2207, but also a lot of competition for them. Get there early.

Loc: FS2207, near FS2207/2209 junction	Road: Gravel, then dirt
L/L: N44 50 704/W122 19 607	Access: DTC, UOP
Cell: OR 22	Tents: 2–3
Nearest H2O: Little N. Santiam R., Dry Cr.	El: 1615
Lndmk: Junction FS2207/2209	RV: Use judgment with small MH

Description: Shade, privacy and solitude in a dry but comfortable camp on an unmarked road heading downhill from FS2207 about 200 yards beyond the junction of FS2207/2209. A small creek about a few hundred yards further on that must be Dry Creek may provide access to water for camp use, though it was just a tiny rill when discovered in early August. Site may need some light housekeeping, however.

Getting there: *(See map pg. 27)* Follow the directions to Site #47 and continue 1.3 miles past the entrance to the Opal Creek Recreation Area. Turn right onto FS2207. Site is on right, about 200 yards from the junction.

Loc: FS2207, about 0.4 mile from FS2209	Road: Gravel, then dirt
L/L: N44 50 617/W122 19 304	Access: Park and carry, 200 yards
Cell: OR 22	Tents: 2–3
Nearest H2O: Possibly Dry Creek	El: 1550
Lndmk: Dry Cr., 0.1 M. NW on FS2207	RV: Small MH

Description: Although I was unable to inspect this site closely, it appeared to be a delightful, secluded site near the river. There is a habitat protection area near the end of the road, which may be Spur 211.

Getting there: *(See map pg. 27)* Follow the directions to Site #47 and continue 1.3 miles past the entrance to the Opal Creek Recreation Area. Turn right onto FS2207. Take Spur 211 to the right at about 0.4 mile past the FS2207/2209 junction shortly after a sign that prohibits parking along FS2207 for the next mile. Tent sites are about 0.2 mile off of FS2207.

Loc: FS2207, 0.6 mile from junction with FS2209	**Road:** Gravel, then dirt
L/L: N44 50 467/W122 19 088	**Access:** Park and carry
Cell: OR 22	**Tents:** 6–10
Nearest H2O: Dry Creek, 0.4 M. NW on FS2207	**El:** 1425
Lndmk: Junction FS2207/2209, 0.6 M. NW	**RV:** Small MH

52

Pools like this one, near Site #52, are common along Cedar Creek and the Little North Santiam River.

Description: Three private and secluded campsites set among the trees and well above the river about 0.1 mile off the road. Each campsite is well-separated from the others and large enough for two to four tents. A wide path about 20 yards long leads down to a beautiful section of the Little North Santiam, though the last 40 to 50 feet are steep enough to require either scrambling or the use of a rope. Because of this difficulty, look to Dry Creek or another small creek for your water needs.

Getting there: *(See map pg. 27)* Follow the directions to Site #47 and continue 1.3 miles past the entrance to the Opal Creek Recreation Area. Turn right onto FS2207 and drive 0.6 mile. Park and go right 0.1 mile on Spur 213 to sites.

Campsites along Cedar Creek are very popular on weekends. Almost all of them are park and carry sites. Because they are mostly sandwiched between FS2207 and the Creek you should practice POYP here if you're going to practice it anywhere. Water for camp use is easily obtained from beautiful Cedar Creek at almost every campsite. The creek has hollowed out numerous picturesque pools in solid rock in its course through this steep canyon country.

Loc: FS2207, near Shady Cove Cg.	**Road:** Gravel
L/L: N44 50 743/W122 17 849	**Access:** Park and carry
Cell: OR 22	**Tents:** 1–2
Nearest H2O: Cedar Creek	**El:** 1445
Lndmk: Shady Cove Cg., 0.1 mile	**RV:** No

53

Description: A hidden, shady, comfortable camp about 30' below the road and close to where Cedar Creek flows into the Little North Santiam. The path to camp may be steep, so check it out first. If you choose this site, respect the fact that nearby Shady Grove Campground is a for-profit venture. If you're not paying for it, don't use it.

Getting there: *(See map pg. 27)* Follow the directions to Site #47 and continue another 1.3 miles beyond the entrance to the Opal Creek Recreation Area. Go right 2 miles on FS2207. Site is on left, just after the bridge over the Little North Santiam, barely a tenth of a mile past Shady Cove Campground.

Loc: On Cedar Creek near the Little N. Santiam R.	**Road:** Gravel, mountain
L/L: N44 50 743/W122 17 304	**Access:** Park and carry
Cell: OR 22	**Tents:** 2–3
Nearest H2O: Cedar Creek	**El:** 1580
Lndmk: Shady Cove Cg., 0.5 M. W	**RV:** No

Description: A comfortable and private camp on Cedar Creek.

Getting there: *(See map pg. 27)* Follow directions to site #50, then follow FS2207. Site is 0.4 mile beyond the Shady Cove Cg.

Loc: FS2207, 0.9 M. beyond Shady Grove Cg.	**Road:** Gravel, mountain
L/L: N44 50 850/W122 16 910	**Access:** Park and carry, short distance
Cell: OR 22	**Tents:** 2–3
Nearest H2O: Cedar Creek	**El:** 1605
Lndmk: Shady Cove Cg.	**RV:** No

Description: A Forest Service signpost marks the path to these picturesque campsites on Cedar Creek, which provide shade and access to several beautiful bedrock pools hollowed out by the creek over the millennia. A narrow shelf running close to the creek for a hundred yards or so would be a good for a larger party, especially if they happen to know each other fairly well.

Getting there: *(See map pg. 27)* Follow directions to site #50, then continue on FS2207. Site is 0.9 mile beyond Shady Cove Cg.

Loc: On Cedar Cr., 1.1 M. from Shady Cove Cg.	**Road:** Gravel, mountain
L/L: N44 50 836/W122 16 713	**Access:** Park and carry
Cell: OR 22	**Tents:** 2
Nearest H2O: Cedar Creek	**El:** 1660
Lndmk: Shady Cove Cg., 1.1 M. W	**RV:** No

Description: Very nice site at a bend in the road with shade and access to more picturesque pools in Cedar Creek. The path to the two tent sites is steep but negotiable. The first site is about 30' from the road.

Getting there: *(See map pg. 27)* Follow directions to site #50, then continue on FS2207. Site is 1.1 miles beyond Shady Cove Cg.

Loc: On Cedar Creek, 1.4 miles from Shady Cove Cg.	**Road:** Gravel, mountain
L/L: N44 50 695/W122 16 327	**Access:** Park and carry
Cell: OR 22	**Tents:** 1–2
Nearest H2O: Cedar Creek	**El:** 1815
Lndmk: Shady Cove Cg., 1.4 M. W	**RV:** No

Description: This campsite is closer to the road than most, but still sufficiently shielded from it by trees and undergrowth to feel private and secluded. Access to Cedar Creek and its enchanting pools is about 100 yards downhill from camp.

Getting there: *(See map pg. 27)* Follow directions to site #50, then continue on FS2207. Site is 1.4 miles beyond Shady Cove Cg., on left, some eight to ten feet below the level of the road.

(58)

Loc: Cedar Cr., 1.5 M. from Shady Cove Cg.	Road: Paved, mountain
L/L: N44 50 655/W122 16 214	Access: Park and carry
Cell: OR 22	Tents: 1–2
Nearest H2O: Cedar Creek	El: 1820
Lndmk: Sullivan Creek, 0.3 M. SE	RV: On road only

Sullivan Creek Falls on FS2207, 1.9 miles from Shady Cove Campground

Description: A short path leads to this small campsite at a bend in the road. Cedar Creek, though not visible from camp, is just a short distance away.

Getting there: *(See map pg. 27)* Follow directions to site #50, then continue on FS2207. Camp is 1.5 mile beyond Shady Cove Cg., on left. Sullivan Creek Falls is about 0.3 miles farther on.

(59)

Loc: On Cedar Creek, 1.7 mile from Shady Cove Cg.	Road: Gravel, mountain
L/L: N44 50 572/W122 16 058	Access: Park and carry, 100 yards
Cell: OR 22	Tents: 1–2
Nearest H2O: Cedar Creek	El: 1900
Lndmk: Sullivan Cr. Falls, 0.2 M. SE	RV: No

Description: A private, secluded and easy-to-reach spot made scenic by the presence of an impressive pool in the creek bed below.

Getting there: *(See map pg. 27)* Follow directions to site #50, then continue on FS2207. Camp is 1.7 miles beyond Shady Cove Cg., on left. Sullivan Creek Falls is about 0.2 mile further on, on the right.

Loc: On Cedar Creek, 0.9 mile past Sullivan Cr. Falls	**Road:** Gravel, mountain
L/L: N44 49 978/W122 15 259	**Access:** DTC, UOP
Cell: OR 22	**Tents:** 1–2
Nearest H2O: Cedar Creek	**El:** 2085
Lndmk: Bridge across Cedar Creek, 0.2 M. SE	**RV:** MH and TT

Description: If you crave a site right on the creek, this site about a hundred yards off the road on a rocky track, is for you.

Getting there: *(See map pg. 27)* Follow directions to site #50, then continue on FS2207. Camp is 2.7 miles beyond Shady Cove Cg., on left and about 0.9 miles past Sullivan Creek Falls.

Loc: On Cedar Cr., 2.8 miles past Shady Cove Cg.	**Road:** Gravel, mountain
L/L: N44 49 942/W122 15 179	**Access:** Park and carry
Cell: OR 22	**Tents:** 1–2
Nearest H2O: Cedar Creek	**El:** 2125
Lndmk: Bridge across Cedar Cr., 0.2 M. SE	**RV:** No

Description: Another small but beautiful site on Cedar Creek.

Getting there: *(See map pg. 27)* Follow directions to site #50, then continue on FS2207. Camp is 2.8 miles beyond Shady Cove Campground, on left and about 1 mile past Sullivan Creek Falls. Campsite is about ten feet below the road along a steep path, about 30' long.

Loc: On Cedar Creek, 0.1 M. past Cedar Creek Bridge	**Road:** Gravel, mountain
L/L: N44 49 854/W122 14 975	**Access:** DTC, UOP
Cell: OR 22	**Tents:** 1–2
Nearest H2O: Cedar Creek	**El:** 2180
Lndmk: Cedar Creek Bridge, 0.1 mile NW	**RV:** Use judgment with MH and TT

Description: Another of the many sites along Cedar Creek. This one appears to have easy access to the creek and provides more seclusion from the road than most.

Getting there: *(See map pg. 27)* Follow directions to site #50, then continue on FS2207. Camp is 3.0 miles beyond Shady Cove Campground, on right and about 1.2 miles past Sullivan Creek Falls.

Loc: FS2207, 0.3 mile past Cedar Cr. Bridge	**Road:** Gravel, mountain
L/L: N44 49 776/W122 14 832	**Access:** DTC, UOP
Cell: OR 22	**Tents:** 1–2
Nearest H2O: Cedar Creek at Bridge	**El:** 2445
Lndmk: Cedar Cr. Bridge, 0.3 mile NW	**RV:** Small MH

Description: Another site that offers almost everything but running water. It would make a nice weekend campsite for those who arrive too late to stake a claim on Cedar Creek.

Getting there: *(See map pg. 27)* Follow directions to site #50, then continue on FS2207. Camp is 3.2 miles beyond Shady Cove Campground and about 1.3 miles past Sullivan Creek Falls, on left. Look for a dirt track leading 100 yards back into the trees.

Loc: OR 22, about 1.6 miles SE of Detroit		**Road:** Paved	
L/L: N44 43 325/W122 07 821		**Access:** Park and carry, about 150'	
Cell: Detroit and possibly around the lake itself		**Tents:** 3–4	
Nearest H20: Either the Santiam R., below camp or Hansen Creek, about 400 feet SE		**El:** 1725	
		RV: No	
Lndmk: Hansen Creek, 400 feet SE			

Description: A well-shaded camp set in scattered tall conifers on the NE arm of Detroit Lake. This area is too desirable and too near to Detroit not to be in demand, so be warned that it attracts a lot of fun seekers.

Getting there: *(See map pg. 27)* Head southeast on OR 22 from the junction at Detroit with FS46. Campsite is off the road to the right at about 1.6 miles and just prior to Hansen Creek, between MP 51 and 52.

Loc: Blowout Rd. (FS10)		**Road:** Gravel, mountain	
L/L: N44 41 942/W122 11 210		**Access:** Park and carry, 100–200 yds.	
Cell: Detroit and around Detroit Lake		**Tents:** 4–5	
Nearest H20: Detroit Lk., Sauers Cr., 1.5 M. NE		**El:** 1659	
Lndmk: Southshore Cg., 0.9 M. NE		**RV:** No	

Description: Here are several tent sites scattered along a steep dirt road meandering downhill through the trees. All sites are shaded but breezy because of their location overlooking the lake. Getting water from the lake back to camp might be difficult. You may choose to fetch it from nearby Sauers Creek, about a mile and a half NE on FS10, and carry it downhill from the road a couple of hundred yards instead.

Getting there: *(See map pg. 29)* Coming from Detroit, turn right onto Blowout Road just after MP 53 and drive 5.3 miles. Park near a large rock barricade on the right and carry gear downhill on a short, steep, dirt road. Find campsites to the right and left of where the road splits, a couple of hundred feet from the rock barricade.

Loc: FS10, just past Site #65		**Road:** Paved	
L/L: N44 41 887/W122 11 250		**Access:** DTC, UOP	
Cell: In camp		**Tents:** 1–2	
Nearest H20: Sauers Cr., 1.6 M. NE		**El:** 1590	
Lndmk: Southshore Cg., 1 M. NE		**RV:** MH and TT	

Description: With its tantalizing view of the lake through the trees, this site, on a bluff overlooking the lake, is ideal for a self-contained RV. There is cell reception in camp. A steep trail (bring a rope) leads downslope about 200 yards to the rocky shore of the lake.

Getting there: *(See map pg. 29)* Coming from Detroit, turn right onto Blowout Road just after MP 53, and drive 5.4 miles. Site is a little over a hundred yards beyond site #65.

Loc: Blowout Rd. (FS10)	Road: Paved
L/L: N44 41 789/W122 11 510	Access: DTC, UOP
Cell: Detroit (and maybe around Lake)	Tents: 1–2
Nearest H20: Sauers Cr., 1.8 mile NE	El: 1595
Lndmk: Southshore Cg., 1.2 M. NE	RV: MH and TT

Description: Though just a few feet off paved Blowout Road, this site is ideal for a self-contained RV. It provides an excellent view of the lake through the trees. As with most of the sites above the lake here, water must be fetched elsewhere.

Getting there: *(See map pg. 29)* Coming from Detroit, turn right onto Blowout Road (FS10) just after MP 53, and drive 5.6 miles to site, on right.

Loc: FS10-130	Road: Gravel
L/L: N44 40 974/W122 11 501	Access: DTC, UOP
Cell: In camp	Tents: 5-6?
Nearest H20: Local creeks	El: 1635
Lndmk: Junction FS10/130	RV: MH and TT

View down south arm of Detroit Lake from site #68

Description: A wide spot in the road on a bluff with a commanding view of the southern arm of the lake. Ideal for an RV. The road here expands to around 100 feet in width.

Getting there: *(See map pg. 29)* Coming from Detroit, turn right onto Blowout Road (FS10) just after MP 53, and drive 6.7 miles to Spur 130, which forks off to the right. Go 0.2 mile to where road widens out to around a hundred feet.

Loc: FS10-130	Road: Gravel
L/L: N44 40 568/W122 10 941	Access: Park and carry, short distance
Cell: Detroit (and possibly around Lake)	Tents: 7-10
Nearest H20: Small creek near camp	El: 1595
Lndmk: FS10/130 Junction, 0.9 miles NW	RV: MH and TT, on road only

Description: *(a twofer)* Two or three comfortable campsites just off the side of lightly traveled Spur 130 that will accommodate a number of tents, with room for a relatively large party to spread out in the largest of the three. A small and possibly intermittent creek near camp may be a source of water for camp use. If not, try the unnamed creek about a half a mile further on.

Getting there: *(See map pg. 29)* Coming from Detroit, turn right onto Blowout Road (FS10) just after MP 53, and drive 6.7 miles to Spur 130, which forks off to the right. Go 0.9 mile to site, on right, about 0.2 mile past Trail #3426.

Loc: North shore of Blowout Creek at the end of spur 068	**Road:** Dirt, primitive
L/L: N44 39 282/W122 08 036	**Access:** DTC, UOP
Cell: Detroit	**Tents:** 2–3
Nearest H20: Blowout Creek	**El:** 1820
Lndmk: Junction FS10-068	**RV:** Small MH or TT

Description: A gem! Someone has taken great care to make this creekside campsite at the end of the road a pleasant place to stay. An excellent and well-made fire ring has been excavated into the center of an eight-foot circular area overlooking the creek that has been flattened to make it possible to sit by the fire and watch the creek slide by. Steps dug into the creek's bank make it easier to get to the water. Trees provide cooling shade and shelter. There is a deeper and slower section of the creek near camp. In short, Shangri-La in the forest. May it be waiting for you.

Getting there: *(See map pg. 29)* Driving south from Detroit on OR 22, turn right onto FS10 just past MP53. Follow FS10 (Blowout Road) approximately 11 miles. Fork right where FS10 splits off from FS1011. Crossing the bridge and driving another 0.6 miles, turn right on Spur 068 and drive north 0.6 mile after crossing a dilapidated old wooden bridge. Site is visible on the right as you approach the creek.

Loc: Spur 068, on Cliff Creek	**Road:** Dirt, primitive
L/L: N44 39 181/W122 08 049	**Access:** DTC, UOP
Cell: Detroit	**Tents:** 1–2
Nearest H20: Cliff Creek, about 0.1 mile	**El:** 1840
Lndmk: Junction FS10/068	**RV:** On road only

Description: This site is a tad uneven, but undeniably pleasant, shady, and private, since Spur 068, which is blocked by a gate a few hundred yards further on, gets very little traffic. It's location on a bluff about fifteen feet above the creek makes access to the water all but impossible.

Getting there: *(See map pg. 29)* Driving south from Detroit on OR 22, turn right onto FS10 just past MP53. Follow FS10 (Blowout Road) approximately 11 miles. Fork right where FS10 splits off from FS1011. Crossing the bridge and driving another 0.6 miles, turn right on Spur 068 and drive north 0.5 mile after crossing a dilapidated old wooden bridge. Site is visible on right, just where Spur 068 starts to curve to the left.

Loc: Blowout Creek, at FS1011/1012 Junction	Road: Gravel
L/L: N44 39 182/W122 07 830	Access: DTC, UOP
Cell: Detroit	Tents: 10–15
Nearest H2O: Blowout Creek	El: 1910
Lndmk: FS1012 bridge over Blowout Cr.	RV: MH and TT

Description: *(a threefer)* At least two of these three sites clustered around the bridge over Blowout Creek are great for RV camping. Of the three, the one on the east side of the creek downstream from the bridge is easily the most appealing, with a densely shaded fire ring close to the creek. The campsite upstream of the bridge is more open to the sun. Campers at all three will enjoy pools deep enough for a summer soak in this creek, which seems to run a little warmer than most mountain creeks in the Forest.

Getting there: *(See map pg. 29)* Driving south from Detroit on OR 22, turn right onto FS10 just past MP53. Follow FS10 (Blowout Road) approximately 11 miles. Sites are on the right and across the bridge, to the left.

Loc: Near bridge at FS1011/1012 junction	Road: Gravel
L/L: N44 39 140/W122 07 792	Access: DTC, UOP
Cell: Detroit	Tents: 5–6
Nearest H2O: Blowout Creek	El: 1860
Lndmk: FS10/1012 Bridge over Blowout Creek	RV: MH and TT

Description: There are two campsites here, one large and one small. Both lack privacy from the road but give access to an entirely charming section of Blowout creek. Sites are somewhat open to the sun, but there is also shade among the maple and alder trees. These are not prime sites. A lot of campers are attracted to this stretch of Blowout Creek during the peak months of summer, and if you find yourself arriving late, this is one of those sites most likely to still be available.

Getting there: *(See map pg. 29)* Driving south from Detroit on OR 22, turn right onto FS10 just past MP53. Follow FS10 (Blowout Road) approximately 11 miles. Sites are on right, a couple of hundred feet past the FS1012 bridge.

Loc: On Blowout Creek	Road: Gravel
L/L: N44 38 877/W122 07 366	Access: Park and carry over berm
Cell: Detroit	Tents: 5–6
Nearest H2O: Blowout Cr., 100'	El: 1805
Lndmk: Junction FS1011/1012, 0.5 mile	RV: No

Description: A sunny, grassy glade separated from the road by a six-foot berm, with room for several tents. The nearby creek, shallow and pleasantly murmuring, is reached through a densely shaded tunnel under tall conifer and maple trees.

Getting there: *(See map pg. 29)* Driving south from Detroit on OR 22, turn right onto FS10 just past MP53. Follow FS10 (Blowout Road) approximately 11 miles, staying to the left on FS1011 another 0.5 mile past where it splits off from FS10. Park where you see the berm and schlep gear to camp, on right.

Loc: FS1011, on Divide Creek	**Road:** Gravel, then dirt
L/L: N44 38 789/W122 07 200	**Access:** DTC, UOP
Cell: Detroit	**Tents:** 5–6
Nearest H2O: Divide Creek	**El:** 1960
Lndmk: FS1011/1012 junction, 0.7 mile NW	**RV:** Small MH

Description: *(a twofer)* There are 2-3 well-shaded campsites scattered among the large conifer trees populating this relatively flat and private area between the road and the creek. Divide Creek provides just the right decibel level of happy, white noise for either sound sleep or contemplative thought. The shore of the creek is mostly smooth, waterworn stones with a bit of sandy beach here and there. A few hundred yards downstream where the creek has cut its course through solid bedrock, there is a clear pool for those hardy few who welcome a cold swim on hot days.

Getting there: *(See map pg. 29)* Driving south from Detroit on OR 22, turn right onto FS10 just past MP53. Follow FS10 (Blowout Road) approximately 11 miles. Stay left on FS1011 where FS1012 turns right and crosses the creek. Continue another 0.7 mile, where a dirt road takes off through the trees to the right for 0.1 mile to camp.

Loc: Where FS1011 crosses Divide Creek	**Road:** Gravel
L/L: N44 38 671/W122 06 792	**Access:** DTC, UOP or park and carry
Cell: Detroit	**Tents:** 6–8
Nearest H2O: Divide Creek	**El:** 2020
Lndmk: FS1011 Bridge over Divide Cr.	**RV:** Steep entry. Use judgment with small MH.

Description: The good and the not so good: There is room for plenty of tents in camp and along the bank of the creek and downstream. The site was relatively clean when discovered in 2013. The breeze can still be heard stirring the trees above the pleasant gurgling of Divide Creek. The downsides are that there may not be much privacy from the cars passing by on the nearby bridge, from which the camp is briefly visible, though FS1011 is not a busy road. The SE to NW orientation of the creek may expose this camp to the sun in July and August. The creek is at the bottom of a ten-foot bank and is not easy to reach from camp.

Getting there: *(See map pg. 29)* Camp is 0.4 mile beyond Site #76. Turn sharply right just after crossing the bridge. The short road into camp is initially steep. It might be a good idea to inspect this camp from the road first or to park and carry your gear.

Loc: OR 22, between MP 56 and 57, by Cooper's Ridge Road Bridge	**Road:** Paved, then dirt track
	Access: Check MVUM
L/L: N44 41 600/W122 02 986	**Tents:** 10–20
Cell: Detroit and in camp (4 bars)	**El:** 1895
Nearest H2O: Small creek on the west end of campsite	**RV:** MH and TT
Lndmk: Coopers Ridge Road Bridge (to FS2234)	

Description: A large camping area with space for several RV's or many tents. A path leads to the Santiam, but clear water for camp use is also available from a lively little rill flowing along the west end of the campsite.

In 2013, this place was surprisingly clean for being so close to the highway, but don't be surprised if that has changed when you get there. The sleepy little town of Idanha is less than a mile away and has a quaint little restaurant and general store that can probably supply you with whatever you forgot to bring from home, including lunch.

Getting there: *(See map pg. 30)* Drive southeast from Detroit on OR 22. Turn right into campsite about 0.3 mile past MP 56 and just past the Cooper Ridge Road (FS2234) Bridge. Campsite is 100 yards off SR22. Check MVUM before driving into this site.

Loc: On Whitewater Creek, 0.7 mile from OR 22	**Road:** Gravel, then path
L/L: N44 48 148/W121 57 928	**Access:** Park and carry
Cell: Detroit and near Coopers Ridge Road Bridge	**Tents:** 15–20
Nearest H2O: Whitewater Creek	**El:** 2110
Lndmk: Junction OR 22/FS2243, 0.6 mile	**RV:** No

Description: On a sunny afternoon this site in a cathedral-like grove of enormous fir and cedar trees near the creek will render you into a state of mute reverence when you first come upon it. It has everything any camper could wish for and can accommodate a large group with its many level tent sites and several comfortable benches scattered around a communal fire pit. Just downstream, there is evidence of an ancient logging operation, though the executioner seems to have spared the giant conifers that make this camp so spectacular. A network of trails allows the hiker to explore up and down the river. Upstream and blocked by a metal gate at the end of the short unmarked road, you will find a lodge that is locked and shuttered but in good condition. There are many flat tent sites in the surrounding woods The downside is that this camp can only be reached via a footpath about 0.1 mile long that leads in from a dirt road where there is limited parking.

Getting there: *(See map pg. 30)* Driving southeast on OR 22 from Detroit, turn left onto FS2243 between MP 60 and 61. Drive 0.6 mile on FS2243 to a short, unmarked road leading off to the right. Park near an opening in the Forest where a trail takes off through the trees. Follow the trail about 0.1 mile to a point where the site will suddenly appear on a shelf above the river below you. The last few feet down to the shelf are very steep, which will make getting gear to the campsite difficult. It would be a good idea to bring a rope.

Loc: On Whitewater Creek, off FS2243	**Road:** Gravel, then dirt
L/L: N44 40 941/W121 57 436	**Access:** DTC, UOP
Cell: Detroit and near Coopers Ridge Road Bridge	**Tents:** 3–4
Nearest H2O: Whitewater Creek	**El:** 2360
Lndmk: Junction OR 22/FS2243, 1.1 mile	**RV:** MH and TT

Description: The slate-gray turbidity and icy temperature of mighty Whitewater Creek give away its source in the Jefferson Park and Russell Glaciers, some eight miles to the east. The creek, which courses swiftly past camp in a more or less straight trajectory toward the Santiam, carries a volume of water more appropriate to a small river and provides enough white noise for sound sleep, but not enough to drown out polite conversation. Water for camp use can be accessed just upstream and at another point about 200' downstream, though some scrambling will be involved in either case. Parties with children should think twice about camping here, due to the swiftness of the water.

Getting there: *(See map pg. 30)* Driving southeast on OR 22 from Detroit, turn left onto SR2243 between MP 60 and 61. A dirt road to the right at about 1.1 miles from OR 22 leads to the site, about 150' from FS2243 and some ten feet above the creek.

Loc: 200 yards off FS2243 and 1.7 miles ENE of OR 22	**Road:** Gravel, then dirt
L/L: N44 41 107/W121 56 842	**Access:** DTC, UOP, Check MVUM
Cell: Detroit and near Coopers Ridge Road Bridge	**Tents:** 1–2
Nearest H2O: Whitewater Creek	**El:** 2460
Lndmk: FS2243/spur430 junction, 0.8 mile NE	**RV:** Small MH

Description: A temptingly private little camp at the end of a short unmarked and primitive little lane curving some 200 yards from FS2243 through alder shrubs and fern to a rustic little sunken fire pit lined with stones. The small size of this well-shaded campsite practically guarantees solitude to whoever is lucky enough to get there first. I noticed very few mosquitoes in the area, possibly because of the swiftness of Whitewater Creek, which is about a hundred yards away through the trees. In spite of the paucity of tent sites here, there is ample room for a small motorhome (though not much room for turning around a travel trailer). Look for a small soaking pool upstream.

Getting there: *(See map pg. 30)* Driving southeast on OR 22 from Detroit, turn left onto SR2243 between MP 60 and 61. Drive 1.7 miles ENE on FS2243 to an unmarked dirt track leading to site, on right.

Loc: Spur 440, about 0.3 miles from FS2243	**Road:** Dirt, primitive
L/L: N44 41 559/W121 56 014	**Access:** DTC, UOP, Check MVUM
Cell: Detroit and near Coopers Ridge Road Bridge	**Tents:** 4–5
Nearest H2O: Whitewater Creek	**El:** 2510
Lndmk: FS2243/spur430 junction, 0.3 mile	**RV:** Use judgment with small MH

Description: A site that is so remote, shaded and private that you won't feel at all shy about talking to the trees or letting out your pent-up silliness in some other way. A trail leading upstream gives access to Whitewater Creek, which probably runs even faster here than it does down below.

Getting there: *(See map pg. 30)* Driving southeast on OR 22 from Detroit, turn left onto SR2243 between MP 60 and 61. Drive 2.4 miles and follow Spur 440 where it splits off to the right for 0.2 mile. At that point, take a primitive dirt track through the trees to the right for 0.1 mile to campsite. Check MVUM before driving. *SR2243 starts to ascend more steeply past its junction with Spur 440.*

Loc: On Whitewater Creek, off spur 460	**Road:** Gravel, then dirt
L/L: N44 41 770/W121 52 682	**Access:** DTC, UOP, Check MVUM
Cell: Detroit and near Coopers Ridge Road Bridge	**Tents:** 3–4, smaller
Nearest H2O: Whitewater Cr., 100 yards	**El:** 3380
Lndmk: Junction 2243/spur460	**RV:** MH and TT, but just off FS2243

Description: A shady campsite with a definite sub-alpine feel at the end of the road and just a few feet from Whitewater Creek, which is much smaller here than below its confluence with Russell Creek, a little less than a mile downstream. This site is about as comfortable, secure and private as any you are going to find in this forest without resorting to a pack animal. A good place for just soaking up the surrounding tranquility, but you probably won't find much to do here beyond what you bring with you. There is a flat spot for a small RV just after you turn onto Spur 460 and a tiny creek on the right side of the road about 0.1 mile from FS2243 for those who would prefer that.

Mount Jefferson from FS2243

Getting there: *(See map pg. 30)* Driving southeast on OR 22 from Detroit, turn left onto SR2243 between MP 60 and 61. Drive on FS2243 for about 5.7 miles to where Spur 460 splits off to the right, then go 0.2 mile on rough road to site, at the end of the road. Check MVUM before driving.

FS2243 starts to climb steeply after Spur 440 at 2.4 miles. **There is room for several tents or a self-contained RV or two at Cheat Creek, around 3.6 miles from OR 22.**

84

Loc: OR 22-047, 0.9 mile S of MP61	Road: Dirt
L/L: N44 40 854/W121 58 327	Access: DTC, UOP
Cell: Detroit and bridge between MP 56 and 57	Tents: 25–50
Nearest H2O: Probably Whitewater Cr., 1.1 miles N	El: 2275
Lndmk: MP 62, 0.1 mile	RV: MH and TT, Use judgment

Description: A huge three-quarter mile-long site offers everything but a drink of water! Many campsites, including at least three multi-tent sites, line the forest road that winds to the back end of the site. All are shaded, private and secluded. Caution should be used when camping with children anywhere near the bluff where Spur 047 ends. For water, I suggest Whitewater Creek, about a mile north on OR 22. The amenities of civilization are close by here: about 12 miles back to Detroit and a little over five to the restaurant at Marion Forks, which has to be experienced if you're in the area.

Getting there: *(See map pg. 30)* Coming south from Detroit on OR 22, turn right onto Spur 047 at 0.9 miles past MP 61, and you are there. Spur 047 meanders about 0.7 mile through tall trees, running parallel to OR 22 to the back of the area overlooking the bluff.

85

Loc: FS2246, 0.4 M. from Pamelia Lk. Trailhead	Road: Gravel
L/L: N44 39 573/W121 59 283	Access: Check MVUM
Cell: Detroit and bridge between MP 56 and 57	Tents: 2–3
Nearest H2O: Milk Cr.	El: 2880
Lndmk: Pamelia Lk. Trailhead, 0.4 M	RV: Small MH or TT

Description: *(Overnight/Emergency)* The lack of privacy and dust from cars passing by on FS2246 render this otherwise charming spot a campsite of last resort. It does offer convenient access to Milk Creek for water, however.

Getting there: *(See map pg. 30)* Coming south from Detroit, turn left (east) onto FS2246 about halfway between MP 62 and 63. Drive 3 miles to site, near the point where Milk Creek crosses under the road.

Loc: FS2255, 1 mile from OR 22	Road: Dirt, steep in one spot
L/L: N44 36 192/W121 56 287	Access: Park and carry
Cell: Detroit and bridge between MP 56 and 57	Tents: 3–4
Nearest H2O: Marion Creek, 2–300 yards through woods	El: 2595
Lndmk: Willis Creek, 0.1 mile south	RV: Road too steep

Description: Camp on a grassy clearing at the end of a dirt track. The site is open to the midday sun, but evening will find it shady and relatively cool. Marion Creek, which is more wild river than creek, especially this close to its confluence with the Santiam, is easily audible through the trees, but not easy to reach. This isn't one of the more memorable camps along the Creek, but it will serve the purpose when you need a place to pitch your tent.

Getting there: *(See map pg. 30)* Coming south from Detroit on OR 22, turn left onto FS2255 at Marion Forks (between MP 66 and 67). Drive 1mile SSE. Look for an unmarked dirt track leading off to the right. Park and carry from this point. Campsite is about 200 yards from FS2255.

Loc: FS2255, between Willis Creek and Spur 713	Road: Gravel
L/L: N44 36 049/W121 56 194	Access: Park and carry
Cell: Detroit	Tents: 3–4
Nearest H2O: Marion Creek or nearby Willis Cr.	El: 2680
Lndmk: FS2255/713 junction, 0.1 miles SSE	RV: Use judgment

Description: A comfortable but waterless camp in a circular clearing enclosing an island of trees. Though the sound of nearby Marion Creek is plainly audible through the trees, no trail leading to the water was in evidence on the day this site was discovered.

Getting there: *(See map pg. 30)* Coming south from Detroit on OR 22, turn left onto FS2255 at Marion Forks (between MP 66 and 67). Drive 1.2 miles and look for an unmarked road leading to the right, toward the Creek. Camp is about 100 yards in from the road.

Loc: FS2255, near Puzzle Cr.	Road: Gravel
L/L: N44 35 614/W121 55 743	Access: Park and carry, 200 yds
Cell: Detroit and bridge between MP 56 and 57	Tents: 3–4
Nearest H2O: Marion Cr.	El: 2730
Lndmk: FS2255/720 split, 0.2 M. N of site	RV: In pull-out near road only

Description: A gem of a campsite that is completely hidden in the trees next to the creek, some 200 yards off the road! You'll want to check this place out if at all possible. There is abundant shade from the large trees overhead, but the camp is still somewhat open to the sun. Flattish rocks near the fire pit serve as tables and work surfaces. Marion Creek announces itself in a pleasant tenor through the trees, but it is neither visible nor easy to reach from camp. Nevertheless, a small offshoot of the creek just feet from camp provides a convenient source of camp water.

Getting there: *(See map pg. 30)* Coming south from Detroit on OR 22, turn left onto FS2255 at Marion Forks (between MP 66 and 67). Drive 1.8 miles to pull-out, on right, just past Spur 720 and 722, which take off to the left. Park in pull-out and schlep gear some 200 yards, crossing a small creek about 100 feet from the pull-out. Follow a faint trail, which curves to the right to campsite.

Loc: FS2255, near Puzzle Cr.	**Road:** Gravel
L/L: N44 35 279/W121 55 053	**Access:** Park and carry
Cell: Detroit and bridge between MP 56 and 57	**Tents:** 2
Nearest H2O: Puzzle or Marion Creek	**El:** 2740
Lndmk: Puzzle Creek Bridge	**RV:** No

Description: A small site sandwiched into the confluence of two powerful and fast-flowing creeks, there is dense shade from the cedar and alder trees that line the campsite all around, almost to the point of claustrophobia. The roar created by the two creeks plunging through steep, mountain terrain creates considerable noise from the right and left.

There is an elevated level spot on the opposite side of the bridge that would be ideal for a tent or two, as well, though there is no fire ring here.

*Due to the fast, strong current of the creeks, parties with young children should probably pass on this site.

Getting there: *(See map pg. 30)* Coming south from Detroit on OR 22, turn left onto FS2255 at Marion Forks (between MP 66 and 67). Drive 2.5 miles to site, on right, just past the bridge over Puzzle Creek. Park on road.

Loc: FS2255, 100 yards from FS2255/730 junction	**Road:** Gravel, then dirt
L/L: N44 35 121/W121 54 901	**Access:** Park and carry
Cell: Detroit and bridge between MP 56 and 57	**Tents:** 4–5
Nearest H2O: Marion Creek near camp or at Spur 820 Bridge	**El:** 2720
Lndmk: FS2225/730 junction, 100 yards	**RV:** Use judgment w/small MH

Description: A dry camp set among colossal, neck-bending fir trees on the opposite side of the road from Marion Creek. Privacy from traffic passing on the road, which is about 100' away, is limited, due to the openness of the forest here.

Getting there: *(See map pg. 30)* Coming south from Detroit on OR 22, turn left onto FS2255 at Marion Forks (between MP 66 and 67). Drive 2.7 miles to site, on left, just before Spur 730 splits off to the left. Park and carry gear.

Loc: FS2255 (Marion Creek Rd.)	Road: Gravel
L/L: N44 34 854/W121 55 070	Access: Park and carry
Cell: Detroit	Tents: 2
Nearest H2O: Marion Creek	El: 2910
Lndmk: Bridge where Spur 820 crosses Marion Cr., 0.1 M. NE	RV: Small MH and TT

Description: Located in a very private clearing near a curve in the road, this is probably the best campsite in the immediate area. Marion Creek, which runs fast and strong here, sounds more river-like than a creek should, but is nevertheless easily reached for camp water. The relatively narrow 40-foot, tree-lined dirt track leading into camp practically guarantees privacy from the few motorists passing by on their way to the trailhead to Marion Lake in the Mount Jefferson Wilderness, a few miles away. If you are too tired to cook, you can always enjoy a good meal at the scenic Marion Forks Restaurant, just three miles back down the road on OR 22.

Getting there: *(See map pg. 30)* Coming south from Detroit on OR 22, turn left onto FS2255 at Marion Forks (between MP 66 and 67). Drive 3.1 miles to site, on right, where road begins to curve left and climb steeply.

Loc: Presley Lk. on FS2257-515-516	Road: Gravel, mountain
L/L: N44 34 961/W121 56 518	Access: Park and carry
Cell: Detroit and bridge between MP 56 and 57	Tents: 1–2, small
Nearest H2O: Somewhere else	El: 3450
Lndmk: Marion Forks, 4 miles N	RV: No

Description: Presley Lake, though picturesque, isn't the mountain lake of everybody's dreams, though making your camp here is probably a guarantee of isolation, solitude, and privacy. Since the lake has was no visible inlet or outlet, those who decide to camp here should procure their water elsewhere.

Getting there: *(See map pg. 30)* Coming south from Detroit on OR 22, turn left onto FS2257 near MP 67 and about 0.5 miles beyond Marion Forks. Drive around 2.8 miles on steeply ascending FS2257, watching for the lake, which can be seen through the trees to the left and below the road. Watch for Spur 515, taking off to the left. Camp is about 0.2 mile from FS2257. Spur 515 is very steep in places. Driving on it with a passenger vehicle is not recommended. Use caution and judgment.

Loc: FS2234, 0.2 mile from OR 22 on Bugaboo Cr.	Road: Paved, then dirt
L/L: N44 35 890/W121 58 264	Access: DTC, UOP, Check MVUM
Cell: Detroit and bridge between MP 56 and 57	Tents: 1
Nearest H2O: Bugaboo Cr.	El: 2270
Lndmk: MP 68 on OR 22, about 0.4 M by road	RV: Small MH or tent camper

Description: An inviting little camp perched on an abrupt bank above Bugaboo Creek under alders and big leaf maple trees. Two pools of clear mountain water, created out of river rock, slow the descent of the creek to a pleasant gurgle. Water is readily available upstream, but the drop to the creek is a sheer ten feet near camp.

Getting there: *(See map pg. 30)* Headed south on OR 22, turn right onto FS2234 about 0.8 miles after MP 67. Drive 0.2 miles to camp, on left, at a curve in the road.

Loc: At junction OR 22/FS11	Road: Paved, gravel, dirt
L/L: N44 34 965/W121 58 993	Access: Check MVUM
Cell: Detroit and bridge between MP 56 and 57	Tents: 25–50
Nearest H2O: North Santiam R.	El: 2670
Lndmk: Junction OR 22/FS11	RV: MH and TT

Description: In 2013, these campsites in a roadside grove of conifer trees were too close to the highway and too trashed to be an appealing destination campsite. Nevertheless, the on and off convenience of the place combined with its easy access to the river might tempt the road-weary traveler to pitch his or her tent or set up an RV here for the night. The area measures roughly 75 yards wide by 150 yards long, front to back. Campsites are not visible from the road, but the noise of the traffic passing by on busy OR 22 is easily audible in camp. There is a smaller camping area with one fire ring on the other side of FS11 for tent camping only, the entrance to which is blocked by large rocks. This site has less privacy from OR 22 than the site on the downstream side of the FS11. If you stay at either of these two sites, please take your trash and a little bit of someone else's with you when you leave.

Getting there: *(See map pg. 30)* Coming south from Detroit on OR 22, turn right (west) onto FS11 between MP 69 and 70. Do not cross the bridge, but turn immediately right and park. You will be able to select from a number of campsites, each with at least one pre-existing fire pit.

Loc: Near FS11/OR 22 junction, just across the bridge	Road: Dirt
L/L: N44 34 756/W121 59 036	Access: Park and carry
Cell: Detroit and bridge between MP 56 and 57	Tents: 20–25
Nearest H2O: N. Santiam R.	El: 2720
Lndmk: Junction FS11/OR 22	RV: MH and TT

Description: Here you will find numerous campsites scattered among the trees along and beyond a rough dirt track that takes off from FS11 (aka the Quartzville Back Country Byway). Some you will find clean and pristine, and some not. Access to the North Santiam is easy from almost all of these campsites. And, while the sounds of the traffic on OR 22 are still audible, these campsites are completely secluded from it by the intervening forest and the river.

Getting there: *(See map pg. 30)* Coming south from Detroit on OR 22, turn right (west) onto FS11 between MP 69 and 70 and go 0.1 mile to a rough dirt road leading off to the left for 0.2 mile to campsites. Park and carry from FS11.

Loc: OR 22, 0.3 mile south of FS11	Road: Paved
L/L: N44 34 678/W121 58 993	Access: Park and carry
Cell: Detroit and bridge between MP 56 and 57	Tents: 2–3
Nearest H2O: Santiam R.	El: 2900
Lndmk: FS 11, 0.3 mile N	RV: MH and TT

Description: Though the site may be cursed with carelessly left litter, the river beyond the habitat railings erected by the Forest Service remains primeval and compelling.

Getting there: *(See map pg. 30)* Coming south from Detroit, continue a little over 0.3 M. past FS11 near MP 70. Site is on right.

Loc: OR 22, about 0.3 miles south of FS11	Road: Paved, then dirt
L/L: N44 34 731/W121 58 978	Access: Park and carry
Cell: Detroit and bridge between MP 56 and 57	Tents: 2–3
Nearest H2O: Santiam R.	El: 2890
Lndmk: OR 22/FS11 junction, about 0.3 mile north	RV: No. Entrance too steep

Description: A campsite that may be too close to busy Route 22 for some. The river can be reached by negotiating a jumble of logs a couple hundred feet away.

Getting there: *(See map pg. 30)* Coming south from Detroit, continue 0.3 M. past FS11 near MP 70. Site is on right, a hundred yards north of Site #97.

Loc: On Downing Cr, off OR 22	Road: Paved, then dirt track
L/L: N44 34 583/W121 58 980	Access: Park and carry
Cell: Detroit and bridge between MP 56 and 57	Tents: 5–10
Nearest H2O: Downing Cr.	El: 2640
Lndmk: Junction FS11/OR 22, 0.4 miles N	RV: Use judgment with small MH

Description: An enchanting site close to Downing Falls and the wide, clear pools below them. You will find room for several good-size tents at this site, just off of busy OR 22. In addition to the beauty of the creek, there is abundant shade and privacy for the group that is lucky enough to commandeer this site. There is evidence that Downing Creek is a popular fishing destination, however, so don't be surprised if you have company. There is a public outhouse nearer the road, but it may not be maintained. Otherwise, this site is definitely POYP.

Getting there: *(See map pg. 30)* Coming south from Detroit on OR 22, continue 0.4 mile past the turn-off to FS11 between MP 69 and 70. Site is on left, where an opening in the trees reveals a dirt track. Park and carry gear to camp.

Loc: OR 22, across from FS2261	**Road:** Paved
L/L: N44 34 456/W121 59 374	**Access:** Park and carry, 200'
Cell: Detroit and bridge between MP 56 and 57	**Tents:** 3-4
Nearest H2O: North Santiam R.	**El:** 2875
Lndmk: MP 70	**RV:** Use judgment

Description: A well-shaded campsite some 40 feet off busy OR 22 that is shielded from passing traffic by trees and shrubs. It features a sturdy but weathered picnic table and homemade bench in front of the fire pit. The site was clean when discovered in 2013 and would have been a comfortable place to spend the night, or even a weekend. Easy access to the North Santiam.

Getting there: *(See map pg. 31)* Coming south from Detroit on OR 22, drive 0.8 mile past FS11. Look for an opening in the trees revealing a dirt track leading downward to an open area. Park and Carry.

Loc: FS1164, 0.2 M. from FS11	**Road:** Gravel
L/L: N44 34 858/W122 01 495	**Access:** DTC, UOP
Cell: Bridge near MP 56 (OR 22) or Tule Lake	**Tents:** 3-4
Nearest H2O: Creek in camp	**El:** 3780
Lndmk: Junction, FS11/1164, 0.2 mile N	**RV:** Small MH, Use judgment with TT

Description: A sunny area punctuated by tall conifers and lined with rhododendron bushes. Abundant wood. Huckleberries in season. A small creek forms a clear, shallow pool behind camp. There is a large, circular turnaround for vehicles.

Getting there: *(See map pg. 30)* Coming south from Detroit on OR 22, turn right (west) onto FS11 between MP 69 and 70. Drive 3.1 miles on FS11, then 0.2 miles on FS1164. Look for an opening in the trees on the right. From OR 20, drive 31.4 miles on FS11, then go right on FS1164.

Loc: North end of Tule Lake	**Road:** Gravel
L/L: N44 33 757/W122 02 705	**Access:** DTC, UOP
Cell: At end of spur 380 and odd places along FS1162 and 1164	**Tents:** 3-4
Nearest H2O: Lynx Cr., about 1 mile south of the lake or	**El:** 3870
Straight Cr., about 1.8 miles north on FS1162	**RV:** Small MH or TT
Lndmk: Tule Lake	

Description: This site on the north end of the lake is probably the prettiest, shadiest and most comfortable campsite anywhere in the area. Again, no water other than lake water, so either bring it from home or fetch it fresh from one of the nearby creeks.

Getting there: *(See map pg. 31)* Heading south on OR 22 from Detroit, turn west onto Forest Service Scenic Route 11 (FS11), about 0.3 mile south of MP 69. Drive approximately 3.2 miles to where FS1164 takes off to the left. Go 4.1 miles on FS1164 to its intersection with FS1162. Turn right and head north on FS1162. Camp is on left at about 0.3 miles, at the north end of the lake. Alternatively, the site can be reached by driving 6.1 miles on FS11 to FS1162, then following that south for several miles to Tule Lake.

Tule Lake on a summer day

Loc: FS1162-380, near Tule Lake	**Road:** Gravel
L/L: N44 33 829/W122 02 631	**Access:** Check MVUM
Cell: At end of Spur 380 and odd places along FS1162 and 1164	**Tents:** 1
Nearest H2O: Lynx Cr., about 1 mile south of the lake or Straight Cr., about 1.8 miles north on FS1162	**El:** 3870
	RV: MH or small TT
Lndmk: Tule Lake	

103

Description: This site boasts a great view of the Santiam Valley below as well as the crest of the Cascades, to the east. Also, you should be able to use your cell phone to order pizza here. Good luck getting delivery. Downsides are the lack of shade and water. For water, try either Lynx Creek, which crosses FS1164 about a mile south of the lake, or Straight Creek, which crosses FS1162 about 1.8 miles north of the lake. A good campsite for star and meteor watching.

Getting there: *(See map pg. 31)* Look for Spur 380 just north of Site #102.

Loc: Tule Lk., off FS1162	Road: Gravel
L/L: N44 33 631/W122 02 720	Access: DTC, UOP
Cell: Spots along FS1162 and FS1164 in vicinity of lake, especially at the end of Spur 380 (Site 103)	Tents: 2–3
	El: 3945
Nearest H2O: Lynx Cr., about 1 mile south of the lake or Straight Cr., about 1.8 miles north on FS1162	RV: Small MH or TT
Lndmk: Tule Lake	

Description: A scenic but waterless site near a spring-fed mountain lake at altitude. The spot is open to the afternoon sun though shade is available nearby. There is a level spot for one larger tent closer to the road and a smaller one near a second fire ring just down the hill. A large log round provides a convenient work surface. The water of the lake, though beautiful, appears to be brackish. Disadvantages are the sheer popularity of the lake and the fact that sound travels so well over water. You'll hear every word spoken by anyone camping on the lake within 300 yards of you, especially at night.

Getting there: *(See map pg. 31)* Site is on the east side of FS1162, about 200 yards south of Site #102.

Loc: On FS1164, near Tule Lake	Road: Gravel, then dirt
L/L: N44 33 680/W122 02 444	Access: DTC, UOP
Cell: On Road near camp	Tents: 3–4
Nearest H2O: Lynx Cr., about 1.1 mile south on FS1164	El: 3790
Lndmk: Tule Lake	RV: Small MH

Description: A wonderfully shaded and private site protected by large second-growth conifers at the end of a dirt track about 200' from the road, despite the fact that it is waterless. Try your cell phone along FS1164 a few hundred yards north of camp.

Getting there: *(See map pg. 31)* Heading south on OR 22 from Detroit, turn west onto Forest Service Scenic Route 11 (FS11), about 0.3 mile south of MP 69. Drive approximately 3.2 miles to where FS1164 takes off to the left. Go 3.9 miles on FS1164 to a dirt track on the right, about 0.2 mile north of the FS1162/1164 junction. Camp is about 200' in from road.

Loc: FS2257, on Fay Lake	Road: Dirt, primitive but drivable
L/L: N44 30 684/W121 58 555	Access: DTC, UOP
Cell: Detroit and bridge between MP 56 and 57	Tents: 5–6
Nearest H2O: N Santiam R., 1.5 miles SW	El: 3890
Lndmk: Fay Lk.	RV: See below

Description: If you love mountain lake camping and are lucky enough to get this place all to yourself, as I did in late July one year, you'll probably want to return to again and again. Fay Lake is small (about 400' x 800'), with a silty bottom. It is not an inviting place to swim, and there are signs posted regarding algae blooms in the area. Still, except for the occasional faint sound of a truck or motorcycle coming up from OR 22, which is about a mile away as the crow flies, there is little to disturb the natural silence of this place. I wasn't surprised to find

Why the road into Fay Lake is so hard for
a mountain biker to resist

First Campsite at Fay Lake

mosquitoes here, but was surprised when they seemed to leave me alone. Watch the fish hawks drop like a stone into the lake to snag a fish, and then fly off again to devour their catch in tree. There are two campsites here. Both are right on the lake. One of them has a picnic table.

Getting there: *(See map pg. 31)* Driving south from Detroit on OR 22, turn left onto FS2267 (Big Meadows Rd.) at 0.9 M. past MP75. Drive 0.6 M. to its junction with FS2257, then go north 2.2 miles, passing the Big Meadows Horse Camp at about 0.2 mile before crossing the now tiny North Santiam River. The road is paved until the Horse Camp and surprisingly drivable in a smaller vehicle, with only a couple of tricky spots along the way. A small motor home might make it into the lake.

Loc: FS11 on Lost Creek	Road: Paved
L/L: N44 34 501/W122 06 696	Access: DTC, UOP
Cell: Tule Lake area	Tents: 1
Nearest H20: Lost Creek	El: 3805
Lndmk: FS11/760 junction, 0.25 M. E	RV: Use Judgment

107

Looking north from the Scenic
Quartzville Back Country Byway.

Description: An excellent overnight waypoint for those traveling the scenic Quartzville Back Country Byway. Lost Creek cascades over a moss-covered rock face to form a two-foot deep V-shaped pool in deep shade. Among other flora, rhododendron and mountain huckleberry bushes line the creek, which can be heard chuckling pleasantly from the campsite. There is room for one small tent at the end of the short, paved entrance to this site. Downsides: lack of privacy from the road and the restricted size of the campsite itself. Be sure to enjoy the incredible vistas of the Willamette National Forest as you travel the Quartzville byway.

Getting there: *(See map pg. 29)* Coming south from Detroit on OR 22, turn right (west) onto FS11 between MP 69 and 70. Go 9.5 miles west on FS11. Site is on left, where the road curves sharply to the south to contour around the drainage formed by Lost Creek. Driving east on FS11 from OR 20, the distance is 25 miles.

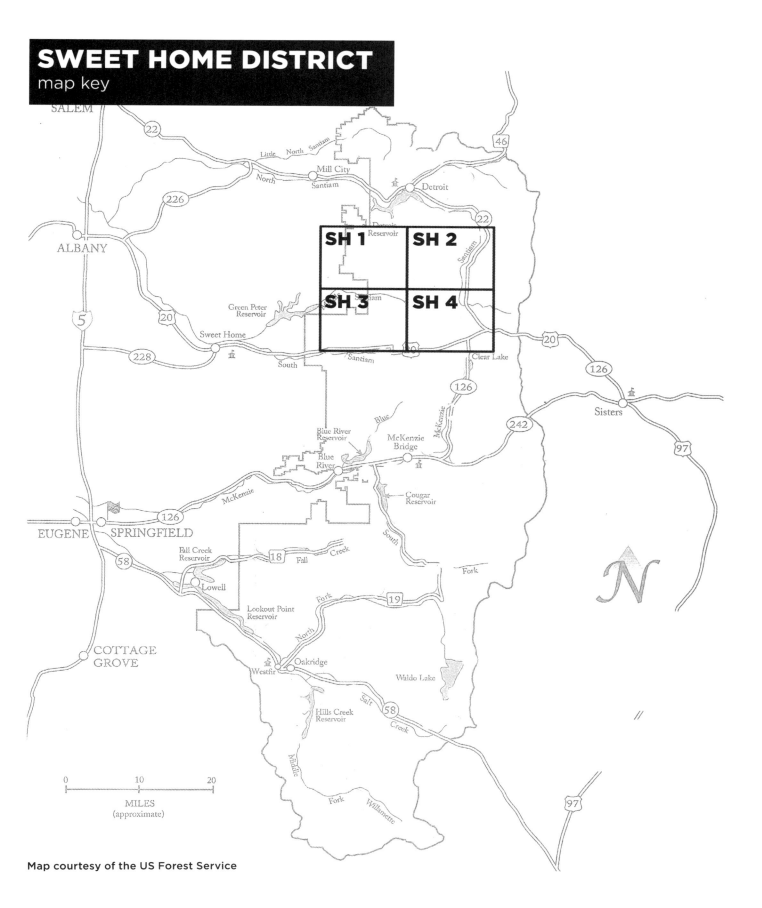

SWEET HOME DISTRICT
map key

SALEM

ALBANY

SH 1   SH 2

SH 3   SH 4

Green Peter
Reservoir

Sweet Home

Mill City

Detroit

Detroit
Reservoir

Clear Lake

Sisters

Blue River
Reservoir

Blue
River

McKenzie
Bridge

Cougar
Reservoir

EUGENE   SPRINGFIELD

Fall Creek
Reservoir

Lowell

Lookout Point
Reservoir

COTTAGE
GROVE

Westfir   Oakridge

Waldo Lake

Hills Creek
Reservoir

0   10   20
MILES
(approximate)

N

Map courtesy of the US Forest Service

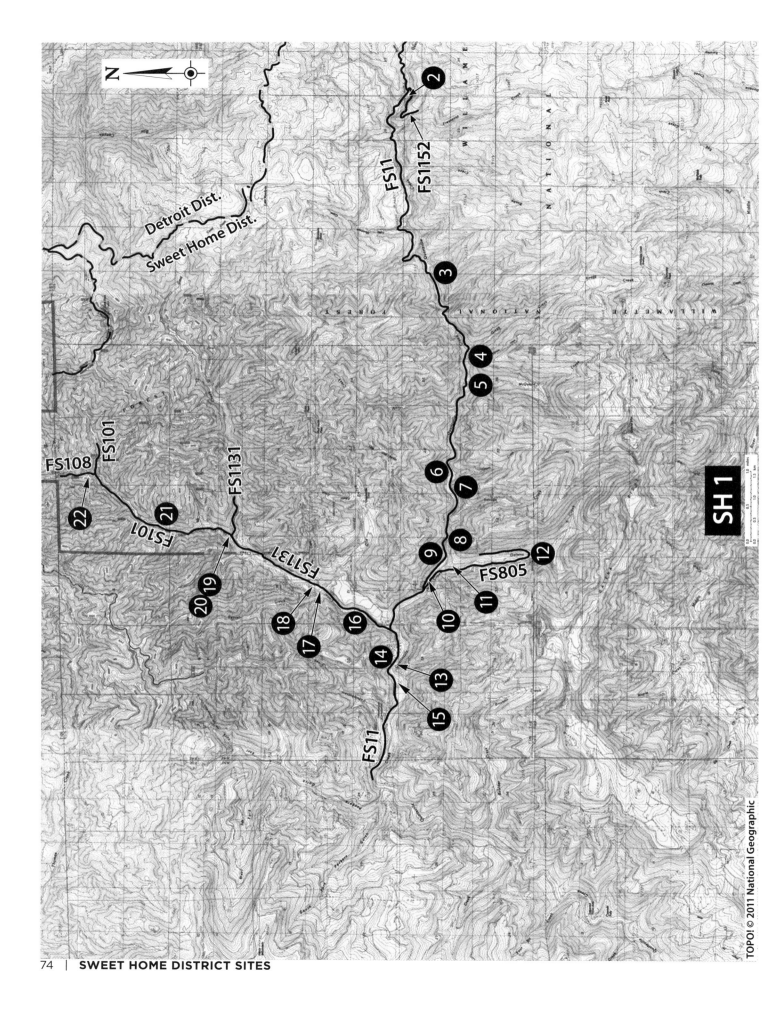

SH 1

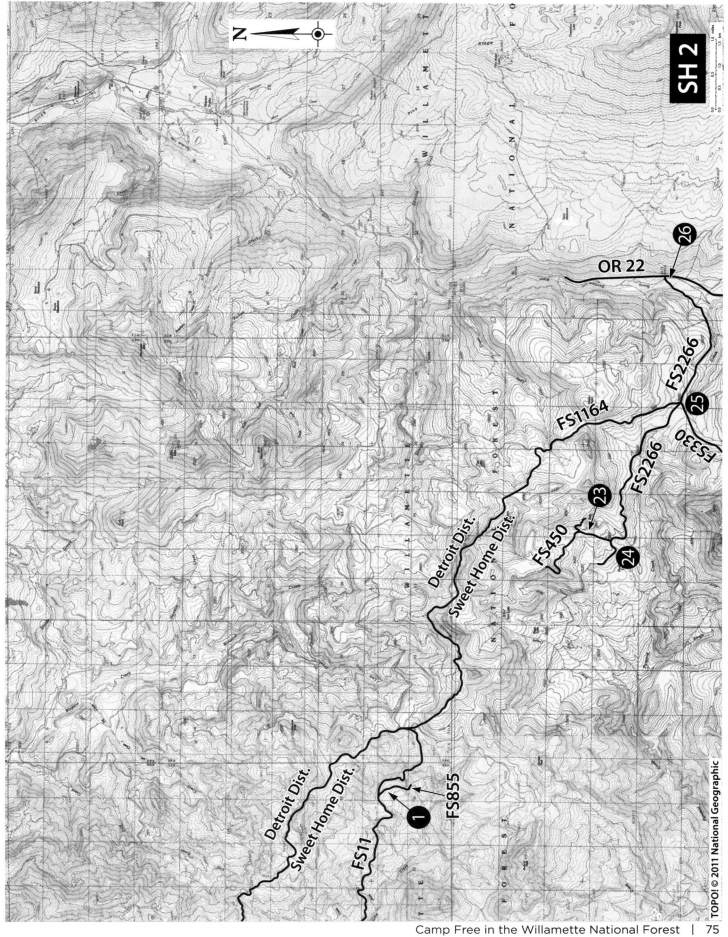

N

OR 22

26

FS2266

25

FS1164

FS330

FS2266

23

FS450

24

Detroit Dist.

Sweet Home Dist.

Willamette National Forest

FS855

1

FS11

Detroit Dist.

Sweet Home Dist.

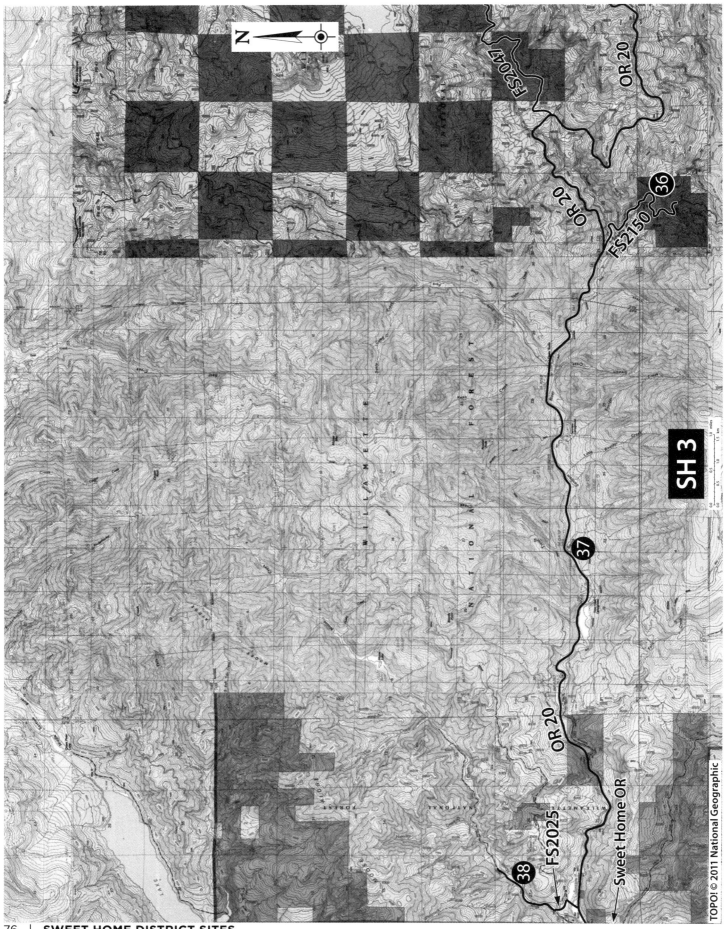

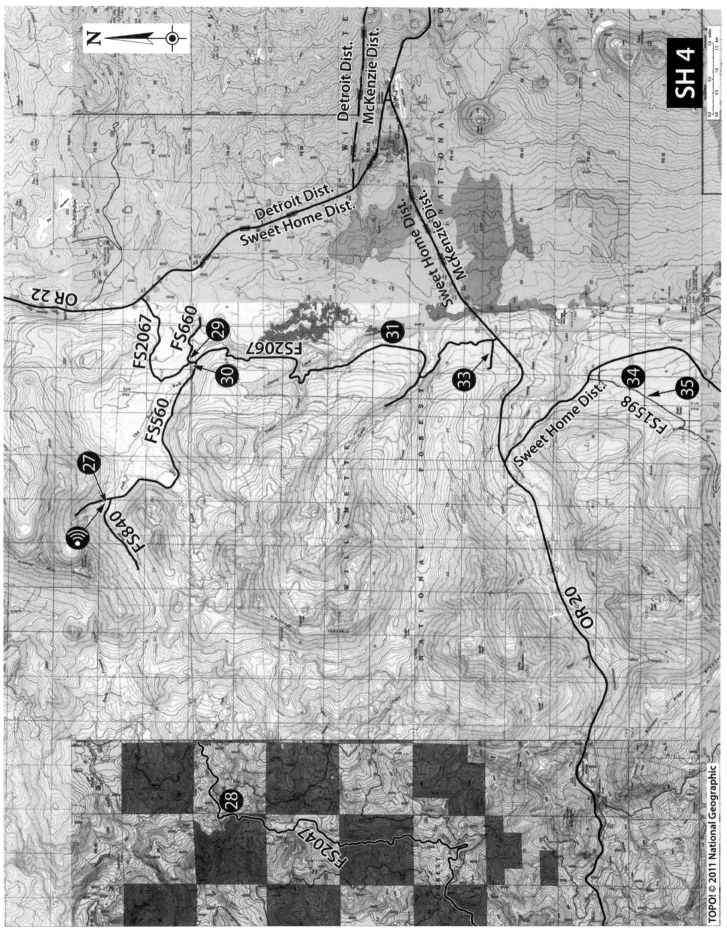

SH 4

SWEET HOME DISTRICT SITES

"The world, we are told, was made especially for man — a presumption not supported by all the facts."
—**John Muir, *A Thousand-Mile Walk to the Gulf***

Telling it like it is: Expect to do some cleanup in most of the campsites along FS11. They are very popular and are often left littered by the people who use them.

Loc: FS11-855, 0.2 mile south of FS11	**Road:** Gravel, mountain
L/L: N44 34 792/W122 08 490	**Access:** DTC, UOP
Cell: Tule Lake and along OR 20	**Tents:** 3–5
Nearest H2O: Nearby creeks	**El:** 3600
Lndmk: Junction 11/855, 0.2 M NW	**RV:** MH and TT

Description: A waterless but nevertheless inviting little campsite set under tall conifers and surrounded by rhododendron and mountain huckleberry bushes that practically begs the passerby to set up camp. Mixed sun and shade during the middle of the day. Traffic on Spur 855 should be minimal, since it is closed 0.8 mile further on.

Getting there: *(See map pg. 75)* Coming south from Detroit on OR 22, turn right (west) onto FS11 between MP 69 and 70 and drive 10.4 miles to Spur 855. Go left (south) 0.2 mile to site, on right. Driving east from OR 20, go 24.1 miles to Spur 855.

Loc: At end of FS11-1152, on Quartzville Creek	**Road:** Gravel
L/L: N44 35 064/W122 11 667	**Access:** DTC or Park and carry
Cell: Tule Lake and along OR 20	**Tents:** 1
Nearest H2O: Quartzville Creek	**El:** 2570
Lndmk: Junction, FS11/1152	**RV:** Small MH or TT

Description: This place, deep in the canyon of Quartzville Creek is both beautiful and popular with the public. There are few tent sites here, so don't be surprised to find the place occupied. The main attraction here is the series of large, deep, slow-moving pools of crystal clear water in the bedrock of the creek, each one of which has several grotto-like nooks. The short road into this site ends at the bridge over the creek.

Getting there: *(See map pg. 74)* Coming south from Detroit on OR 22, turn right (west) onto FS11 between MP 69 and 70 and drive 15.1 miles west, where you will suddenly see the deep canyon of the creek materialize beneath you to the left. Turn sharply left onto Spur 1152 and drive a couple of hundred yards to the bottom of the hill and the bridge. Good luck finding this campsite unoccupied. Traveling east on FS11, it's 19.4 miles to FS1152.

Loc: FS11, at the end of the bridge over Quartzville Creek	Road: Paved
L/L: N44 34 790/W122 14 712	Access: DTC, UOP
Cell: Tule Lake, Sweet Home	Tents: 1–2
Nearest H2O: Quartzville Creek, 20'	El: 1885
Lndmk: Quartzville Cr. Bridge	RV: Small MH and TT

Description: A larger site (about 40 feet by 75 feet) on a ledge above the beautiful Quartzville Creek. Campers will find easier access to the creek by following a wide, rocky track from camp. Site needed some clean-up in 2013.

Getting there: *(See map pg. 74)* Coming south from Detroit on OR 22, turn right (west) onto FS11 between MP 69 and 70 and drive 18.4 miles west to site, on left, just past the bridge over Quartzville Creek. The site is 3.4 miles east of the turn-off to site #2. Coming from OR 20, drive 16.1 miles to site, on right, just before crossing the bridge over the creek.

Loc: Quartzville Cr., 0.1 M from bridge	Road: Paved, then dirt
L/L: N44 34 367/W122 16 060	Access: DTC, UOP
Cell: Tule Lake and along OR 20	Tents: 1–2
Nearest H2O: Quartzville Cr.	El: 1960
Lndmk: Spur 720, 0.5 M. W	RV: Use judgment w/small MH

Description: This camp on Quartzville Creek is directly across from where Gregg Creek forms a pool about five feet higher than the surface of Quartzville Creek. A path leading downhill from camp to the creek provides fairly easy access to the water. Expect to have to do some cleanup if you camp along Quartzville Creek.

Getting there: *(See map pg. 74)* Coming south from Detroit on OR 22, turn right (west) onto FS11 between MP 69 and 70 and drive 19.8 mile west to site, on left, about 0.1 mile past the bridge over Quartzville Creek. Driving east from OR 20, go 14.7 miles to site, on right, just before crossing the bridge over the creek.

Loc: FS11, near Spur 720	Road: Paved
L/L: N44 34 376/W122 16 628	Access: Park and carry, 0.1 mile downhill
Cell: Tule Lk. and along OR 20	Tents: 4–6
Nearest H2O: Quartzville Creek	El: 2090
Lndmk: FS11/720 junction, 100 yds	RV: No

Description: Here is a large, beautiful, shady and secluded, circular campsite centered around a huge fir tree. It overlooks and provides easy access to a broad, braided section of the creek. The site is also located on a mining claim. If work is going on here, you will find another site just another hundred yards west on FS11. This second site is too far above the creek to provide easy access to water, however.

Getting there: *(See map pg. 74)* Coming south from Detroit on OR 22, turn right (west) onto FS11 between MP 69 and 70 and drive 20.3 miles west to sites, on left, just past Spur 720. Coming from OR 20, drive 14.2 miles to site, on right.

Loc: FS11, 21.7 miles from OR 22	Road: Paved
L/L: N44 34 580/W122 18 069	Access: DTC, UOP
Cell: Tule Lk. and along OR 20	Tents: 8–10 or more
Nearest H2O: Quartzville Creek	El: 1800
Lndmk: FS11/1142 junction, 0.1 mile west	RV: MH and TT

Description: *(A twofer)* There are two large sites here: The larger is a 50 x 100 yard flat area under big leaf maple trees. It is centered around a communal steel fire pit some fifteen feet above Quartzville Creek. A rope over the bank would be handy here, as access to the creek is difficult. A somewhat smaller site that is still capable of hosting several tents is to be found adjacent to this site. In late July, the creek below had a dank, but not unpleasant smell, probably caused by algae on the rocks left exposed to the air and heat as the water level dropped from its spring high.

Getting there: *(See map pg. 74)* Coming south from Detroit on OR 22, turn right (west) onto FS11 between MP 69 and 70 and drive 21.7 miles. Site is on right, just after crossing a bridge over Quartzville Creek that replaces a bridge washed away in a previous flood. The remnants of the old bridge are still visible to the right as you cross the new bridge. Coming from OR 20, drive 12.8 miles on FS11 to site, on left, just prior to crossing the bridge.

Loc: FS11, 22 M. west of OR 22	Road: Paved
L/L: N44 34 538/W122 18 471	Access: DTC, UOP
Cell: Tule Lk. and along OR 20	Tents: 5–8
Nearest H2O: Quartzville Creek	El: 1695
Lndmk: Between Green and Savage Creeks	RV: MH and TT

Description: *(A twofer)* Two relatively large and comfortable campsites within a few hundred yards of each other on a shaded bluff overlooking Quartzville Creek. Unfortunately, both were occupied at the time of discovery, and there was no opportunity for inspection.

Getting there: *(See map pg. 74)* Coming south from Detroit on OR 22, turn right (west) onto FS11 between MP 69 and 70 and drive 22 miles to sites, on right. Coming from OR 20, drive 12.5 miles. Start looking for sites, on left after crossing the bridge over the creek at around mile 11.

Loc: Bridge over Quartzville Cr.	Road: Paved
L/L: N44 34 602/W122 19 275	Access: DTC, UOP
Cell: Tule Lk. and along OR 20	Tents: 3–4
Nearest H2O: Quartzville Creek	El: 1675
Lndmk: Bridge over Quartzville Cr.	RV: MH and TT

Description: Two campsites on the north side of the bridge and opposite sides of the road. Access to the creek is not easy, however, since the sites are 25–30' above the creek. A path from one camp leads down to the creek ends in a ten foot drop to the water. Bring your garbage glompers.

Getting there: *(See map pg. 74)* Coming south from Detroit on OR 22, turn right (west) onto FS11 between

MP 69 and 70 and drive 22.8 miles to bridge. Sites are on right and left on the north side of the bridge. Coming from OR 20, drive 11.7 miles to bridge.

Loc: FS11, 0.5 M. SE of Spur 805	**Road:** Paved
L/L: N44 36 674/W122 19 662	**Access:** DTC, UOP
Cell: Tule Lk. and along OR 20	**Tents:** 5–6
Nearest H20: Quartzville Creek	**El:** 1589
Lndmk: Junction FS11/805, 0.5 M. NW	**RV:** MH and TT

Description: A pleasant and shady campsite above the river.

Getting there: *(See map pg. 74)* Coming south from Detroit on OR 22, turn right (west) onto FS11 between MP 69 and 70 and drive 23.2 M. to site, on left. Coming from OR 20, drive 11.3 miles. Site is approximately 150 feet from road.

*****Note:** *Sites 10 through 18 are on BLM land, where the following restrictions apply:*

- *Camping is allowed only where there is a metal fire ring.*
- *Fires are allowed only in the metal fire rings provided.*
- *Fourteen-day stay limit, after which campers must move at least 25 miles away.*

Loc: On Quartzville Cr., 0.2 M. from FS11	**Road:** Gravel, mountain
L/L: N44 34 828/W122 20 042	**Access:** Park and carry, steep path
Cell: Tule Lk and along OR 20	**Tents:** 10–15
Nearest H20: Quartzville Creek	**El:** 1580
Lndmk: Spur 805 Bridge over Quartzville Cr.	**RV:** On road only

Description: *(BLM Land)* This site is perched on a 100-yard-long ledge above a particularly beautiful section of the creek and offers several separate campsites. Beautiful, swimmable pools of crystalline water beckon just below camp Access is via a steep fifteen-foot-path from the road. The site, which was badly in need of a cleanup in 2013, would be ideal for a group. A small group, working together, could restore this to its pristine and beautiful natural state in short order.

Getting there: *(See map pg. 74)* Coming south from Detroit on OR 22, turn right (west) onto FS11 between MP 69 and 70 and drive 23.6 miles west. Take Spur 805 south 0.2 miles to site, on left. Headed east on FS11, drive 10.9 miles to Spur 805. Park on the road and ferry gear down the steep path to the level ground below. A rope would help a lot here.

Loc: Galena Cr., 0.5 M. from FS11	**Road:** Gravel, mountain
L/L: N44 34 532/W122 19 790	**Access:** DTC, UOP
Cell: Along OR 20	**Tents:** 3–4
Nearest H20: Galena Cr.	**El:** 1720
Lndmk: FS11 bridge across Quartzville Cr., 0.5 M	**RV:** MH and TT

Description: *(BLM Land)* Plan on putting your garbage glompers to use here. Like so many sites along Quartzville Creek, some cleanup is the price of admission to this camp. Once the site is cleaned up, you will have turned it into an utterly beguiling little campsite with streamside tranquility, shade, and privacy. The campsite is visible briefly from cars passing by above on Spur 805, which should be very lightly traveled.

Getting there: *(See map pg. 74)* Coming south from Detroit on OR 22, turn right (west) onto FS11 between MP 69 and 70 and drive 23.6 miles west. Take Spur 805 south 0.5 miles to site, on left, where a dirt track cuts off at an angle and heads downhill about a hundred yards to camp. Headed east on FS11, drive 10.9 miles to Spur 805.

Loc: FS1100-805	**Road:** Gravel
L/L: N44 30 630/W122 19 554	**Access:** DTC, UOP
Cell: Along OR 20	**Tents:** 1–2
Nearest H2O: Galena Cr.	**El:** 1624
Lndmk: FS11 bridge across Quartzville Cr., 1.8 M. N	**RV:** Small MH only

Garbage left at Site # 12 on Galena Creek

Description: *(BLM Land, a pool to remember)* When discovered, this site had been severely trashed. It would not be included in this book were it not for the exceptionally seductive pool of clear water formed by Galena Creek just downstream from camp, which looks to be about 30' across and some 8-10 feet deep. The pool's very beauty seems to have attracted people in need of adult supervision, who then left their mark on the camp just upstream. Unfortunately, the Trash plus ten percent concept won't go far toward making this place habitable again, but you might want to visit the pool. Look for a path covered by loose rock on the north side of Spur 805.

Getting there: *(See map pg. 74)* Coming south from Detroit on OR 22, turn right (west) onto FS11 between MP 69 and 70 and drive 23.6 miles west. Take Spur 805 south 1.8 miles to site, on right, where the road curves sharply just after crossing Galena Creek. Headed east on FS11, drive 10.9 miles to Spur 805.

Loc: FS11, near the Old Miner's Meadow Group Camp	**Road:** Paved
L/L: N44 35 240/W122 21 398	**Access:** DTC, UOP
Cell: Along OR 20	**Tents:** 5–10
Nearest H2O: Quartzville Cr.	**El:** 1470
Lndmk: Old Miner's Meadow Group Camp, 0.2 M. SE	**RV:** MH and TT

Description: *(BLM Land)* A large, comfortable site with easier access to the creek than most of the upstream sites along Quartzville Creek.

Getting there: *(See map pg. 74)* Coming south from Detroit on OR 22, turn right (west) onto FS11 between MP 69 and 70 and drive 25 M. to site, on left, 0.2 M. past the Old Miner's Meadow Group Camp. Coming from OR 20, drive 9.5 miles.

Loc: FS11, 0.3 M. west of the Old Miner's Group Camp	Road: Paved
L/L: N44 35 301/ W122 21 508	Access: Park and carry
Cell: Along OR 20	Tents: 3–5
Nearest H2O: Quartzville Cr.	El: 1480
Lndmk: Old Miner's Meadow Grp. Camp., 0.3 mile SE	RV: No

Description: *(BLM Land)* A comfortable-looking camp sandwiched between the road and Quartzville Creek that appears to have easy creek access. Unable to inspect thoroughly.

Getting there: *(See map pg. 74)* Coming south from Detroit on OR 22, turn right (west) onto FS11 between MP 69 and 70 and drive 25.1 M. to site, on left, 0.3 M. past the Old Miner's Meadow Group Camp. Coming from OR 20, drive 9.4 miles.

Loc: FS11, 0.6 M. E of Yellowbottom Campground	Road: Paved
L/L: N44 35 218/W122 21 740	Access: DTC, UOP
Cell: Along OR 20	Tents: 40–50
Nearest H2O: Quartzville Cr.	El: 1445
Lndmk: Yellowbottom Campground, 0.6 M. W	RV: MH and TT

Description: *(BLM Land)* A very large campsite capable of handling many campers and casual sightseers. Expect a crowd and the same kinds of problems you'd encounter in a large public campground.

Getting there: *(See map pg. 74)* Coming south from Detroit on OR 22, turn right (west) onto FS11 between MP 69 and 70 and drive 25.3 M. to site, on left, 0.5 M. past the Old Miner's Meadow Group Camp. Coming from OR 20, drive 9.2 miles.
Note: Driving west on FS11 from this site to Highway 20, you will find numerous roadside BLM campsites on both sides of the road.

Loc: Canal Cr., 0.5 M. N of FS11	Road: Gravel, mountain
L/L: N44 35 606/W122 20 547	Access: Park and carry
Cell: Along OR 20	Tents: 1
Nearest H2O: Canal Cr.	El: 1660
Lndmk: Junction FS11/1131, 0.5 M. S	RV: On road only

Description: *(BLM Land)* Here you will find a very private and isolated campsite with room for one modest-size tent in the shelter of a large log tossed up when the stream was on a rampage some previous winter. Downstream, you will find several tantalizing pools to explore. You will probably also find some light housekeeping to be necessary. Otherwise, the spot is lovely.

Getting there: *(See map pg. 74)* Coming south from Detroit on OR 22, turn right (west) onto FS11 between MP 69 and 70 and drive 24.5 miles to FS1131. Headed east from OR 20, drive 10 miles. Go north 0.5 mile on FS1131 to site, on left. Park in pullout and schlep gear a hundred yards along path to Canal Creek.

Loc: FS1131, 1.1 miles from FS11	Road: Gravel, mountain
L/L: N44 36 119/W122 20 138	Access: Park and carry
Cell: Along OR 20	Tents: 2–3
Nearest H2O: Canal Cr.	El: 1580
Lndmk: Junction FS1131/101/105	RV: Entry too steep

Description: *(BLM Land)* Find shade, privacy and a view of Canal Creek at this site. A steep but walkable (in dry weather) path leads from camp to a beautiful pool below a huge, silvered, old-growth log stretching across the stream.

Getting there: *(See map pg. 74)* Camp is 0.6 miles north of Site #16. The path to camp is about 100 feet up the road from a pull-out that will accommodate about two cars.

Loc: On Canal Cr., 50 yards off FS1131	Road: Gravel, mountain
L/L: NN44 36 209/W122 20 128	Access: Park and carry
Cell: Along OR 20	Tents: 3–4
Nearest H2O: Canal Cr.	El: 1725
Lndmk: Junction FS11/1131, 1.2 M. S	RV: No

Pool in Canal Creek below Site #18

Description: *(BLM Land)* Here you'll find an appealing site on the creek, with picturesque pools just downstream. As with many sites in this area, expect to do some housekeeping.

Getting there: *(See map pg. 74)* Coming south from Detroit on OR 22, turn right (west) onto FS11 between MP 69 and 70 and drive 24.5 miles to FS1131. Headed east from OR 20, drive 10 miles. Go north 1.3 miles on FS1131. Park at N44 36 151/W122 20 067, where you will find a pullout created by a dirt track on the left that has been barricaded by a berm. Carry gear downhill about 150 yards to camp.

Loc: At junction of FS1131/101/105	Road: Gravel, mountain
L/L: N44 37 164/W122 19 236	Access: DTC, UOP
Cell: Along OR 20	Tents: 3–4
Nearest H2O: Canal Cr.	El: 1695
Lndmk: Junction FS1131/101/105	RV: Entry too steep

Description: Camp near the bridge where Elk Creek joins Canal Creek under a canopy of large alder trees. In late summer, both creeks flow over bedrock and are so shallow that it is possible to walk across them on the exposed rock though there is a deeper pool below camp. This site is on a mining claim, so make sure that it is not being actively worked by the claim owners before staking down your tent.

Getting there: *(See map pg. 74)* Coming south from Detroit on OR 22, turn right (west) onto FS11 between MP 69 and 70 and drive 24.5 miles to FS1131. Headed east from OR 20, drive 10 miles. Go north 2.6 miles on FS1131. Camp is on the left, just after crossing the bridge.

Loc: Elk Creek, off FS1131-101, 0.1 mile from bridge	**Road:** Gravel, mountain
L/L: N44 37 227/W122 19 187	**Access:** DTC, UOP
Cell: Along OR 20	**Tents:** 3–5, total
Nearest H2O: Elk Cr.	**El:** 1635
Lndmk: Junction FS1131/101/105, 0.1 M. S	**RV:** MH and TT

Description: *(a twofer)* Two separate campsites at opposite ends of a large and densely shaded clearing. Both camps have meticulously constructed fire pits. The larger of the two is on the downstream end of the clearing. The upstream site may be dusty later in the summer. There is plenty of room to drive a small motor home completely around the island of trees in the center of camp. A steep path taking off between the two camps leads to Elk Creek, about 200 feet below, the last ten feet of which require scrambling over roots to get to the creek. Someone has artfully built a small dam to contain the creek in a kind of a warming pool just below where it slides over a wide shelf of solid rock. Because of the steepness of the path to the creek, you are going to want to get your water elsewhere.

Getting there: *(See map pg. 74)* Coming south from Detroit on OR 22, turn right (west) onto FS11 between MP 69 and 70 and drive 24.5 miles to FS1131. Headed east from OR 20, drive 10 miles to FS1131. Go north 2.6 miles on FS1131. Follow Spur 101 to the left after bridge. Watch for a turn-off to the left about a tenth of a mile past the bridge. Site is about 100' off of Spur 101.

Loc: Elk Cr., 1.1 M. from FS1131/101 junction	**Road:** Gravel, mountain
L/L: N44 37 977/W122 19 063	**Access:** DTC, UOP
Cell: Along OR 20	**Tents:** 1–2 small
Nearest H2O: Elk Cr.	**El:** 1705
Lndmk: Bridge over Canal Cr, 1.1 M. S	**RV:** No

Description: A small campsite sandwiched between the creek and the road about fifteen feet above pleasantly chuckling Elk Creek with space for a couple of small tents. Look for a few mountain huckleberry bushes among the surrounding fir and alder trees. A relatively easy trail provides creek access.

Getting there: *(See map pg. 74)* Coming south from Detroit on OR 22, turn right (west) onto FS11 between MP 69 and 70 and drive 24.5 miles to FS1131. Headed east from OR 20, drive 10 miles to FS1131. Go north 2.6 miles on FS1131 to bridge where Spur 101 splits to the left. Go 1.1 miles to site, on right, about a tenth of a mile past a bridge over Elk Creek.

There is a very secluded camp at the end of a rough track that takes off from Spur 101 about 0.2 miles south of Site #21. A small creek flowing nearby provides this camp with water. Unfortunately, this track is not drivable, and the author was not able to inspect the camp when it was spotted from the road.

Loc: Junction FS1131-101/108	Road: Gravel, mountain
L/L: N44 38 798/W122 18 182	Access: DTC, UOP
Cell: Along OR 20	Tents: 1–2
Nearest H2O: Near Spur 101/108 junction	El: 2015
Lndmk: Bridge over Canal Cr, 2.3 M. S	RV: MH and TT

Description: This camp is just off the road near the end of Spur 101 on a ledge about fifteen feet above an unnamed little tributary that joins Elk Creek a few hundred yards downstream. This is rugged country. Getting to the creek below camp would be difficult at best. Draw water for camp use downstream near Spur 101 or from Elk Creek.

Getting there: *(See map pg. 74)* Coming south from Detroit on OR 22, turn right (west) onto FS11 between MP 69 and 70 and drive 24.5 miles to FS1131. Headed east from OR 20, drive 10 miles to FS1131. Go north 2.6 miles on FS1131 to bridge where Spur 101 splits to the left. Go 2.6 miles on Spur 101, then take Spur 108 uphill about a hundred feet to site, on left. Site is about a hundred feet off the road.

Loc: Daly Lake	Road: Gravel
L/L: N44 32 444/W122 04 030	Access: Park and carry
Cell: Tule Lake, via FS2266 and 1164	Tents: 3–6
Nearest H2O: Daly Lake and Creek	El: 3610
Lndmk: Daly Lake	RV: No

Description: *(A walk-in)* The view of the Daly Lake shimmering in the afternoon sun as you set up your tent will make your heart race. This is the full meal deal of camping in the Willamette National Forest. Not only is Daly Lake one of the most stunningly beautiful mountain lakes that you can reach by car, but it comes with campsites equipped with steel fire rings and picnic tables that are wheelchair accessible! And if that isn't enough, there is a well-maintained outhouse near the road a couple of hundred yards from camp. Campsites 1 and 2 have a commanding view of the lake. Water is available from the lake or the creek that feeds it. Both are at the bottom of a steep 20' slope that is negotiable with care. The only other downside may be the number of people who walk down the trail from the parking lot to see and photograph the lake. A Northwest Forest Pass is required to camp here. Be sure to do the hike into nearby Parish Lake while you're here.

Getting there: *(See map pg. 75)* Headed south from Detroit on OR 22, take FS2266 to the right near MP 74 and drive 4.8 miles to its junction with Spur 450. Drive 0.4 mile north on Spur 450 to Daly Lake campsites, on right. Site is well marked. Park and carry gear to campsites.

Loc: Parish Lk.	Road: 0.7 mile forest trail
L/L: N44 31 965/W122 04 487	Access: Park and carry on rough trail, 0.7 mile
Cell: Tule Lk.	Tents: 2–3
Nearest H2O: Parish Lk.	El: 3723
Lndmk: FS2266/450 junction	RV: No

Description: Parish Lake is a beautiful little gem of a mountain lake that, if you're lucky, you can enjoy in solitude. With an elevation drop of a mere 170 feet from the road, it's a relatively easy hike to the lake. The trail is narrow, rocky and overgrown with roots in several places, and there are a few downed logs to negotiate as well. Campsites are limited, and it might be necessary to fight your way through the brush around the lake to find one that satisfies your needs. Campers I found there when I explored the place in 2013 reported that the fishing was good.

Getting there: *(See map pg. 75)* Headed south from Detroit on OR 22, take FS2266 to the right near MP 74 and drive 5.3 miles to the trailhead on the left side of the road, about a half-mile beyond where Spur 450 takes off to the north to Daly Lake. Park and walk to lake.

Loc: Camp Cr., 0.1 M. from FS2266/1164 junction	**Road:** Paved, then dirt
L/L: N44 31 268/W122 01 918	**Access:** DTC, UOP
Cell: Tule Lake, via FS1164	**Tents:** 3–5
Nearest H2O: Camp Cr.	**El:** 3575
Lndmk: Junction FS2266/1164, 0.1 mile	**RV:** Small MH and TT

Description: Aptly named Camp Creek sings with the gentle lullaby of a tranquility fountain as it slides by this initially unprepossessing little campsite tucked away just off paved FS2266. There is a fire ring under three tall conifers near the center of a large clearing in the forest. Huckleberries abound in early August. Not all tents sites here are perfectly level, and you may decide to locate your tent on the softer forest duff under the trees upstream of the clearing. Just remember not to build any fires there. Forest duff is quite flammable when it is dry. Spur 310 formerly crossed the creek to another, smaller and somewhat rocky campsite on the opposite shore of the creek, but the bridge was carried away during some past storm. It may be possible to reach this campsite via Scar Mountain Road.

Getting there: *(See map pg. 75)* Headed south from Detroit on OR 22, take FS2266 to the right near MP 74 and drive 2.2 miles to the FS 2266/1164 Junction. Here Spur 310 cuts off from Spur 330 a hundred feet, or so from FS2266. At 0.1 mile from the intersection on Spur 310, you will come to the campsite, where the former bridge over Camp Creek has been washed out.

Loc: Where FS2266 crosses the North Santiam	**Road:** Paved, then gravel
L/L: N44 31 444/W121 59 799	**Access:** Park and carry, 100 yds.
Cell: Detroit and Tule Lake area	**Tents:** 1–2, smaller
Nearest H2O: Santiam R.	**El:** 3093
Lndmk: Junction FS2266/OR 22, 0.1 mile east	**RV:** On road only

Description: A comfortable, shady camp near the North Santiam where a small party could settle in for a night or two. The river here is relatively narrow and shallow.

Getting there: *(See map pg. 75)* Coming south on OR 22 from Detroit, turn right onto FS2266 about half a mile after MP 73. Go west a bit more than 0.1 mile. After crossing the bridge, make an immediate and sharp U-turn to the left onto the gravel ramp leading a hundred feet or so toward the river. Park and carry gear 100 yards into the woods to campsites, near a fire ring.

Loc: Junction of 2067-560/840	Road: Gravel, mountain
L/L: N44 29 537/W122 03 489	Access: DTC, UOP
Cell: In camp	Tents: 3–4
Nearest H2O: Tributary to N. Fk. Park Cr., near Camp	El: 3665
Lndmk: Junction Spur 560/840	RV: MH and TT

Description: A surprisingly comfortable camp located at the junction of two lightly traveled spur roads where you will find shade and, if you have the right cell phone carrier, be able to call home. The path leading out of the back of camp some hundred odd feet will bring you to a source of abundant clear water from a tiny, unnamed tributary to the North Fork of Park Creek.

Getting there: *(See map pg. 77)* Driving south from Detroit on OR 22, turn right onto FS2067, near MP 76. Drive 2 miles to the bridge across Park Creek. Go 3.0 miles on Spur 560 to site, on left, just past the junction with Spur 840. Look for a dirt track curving back into the trees. Traveling east on OR 20, turn left onto FS2067 between MP 70 and 71. Drive 5.7 miles north on FS2067 to Junction with Spur 560, near bridge and site #30, then take Spur 560 three miles to site, on left.

Loc: Where FS2047 crosses the Middle Fork of the Santiam	Road: Gravel, mountain
L/L: N44 28 010/W122 08 860	Access: Park and carry
Cell: Site 27	Tents: 1
Nearest H2O: Middle Fk. Santiam R.	El: 2395
Lndmk: FS2047 Bridge over the MFS	RV: No

Description: The only decent campsite with water that I found between the northern terminus of FS2047 and where it joins OR 20 on its southern end. This site, at the bottom of a steep 15-foot-long path leading down to the river, offers comfort and access to a couple of beautiful pools in the river. Bear in mind that, though the road here is sparsely traveled, the site can be seen from a passing vehicle. Consider using a rope when transporting gear down the path to camp.

For those who like to explore, FS2047, winding some 21 miles along the north-south ridges of the Cascades, offers beautiful vistas to admire and interesting places to explore. A good map is essential to keep you from getting confused at the many intersections along the way. A GPS would also be handy.

Getting there: *(See map pg. 77)* Headed south from Detroit on OR 22, take FS2266 to the right near MP 74 and drive 3.2 miles to FS2047 (aka Sheep Creek Rd.). Go south 12 miles to site, located where FS2047 crosses the Middle Fork of the Santiam. Park at the side of the road and carry gear down to camp. Driving east on OR 20, turn north onto Sheep Creek Road about 1.9 miles past MP55 and Storm Creek, and then drive 8.7 miles to site.

Loc: FS2067-660, about 200 yards from Site #30	Road: Gravel, then dirt
L/L: N44 28 598/W122 01 072	Access: DTC, UOP
Cell: Site #27 and near OR 20/2067 junction	Tents: 4–5
Nearest H2O: Park Cr.	El: 3600
Lndmk: FS2067 bridge over Park Cr.	RV: MH and TT

Description: A waterless but pleasing and private site in a shady grove of tall conifers about a hundred yards off 2067.

Getting there: *(See map pg. 77)* Follow the directions to site #30. Turn left (east) onto Spur 660 about a hundred yards north of the bridge over Park Creek. Site is in clearing about a hundred or so yards from FS2067, on the left.

Loc: Where FS2067 crosses Park Creek	Road: Gravel
L/L: N44 28 512/W122 01 126	Access: DTC, UOP
Cell: Site #27 and near OR 20/2067 junction	Tents: 1–2, smaller
Nearest H2O: Park Cr.	El: 3600
Lndmk: Bridge over Park Creek	RV: MH and TT

Looking upstream from the Park Creek Bridge

Description: The upstream view of slow-running Park Creek under the late afternoon sun is something you won't soon forget. In spite of the surrounding beauty, however, this offers only one or two level tent sites and is actually more suitable for RV camping. One downside is that the site is exposed to traffic driving across the bridge on FS2067. Park Creek runs clear but has its origins in a large, marshy meadow just upstream, so boil your water well.

Getting there: *(See map pg. 77)* Driving south from Detroit on OR 22, turn right onto FS2067 near MP 76. Drive 2 miles to the bridge across Park Creek. Campsite is on right, at the end of the bridge.

Loc: FS2067, 2.2 M. N of OR 20	Road: Gravel, then dirt
L/L: N44 26 180/W122 00 789	Access: DTC, UOP
Cell: Site #27 and maybe at Sno-Park along OR 20	Tents: 15–20
Nearest H2O: Crescent Cr., 0.9 mile S	El: 3450
Lndmk: Junction FS2067/OR 20, 2.2 M. S	RV: MH and TT

Description: There are two large, dry campsites here that are worth considering as destination campsites. Both offer shade and privacy and a steel fire pit for convenience and safety. The first site, about twenty-five yards off the road in a clearing some hundred yards long by forty feet wide, will accommodate many tents. The second site is about 200 yards beyond on a dirt track through the forest. There is a large rock which must be avoided along the road to the second site, some 200 yards further on. Campers traveling in or with RVs should exercise caution here.

Getting there: *(See map pg. 77)* Coming south from Detroit on OR 22, turn right onto OR 20 around MP 81. Drive west 4 miles, then go right (north) 2.2 miles on FS2067 to site, on right. Traveling east on OR 20, turn left onto FS2067 between MP 70 and 71. Go north 2.2 miles. Site is 3.5 miles south of the bridge over Park Cr.

Loc: FS2067-504, 0.1 mile from FS2067	**Road:** Gravel
L/L: N44 24 972/W122 00 885	**Access:** Park and carry
Cell: Site #27 and maybe at Sno-Park along OR 20	**Tents:** 6–10
Nearest H2O: Probably Crescent Cr.	**El:** 3485
Lndmk: Lava Lake Snow Park	**RV:** ?

Description: A dry camp in a clearing along Spur 504, which takes off from the Lava Lake Sno-Park parking lot. Its tall trees provide pleasant shade and privacy, even though the site is within earshot of OR 20.

Getting there: *(See map pg. 77)* Coming south from Detroit on OR 22, turn right onto OR 20 around MP 81. Drive west about 4 miles to the Lava Lake Sno-Park, on right. Traveling east on OR 20, turn left into the Lava Lake Sno-Park between MP 70 and 71. Look for Spur 504 taking off from the west side of the parking lot. Park and carry.

Loc: FS1598, 0.7 M. from FS2672	**Road:** Gravel, mountain
L/L: N44 23 266/W122 01 569	**Access:** DTC, UOP
Cell: Site #27 and maybe at Sno-Park along OR 20	**Tents:** 4–5
Nearest H2O: Hackleman Cr., near OR 20	**El:** 3490
Lndmk: FS1598/2672 junction, 0.7 M. N	**RV:** MH and TT

Description: A waterless, secluded, and private site on Smith Prairie which I was unable to inspect because it was occupied at the time of discovery. It is well hidden in the trees. Ideal for RV camping.

Getting there: *(See map pg. 77)* On OR 20, turn south onto FS2672 near MP 68, 2.7 miles from the OR 20/126 junction. Drive 1.7 miles. Turn right (south) onto FS1598 and go 0.7 miles to site, on left where you will see a dirt track leading off into the trees. Camp is about 100 yards off the road.

Loc: FS1598, on Smith Prairie	**Road:** Gravel, then dirt track
L/L: N44 22 885/W122 01 795	**Access:** Check MVUM
Cell: Site #27 and maybe at Sno-Park along OR 20	**Tents:** 10–15
Nearest H2O: Smith River or Hackleman Cr.	**El:** 3513
Lndmk: Junction FS2672/1598, 0.9 mile N	**RV:** MH and TT (Check road first)

Description: *(Two waterless sites on Smith Prairie)* Concealed in the trees of Smith Prairie within a few tenths of a mile of each other are two nice waterless sites just off of FS1598. The first is set under the trees at the end of a dirt track about a hundred yards off the road. The second is about a tenth of a mile south of FS1598 in the center of a stand of mammoth conifers surrounded by a cone-strewn dirt track. This site has obviously been used as a hunters' camp in the past.

Getting there: *(See map pg. 77)* On OR 20, turn south onto FS2672 near MP 68, 2.7 miles from the OR 20/126 junction. Drive 1.7 miles. Turn right (south) onto FS1598 and go 0.9 miles to first site, on left, where you will see a dirt track leading off into the trees. Camp is about 100 yards off the road. The road to the second site is about 0.2 to 0.3 M. southward on FS1598, where an unnamed dirt track leads about 0.1 mile off into the forest to the left of the road. Campers with RVs should check out the road before attempting to drive any part of it.

Loc: Where FS2044 crosses the South Santiam R.	**Road:** Gravel, mountain
L/L: N44 23 121/W122 14 055	**Access:** DTC, UOP & park and carry
Cell: Site #27, town of Sweet Home	**Tents:** 6–10
Nearest H20: South Santiam R.	**El:** 1900
Lndmk: House Rock Cg., 1.2 M. N	**RV:** MH and TT

This balanced rock cairn near Site #36 suggests a more benign and creative way for campers to leave their mark.

Description: *(a threefer)* Here are three good destination campsites scattered along a beautiful stretch of the South Santiam. The one closest to the road and bridge will work well for those camping in a motorhome or other RV. A second campsite can be found a bit downstream on a grassy knoll near a gravel turnaround. The third, a park and carry site is located along a trail taking off from the opposite side of the road. This site is the most private and shadiest of the three. All sites offer access to river beaches and pools for soaking and bathing. Be sure use a bucket to do your bathing well away from the river so as not to contaminate it with soap.

Getting there: *(See map pg. 76)* From OR 20 near MP 55, go south 1.4 miles on FS2044 (road to House Rock Campground). Camp is on the south side of the bridge over the South Santiam River, on right.

Loc: Along Old Santiam Wagon Rd., near Yukwah Rec. Area	**Road:** Gravel
L/L: N44 24 113/W122 20 117	**Access:** Check MVUM
Cell: Town of Sweet Home	**Tents:** 5–6
Nearest H20: Santiam R., 100 feet	**El:** 1049
Lndmk: Trout Cr. Cg., 1 mile W	**RV:** Small MH

Description: This campsite by the river would have been a welcome site to weary pioneer travelers who had just suffered the hardships of coming across the spine of the Cascades in wagon trains in the late 19th century. Indeed, it seemed so to me when I stumbled upon it by bicycle in the summer of 2013, some hundred years and several decades later. It offers solitude, privacy, beauty, shade, water, and even a bit of a beach on which to admire the river from the comfort of your chaise lounge. There are a couple more tent sites along the road leading into camp. An easy path leads to a rocky beach, about 40 feet from camp, where the water slows to a wide, deep pool beneath a wall of solid rock on the opposite shore.

Getting there: *(See map pg. 76)* Driving east on OR 20, go right and cross the bridge on the Old Santiam Wagon Road, just past the Yukwah Recreation Area. Cross the river on the bridge, then bear left on Spur 600. At 0.5 mile, keep left where Spur 610 splits off from 600. Camp is at the end of a 0.1 mile-long gravel track that takes off toward the river to the left near the 600/610 split. Spur 600 is blocked by a gate and private property ahead.

Loc: FS 2025, confluence of Whiterock and Moose Creeks	**Road:** Gravel, mountain
L/L: N44 24 775/W122 25 774	**Access:** Park and short carry
Cell: Town of Sweet Home	**Tents:** 2
Nearest H2O: Moose Creek	**El:** 960
Lndmk: MP 52 on OR 20	**RV:** No

38

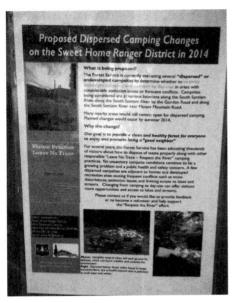

When campers become part of the problem

Description: An old hunters' camp under towering alder and big leaf maple trees that would be unremarkable were it not for its location at the junction of these two good-sized creeks. A rough path winds downhill through the brush to Moose Creek and some deep pools in the bedrock of the creek canyon. Depending on season and temperature, you might notice a dank smell near the creek, which is typical of creeks at lower elevations in late summer. The water of both creeks is somewhat turbid. Unless you prefer your coffee chewy, you might want to let the sediment settle out of the water before boiling it for cooking or drinking.

Getting there: *(See map pg. 76)* From Sweet Home on OR 20 near First St., drive east 16.5 miles. Go left on the Moose Mountain Road, near MP 52. At 0.2 mile, the road splits into FS2025 and 2027. Follow FS2025 one mile to site, on right, near a cleared parking area, just past Whiterock Creek. Camp is about 40 feet from the road.

*Note: In 2013, there was a large, dispersed camping site in use near the Moose Mountain Road bridge over the Santiam River that had been turned into an overcrowded squatters' camp. The Forest Service is moving to close it and others like it. Do not become part of the problem. Avoid this area.

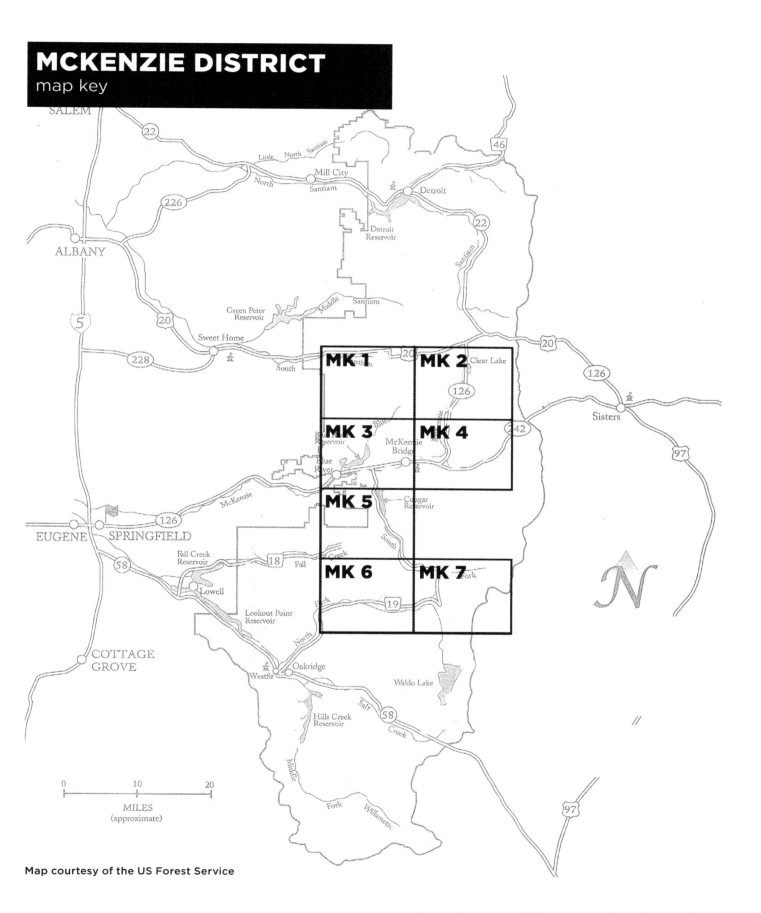

SALEM

22

Little North Santiam

Mill City

226

North Santiam

Detroit

46

Detroit Reservoir

22

ALBANY

5

20

Green Peter Reservoir

Middle Santiam

Santiam

Sweet Home

228

South

MK 1 Santiam

20

MK 2 Clear Lake

126

20

126

Sisters

MK 3 Blue River Reservoir

Blue River

MK 4 McKenzie Bridge

242

97

EUGENE SPRINGFIELD

126

McKenzie

MK 5 Cougar Reservoir

Fall Creek Reservoir

58

18 Fall

Creek

South

MK 6 Fork

MK 7 Fork

N

Lowell

Lookout Point Reservoir

North Fork

19

COTTAGE GROVE

Westfir Oakridge

Hills Creek Reservoir

Salt Creek

58

Waldo Lake

97

Middle

Fork

Willamette

0   10   20

MILES
(approximate)

Map courtesy of the US Forest Service

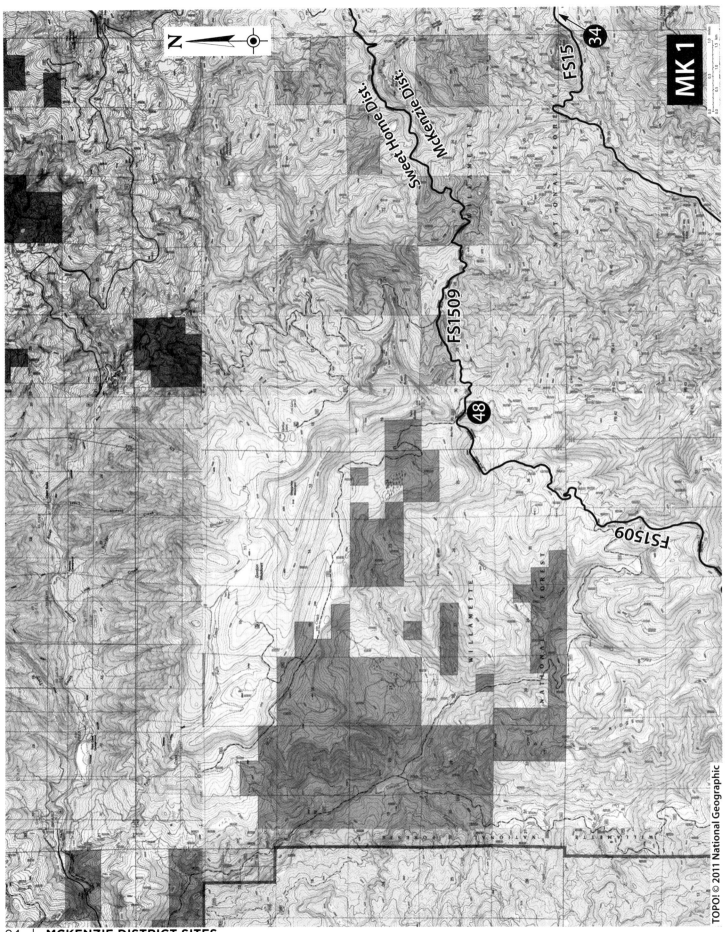

TOPO! © 2011 National Geographic

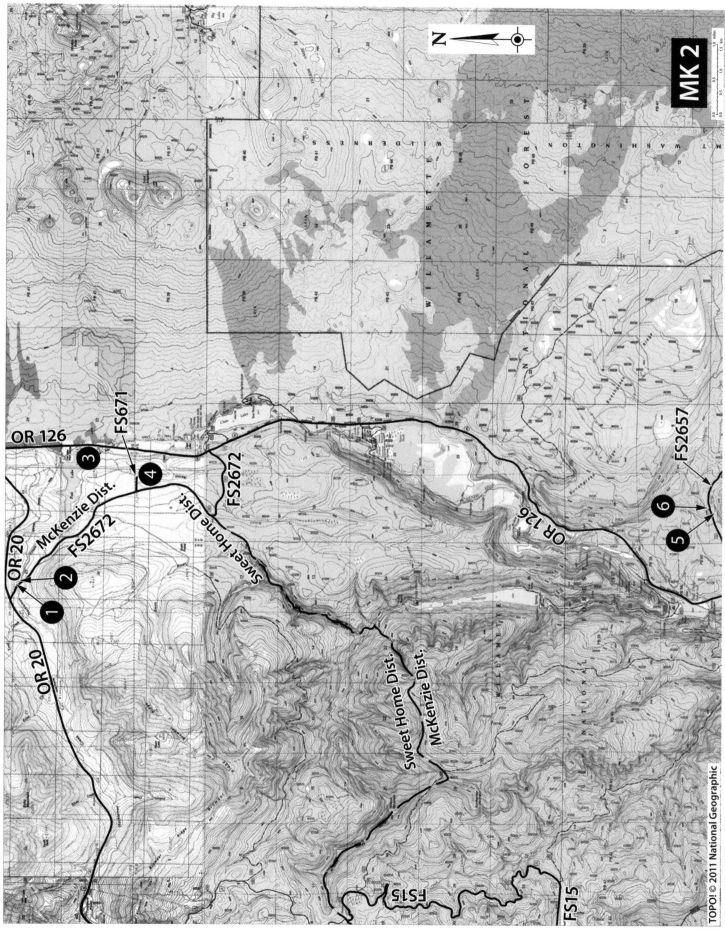

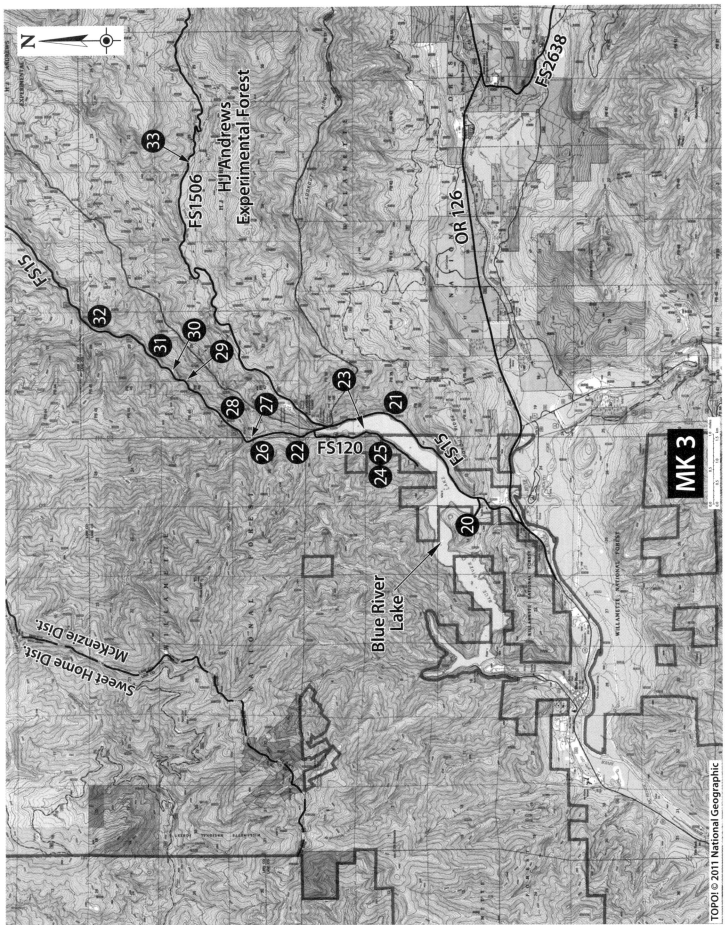

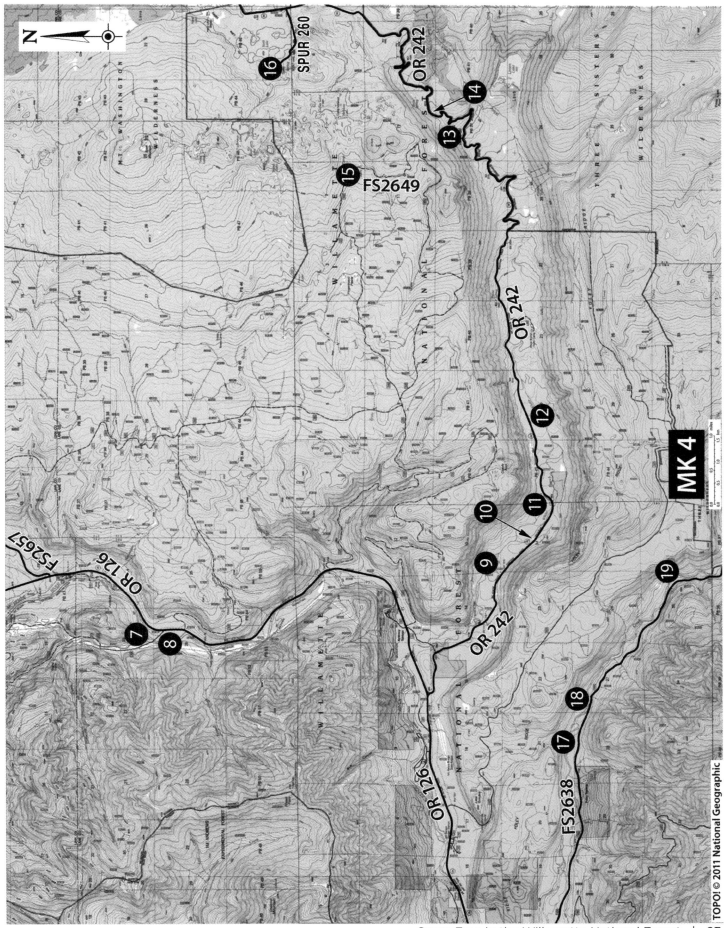

TOPO! © 2011 National Geographic

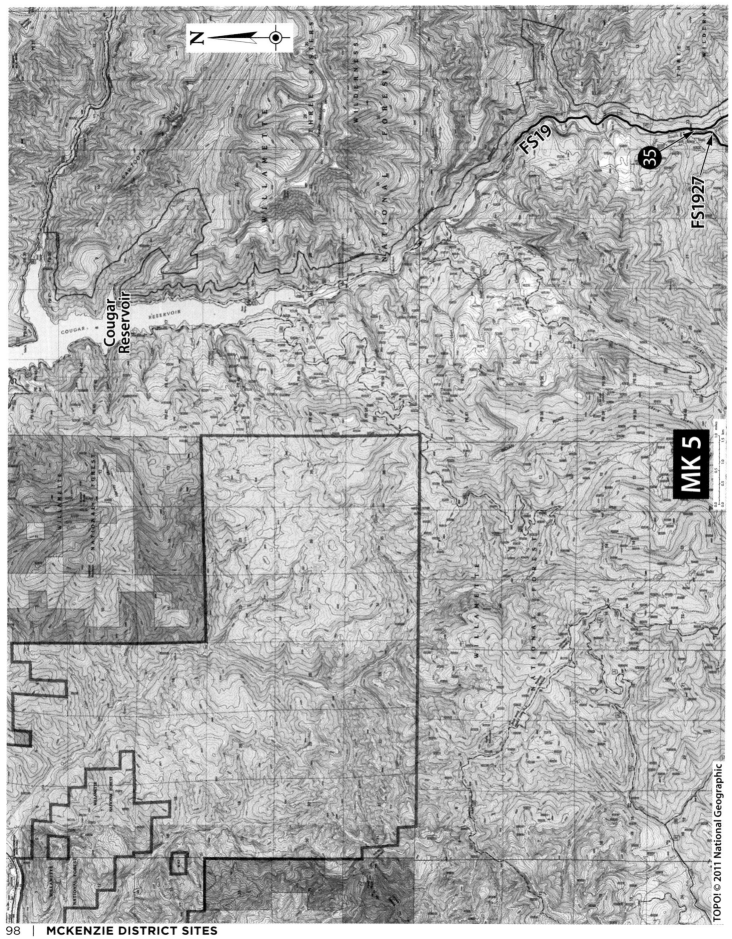

Cougar
Reservoir

FS19

FS1927

35

MK 5

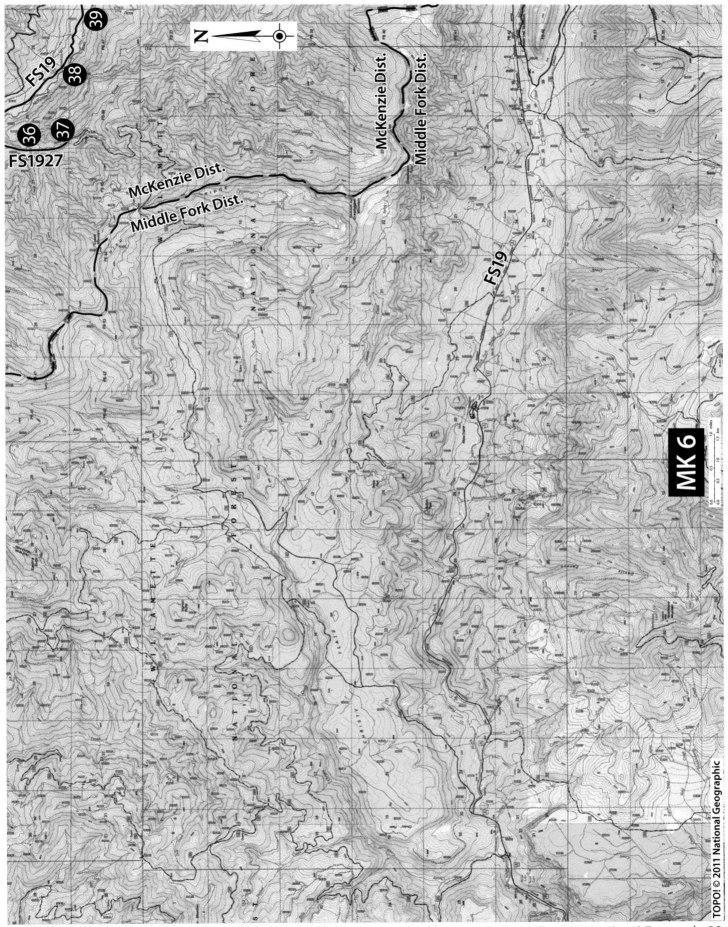

39

FS19

38

36 37

FS1927

McKenzie Dist.

Middle Fork Dist.

McKenzie Dist.

Middle Fork Dist.

FS19

MK 6

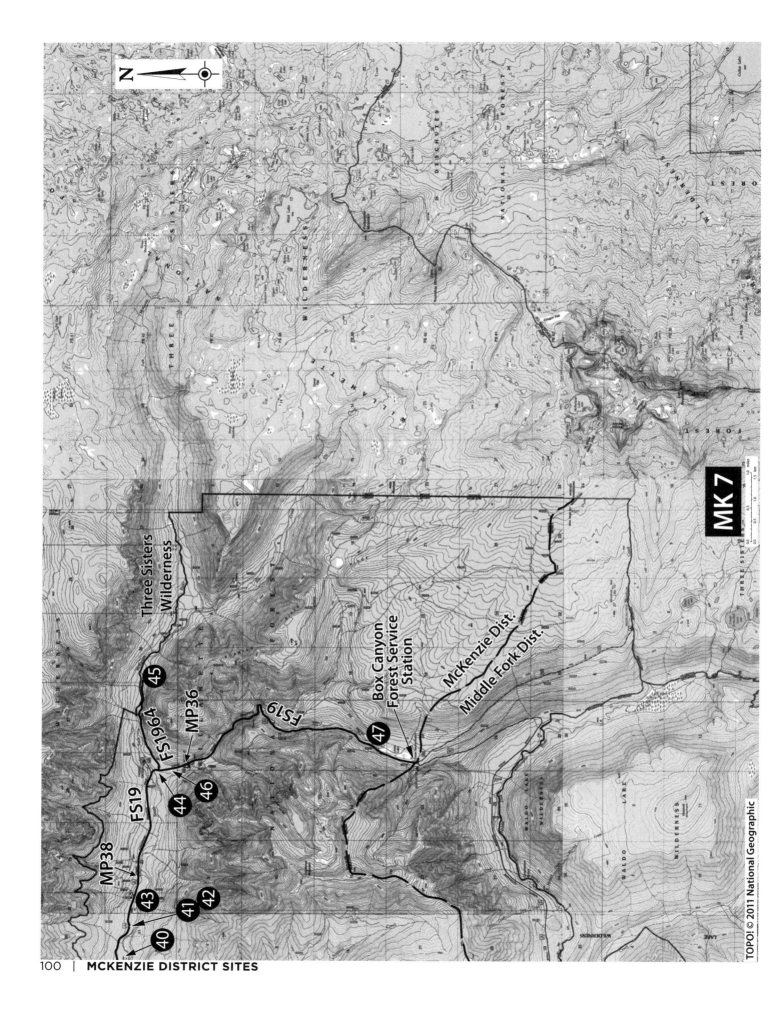

N

Three Sisters
Wilderness

FS1964

MP36

45

44 46

FS19

MP38

FS19

43 41 42

40

Box Canyon
Forest Service
Station

47

McKenzie Dist.

Middle Fork Dist.

MK7

TOPO! © 2011 National Geographic

MCKENZIE DISTRICT SITES

"We need the tonic of wildness...At the same time that we are earnest to explore and learn all things, we require that all things be mysterious and unexplorable, that land and sea be indefinitely wild, unsurveyed and unfathomed by us because unfathomable. We can never have enough of nature."
—Henry David Thoreau, *Walden: Or, Life in the Woods*

Loc: Hackleman Cr., 0.2 M. from OR 20	**Road:** Gravel, then dirt
L/L: N44 24 736/W122 02 544	**Access:** DTC, UOP
Cell: Site #27, Sweet Home Dist	**Tents:** 6–8
Nearest H2O: Hackleman Cr.	**El:** 3170
Lndmk: OR 20/126 junction, 2.7 M. ENE	**RV:** MH and TT

Description: A choice site. One that is easy to reach, yet both far enough from OR 20 to offer solitude and tranquility beside the creek and far enough from FS2672 to be protected from the dust from passing cars. It is blessed with abundant large conifers for shade. Hackleman Creek, about 75 yards away, is easy to get to for water, fishing or for cooling off on a hot day. Its gentle susurration will be as good as a glass of warm milk for putting you to sleep at night.

Getting there: *(See map pg. 95)* On OR 20, turn south onto FS2672 near MP 68, 2.7 miles from the OR 20/126 junction. Drive 0.2 miles, then, just after crossing over Hackleman Creek, follow a dirt track to the left for a hundred yards into the trees.

Loc: Off FS2672, 0.3 mile from OR 20	**Road:** Gravel, then dirt
L/L: N44 24 677/W122 02 487	**Access:** Check MVUM
Cell: Site #27, Sweet Home Dist	**Tents:** 1–2
Nearest H2O: Hackleman Cr.	**El:** 3170
Lndmk: OR 20/126 junction, 2.7 M. ENE	**RV:** Small MH and TT

Description: Though neither as spacious nor as alluring as Site #1, this site will still serve as a decent weekend base camp and jumping-off place for taking advantage of the recreational possibilities of the surrounding area. Hackleman Creek can be seen beckoning through the trees, but looks to be on the other side of a brushy hike of 100 to 150 yards down a moderately steep grade. Water for camp use might be easier to obtain near the bridge, about a tenth of a mile back toward OR 20. Beware of building a fire here. The forest duff under your feet is flammable, and the fire ring left here by a previous camper may not have been excavated down to mineral earth.

Getting there: *(See map pg. 95)* On OR 20, turn south onto FS2672 near MP 68, 2.7 miles from the OR 20/126 junction. Drive 0.3 mile. Camp is on the left, at the end of a dirt track taking off from FS2672 at an angle.

Loc: East end of Fish Lake	Road: Paved
L/L: N44 23 879/W122 00 201	Access: Check MVUM
Cell: Site #27, Sweet Home Dist	Tents: 25–50
Nearest H2O: None	El: 3200
Lndmk: Fish Lake and OR 126	RV: MH and TT

Description: A large, waterless area with multiple campsites well separated from each other for privacy. Many are open to sunlight, but ample tree cover provides shade when needed. Disadvantages for the solitude seeker might be the proximity of OR 126, which can be busy on weekends, though there are more peaceful campsites to be found to the rear of the area. Horse campers also use this site. Hikers and mountain bike riders should consider traveling back in time on the nearby Old Santiam Wagon Road and the trail to Clear Lake. Both can be picked up on the east side of OR 126. Look for Fish Lake Creek crossing under the road about a tenth of a mile southwest.

Getting there: *(See map pg. 95)* Headed east on US 20, turn south onto OR 126 near milepost 70. Headed south on OR 22, go right on Route 20 about three miles to the 20/126 junction, then south on OR 126 to Fish Lake. Site is about 0.1 mile south of the Fish Lake Interpretive Center, on right.

Loc: FS2672, 2.7 M. S of SR20	Road: Gravel, mountain
L/L: N44 23 167/W122 00 853	Access: Check MVUM
Cell: Site #27, Sweet Home Dist, Sno-Park	Tents: 4–5
Nearest H2O: Ikenich Cr.	El: 3253
Lndmk: FS 2672/1598 junction, 0.9 M. N	RV: MH and TT

Description: Set well back from the road on a dirt track and located in a large clearing interspersed with soaring, old growth conifers, this site guarantees privacy and solitude. Ikenich Creek, about 200 yards away through the woods, runs sluggishly between two modest slopes. It is accessible via a tortuous trail, but better water is available from Hackleman Creek, less than 2.5 miles north on FS2672.

Getting there: *(See map pg. 95)* On OR 20, turn south onto FS2672 near MP 68, 2.7 miles from the OR 20/126 junction. Drive 2.7 miles. Camp is on the left, at the end of a dirt track, about 100 yards off of FS2672.

Loc: FS2657 (Ollalie Cr. Rd.), 1.4 M east of OR 126	Road: Gravel
L/L: N44 16 344/W122 01 258	Access: Check MVUM
Cell: Along OR 126 near Blue River Res.	Tents: 4–6
Nearest H2O: Ollalie Cr. (in camp)	El: 2494
Lndmk: FS2657/830 junction, 100 yds. east	RV: MH and TT

Description: Taking the road less traveled to this happy little creek chuckling through a stand of second growth conifer trees will put things right for you in no time. There is ample shade here, with room for three to four tents near a circular turnaround and another two or three near the creek.

Getting there: *(See map pg. 95)* Traveling north or south on OR 126, between Trail Bridge and Ollalie Campgrounds and near MP 13, turn east onto FS2657. Drive 1.4 miles from OR 126 to site, on right. FS 2657 was in excellent condition in the summer of 2014.

Loc: FS2657, 1.6 miles east of OR 126	**Road:** Gravel (very good)
L/L: N122 16 413/W122 01 106	**Access:** Park and carry
Cell: Along OR 126 near Blue River Res.	**Tents:** 7–8
Nearest H2O: Ollalie Creek (across road)	**El:** 2388
Lndmk: FS2657/830 junction, 100 yards west	**RV:** MH and TT

Description: This shaded and breezy but waterless site is about a hundred yards off the road in a clearing surrounded by tall second growth conifers. It offers ample shade and only a few mosquitoes. Be careful of the meadow, which is home to numerous wildflowers during the summer. Find water for camp use near site #5, about a tenth of a mile west of the junction with Spur 830.

Getting there: *(See map pg. 95)* Follow the directions to Site #5, then continue another 0.2 mile on FS2657. Site is on left.

Loc: FS 2654-650, 0.1 mile west of OR 126	**Road:** Dirt, one lane
L/L: N44 14 150/W122 03 03 458	**Access:** Park and carry
Cell: Along OR 126 near Blue River Res.	**Tents:** Many
Nearest H2O: McKenzie R.	**El:** 1900
Lndmk: Junction FS2654/OR 126	**RV:** MH, yes, TT?

Description: A delightfully secluded prime campsite located in a large clearing next to a swift section of the McKenzie.

Getting there: *(See map pg. 97)* Driving on OR 126, turn onto FS2654 just north of MP 15 and go 0.1 mile northwest. Take Spur 650 two-tenths mile south to camp, on right.
A third (waterless) campsite can be found about a hundred yards north of FS2654

Loc: FS2654-650 off OR 126	**Road:** Dirt, one lane
L/L: N44 14 112/W122 03 444	**Access:** Check MVUM
Cell: Along OR 126 near Blue River Res.	**Tents:** 10–15
Nearest H2O: McKenzie R (in camp)	**El:** 1900
Lndmk: OR 126/FS2654	**RV:** No

Description: This large, comfortable and shady camp is located on a fast-moving section of the McKenzie River, so care should be taken when camping here with small children.

Getting there: *(See map pg. 97)* From OR 126, turn onto FS2654 just north of MP 15. Drive 0.1 mile northwest, then take Spur 650 south 0.25 mile to a rock barricade. Park and carry gear the last one hundred yards on level track to camp near the shore of the McKenzie.

Loc: Lost Creek, end of Spur 220, off Scenic Byway 242	Road: Paved, then dirt
L/L: N44 10 294/W122 02 212	Access: Check MVUM
Cell: Unincorporated town of Rainbow off OR 126	Tents: 3–5
Nearest H2O: Lost Cr.	El: 1795
Lndmk: Limberlost Cg., 1 mile NW	RV: Use judgment with small MH

Description: This shady and comfortable camp is about a hundred feet from Lost Creek, which runs more like a small river through overhanging alder brush. There is good access to the creek for water for camp use and fishing, if allowed, via a curving path leading out of the rear of camp. Except for a few drink cans in the fire pit, this camp was clean when discovered. The noise of the creek is not so loud as to be intrusive.

Getting there: *(See map pg. 97)* From OR 126, turn south onto the McKenzie Pass-Santiam Pass Scenic Byway at MP 55. At 2.3 miles, look for Spur 220 taking off to the left. Camp is at 0.2 mile, where the road ends. The road is traversable but may be too overgrown and narrow for an RV.

Loc: Lost Creek, off Scenic Byway 242	Road: Paved, then dirt
L/L: N44 09 769/W122 01 762	Access: Check MVUM
Cell: Along OR 126 near Blue River Res.	Tents: 6–10
Nearest H2O: Lost Creek	El: 1895
Lndmk: Spur 205-295, across road	RV: Use judgment

Description: A charming little camp on forest duff under tall conifer trees that will make a good base camp for a weekend of exploring. Camp fifteen feet above a swift section of Lost Creek. A relatively steep but negotiable trail allows access to the creek, but be careful when camping with children here.

Getting there: *(See map pg. 97)* From OR 126, turn south onto the McKenzie Pass-Santiam Pass Scenic Byway at MP 55. At 3 miles, turn left on an unmarked dirt track. Camp is 100 yards off the road.

Loc: Scenic Byway 242	Road: Paved, then dirt
L/L: N44 09 591/W122 01 104	Access: Check MVUM
Cell: Along OR 126 near Blue River Res.	Tents: 8–10
Nearest H2O: Lost Cr.	El: 1955
Lndmk: MP 59, 100 yds.	RV: MH and TT

Description: This waterless site in the trees about a hundred yards off the Scenic Byway is visible from the road but would be a good site for a large group. There is a house a couple of hundred yards west of the location, so make sure you can camp here before you drive a tent stake. Water can be obtained from Lost Creek on the other side of 242 near MP 59.

Getting there: *(See map pg. 97)* From OR 126, turn south onto the McKenzie Pass-Santiam Pass Scenic Byway at MP 55. At 3.6 miles, turn left on an unmarked dirt track where you see a grove of tall trees behind a small meadow.

Loc: Scenic Byway 242	**Road:** Paved, then dirt track for 0.2 M.
L/L: N44 09 846/W121 59 593	**Access:** Check MVUM
Cell: Along OR 126 near Blue River Res.	**Tents:** 2–3
Nearest H2O: White Branch Creek	**El:** 2110
Lndmk: White Branch Youth Camp, 1 M. E	**RV:** Use judgment

Description: A delightful little camp in a clearing surrounded by large mixed conifers. Nearby is robust but unpretentious little White Branch Creek, which offers a bottom of sand and pebbles and, downstream, a double-log bridge to the other side.

Getting there: *(See map pg. 97)* From OR 126, turn south onto the McKenzie Pass-Santiam Pass Scenic Byway at MP 55. At 4.9 miles, turn right onto Spur 247. Camp is near where Spur 248 splits off from 247, 0.2 mile south of the Scenic Byway.

Loc: Alder Springs Cg./Linton Lk. T.H.	**Road:** Paved
L/L: N44 10 627/W121 54 829	**Access:** DTC, UOP
Cell: Along OR 126 near Blue River Res.	**Tents:** 5–10
Nearest H2O: Spring above camp, local creeks	**El:** 3565
Lndmk: Alder Springs Rest Stop, near Camp	**RV:** MH and TT

Sign near the White Branch Youth Camp on the Santiam Pass-McKenzie Pass Scenic Byway

Description: Camp at this convenient Forest Service campground and don't pay a dime! It's clean. There are five solid picnic tables with fire rings and a nearby pit toilet that also serves as a roadside rest stop. Hike to Linton Lake on the nearby trail. Though its namesake Alder Springs is a couple of hundred yards uphill from camp, I found the amount of water it provides to be minimal, so make sure you have some aboard before camping here.

Getting there: *(See map pg. 97)* From OR 126, turn south onto the McKenzie Pass-Santiam Pass Scenic Byway at MP 55. At 10.5 miles, a sign will announce the camp and rest stop, on left. *Note: Vehicles over 35 feet in length are prohibited from driving this highway past the White Branch Youth Camp.*

Loc: Scenic Byway 242	**Road:** Paved
L/L: N44 10 976/W121 54 409	**Access:** Check MVUM
Cell: Along OR 126 near Blue River Res.	**Tents:** 3–4
Nearest H2O: Local Creeks	**El:** 3834
Lndmk: Alder Springs Cg., 1.3 M. downhill	**RV:** MH and TT, under 35'

Description: *(Overnight/Emergency)* A camp of last resort that offers privacy, but little else. Make sure you're carrying your own water.

Getting there: *(See map pg. 97)* This site is a little over a mile up the hill from the Alder Springs Campground. Between two sharp S-curves at 11.8 miles, where the road curves eastward around an open, flat area screened from the road by a stand of thickly growing maple trees.

Loc: Irish Camp Lk, FS2649	**Road:** Gravel
L/L: N44 11 950/W121 55 459	**Access:** Park and carry, UOP
Cell: Along OR 126 near Blue River Res.	**Tents:** 1
Nearest H2O: Irish Camp Lake or nearby creeks	**El:** 4640
Lndmk: Spur 676 to Prince Lk. Tr., 1 M. W	**RV:** On road only

15

Late summer afternoon along the north shore of Irish Camp Lake

Description: Those who can stake their claim here will have this whole picturesque and serene little mountain lake to themselves for the simple reason that this is the only place to camp around the lake. Haul your gear from road to campsite on a gently-sloping 100-yard-long trail. The single tent site near the fire pit slopes gently to the lake. FS2649 is very lightly traveled.

Getting there: *(See map pg. 97)* Driving east on OR 126 (McKenzie R. Hiway), turn right onto FS2649 between MP 57 and 58 (1.5 miles past the Belknap Springs Road). Go 8.5 miles to lake, staying to the left where FS2649 splits into two roads at around 4.5 miles. About a mile after Spur 676 takes off to the left to Trailhead #3508, you will see the lake on your left. Park on the road and carry gear about a hundred yards down a rough trail to the single campsite on the south shore of the lake. As mountain roads go, most of FS2649 is smooth and fast. Just a few of the steeper sections are washboarded.

Loc: Scott Lake	**Road:** Paved, then dirt
L/L: N44 12 647/W121 53 240	**Access:** Mostly park and carry
Cell: OR 126 near town of Rainbow, or try around Lake	**Tents:** 17–34
Nearest H2O: Scott Lake	**El:** 4800
Lndmk: Turn-off to Frog Camp, about 0.5 M. S	**RV:** Sites along road only

16

Description: When it comes to camping, Scott Lake is definitely one of the crown jewels of the Willamette National Forest. There are maintained facilities here, including picnic tables and outhouses, yet camping is free with the purchase of an Interagency Access Pass, a Northwest Forest Pass, National Forest Recreational Pass or a Golden Age Passport. Otherwise, there is a five dollar day use fee required. This lake has a fan base of people who camp here regularly and are almost fiercely protective of the place. Many of them use the collapsible

Camping at Scott Lake

carriers made for jogging with small children to ferry their gear to preferred spots well away from the road. The bottom of the lake is sandy and inviting for swimming. There is a boat launch for canoes and small boats. You will need to get here early in the week to claim your campsite, especially during the peak camping months of summer.

Getting there: *(See map pg. 97)* From OR 126, turn right onto the McKenzie Pass-Santiam Pass Scenic Byway at MP 55. At 16 miles (around the 71 mile marker) and about a half a mile past the turn-off to Frog Camp, turn left onto Spur 260. Drive 0.6 miles to lake, where you will begin to see the first campsites on the right.

17

Loc: Horse Creek Road (FS 2638)	**Road:** Gravel, then dirt
L/L: N44 09 231/W122 05 280	**Access:** Check MVUM, P&C
Cell: Along OR 126 near Blue River Res.	**Tents:** 1–2
Nearest H20: Horse Creek	**El:** 1645
Lndmk: End of paved road, 0.4 M. W	**RV:** No

Description: A small, well-shaded destination site in the trees near Horse Creek.

Getting there: *(See map pg. 97)* From OR 126, head south on Horse Creek Road (FS2638) after crossing the bridge over the McKenzie at the little town of McKenzie Bridge. Go 4.8 miles in a southeasterly direction. Follow an unnamed dirt track about 0.1 mile through the trees to the left.

18

Loc: Horse Creek	**Road:** Gravel, then primitive dirt
L/L: N44 09 078/W122 04 514	**Access:** Check MVUM, P&C
Cell: Along OR 126 near town of Rainbow and Blue R. Res.	**Tents:** 1–2
Nearest H20: Horse Creek	**El:** 1616
Lndmk: Spur 460, 0.2 mile ESE	**RV:** Use judgment

Description: A cool, shaded site located directly on Horse Creek.

Getting there: *(See map pg. 97)* From OR 126, just after crossing the bridge over the McKenzie at the little town of McKenzie Bridge, go 5.5 miles in a southeasterly direction on Horse Creek Road (FS2638). Then follow an unnamed dirt track about 0.1 mile through the trees to the left.

Loc: FS2638 on Horse Creek	Road: Gravel, then dirt
L/L: N44 08 031/W122 02 501	Access: Check MVUM, P&C
Cell: Town of Rainbow on OR 126 (unincorporated)	Tents: 1–2
Nearest H2O: Horse Creek	El: 2082
Lndmk: Spur 352, 0.1 mile NW	RV: No

Description: A cool and densely shaded destination site in a small clearing very near fast-moving Horse Creek. Privacy, shade, shelter, and easy access to the creek.

Getting there: *(See map pg. 97)* From OR 126, go south on Horse Creek Road (FS2638) just after crossing the bridge over the McKenzie at the little town of McKenzie Bridge. Go 7.7 miles in a southeasterly direction. Park and carry gear along an unnamed dirt road through the trees to the left to site.

Loc: FS15-105 at the end of SE arm of Blue R. Lk.	Road: Gravel
L/L: N44 10 496/W122 17 237	Access: Check MVUM
Cell: Some reception along FS15	Tents: 1–2, at least
Nearest H2O: Blue River Lk., local creeks	El: 1400
Lndmk: FS15/1501 junction, 0.1 mile S	RV: Use judgment with MH and TT

Looking north from Site #20

Description: This site, at the end of the shorter southeastern arm of Blue River Lake, offers seclusion, privacy, shade, and access to a rocky beach for swimming and boating. Expect competition for this site.

Getting there: *(See map pg. 96)* From OR 20, take FS15 south from a point about 0.6 miles west of the Tombstone Sno-Park and drive 11 miles to FS15/2656 junction, then continue another 15 miles on FS15. Turn right onto Spur 105 (aka the Saddle Dam Road). Site is 0.3 mile from FS15, on right, about a hundred yards off the road.
From OR 126 (the McKenzie River Hiway) near MP 41, go north 0.7 mile on FS15, then left 0.25 mile on Spur 105 to site, on right, overlooking the Lake.

Loc: Spur124	Road: Paved
L/L: N44 11 512/W122 15 456	Access: Park and carry
Cell: Along OR 126 near Blue River Res.	Tents: 2
Nearest H2O: Blue R. Lk., local Creeks	El: 1400
Lndmk: Bridge to Mona Lk. Cg., 1.2 M. N	RV: No

Description: A campsite at the end of a short road (#124) leading off of FS15 toward the reservoir. I was unable to inspect the site, and can't report as to lake access from it, although campers I encountered in the area later told me that there is a beach below this campsite. Use judgment when camping here. FS15 gets a lot of traffic during the summer months.

Getting there: *(See map pg. 96)* From OR 20, take FS15 south from a point about 0.6 miles west of the Tombstone Sno-Park and drive 11 miles to FS15/2656 junction, then continue another 12.9 miles on FS15 to site, on right.

From OR 126 (the McKenzie River Hiway) near MP 41, go 2.7 miles north on FS15 to site, on left. The gravel apron at the turn-off has been considerably chewed up by overuse and/or heavy vehicles. Use judgment.

Loc: Blue R., very near Blue R. Lk.		**Road:** Paved	
L/L: N44 12 612/W122 15 813		**Access:** Check MVUM	
Cell: Along OR 126 near Blue River Res.		**Tents:** 2–3	
Nearest H2O: Blue R.		**El:** 1490	
Lndmk: Bridge over Blue R. to Mona Cg., 0.2 M. S		**RV:** No	

Description: A nice family-size campsite about a hundred feet off the road and a quarter of a mile from the north end of Blue River Lake. Moderate privacy.

Getting there: *(See map pg. 96)* From OR 20, take FS15 south from a point about 0.6 miles west of the Tombstone Sno-Park and drive 11 miles to FS15/2656 junction, then continue another 11.6 miles on FS15 to site, on right.

From OR 126 (the McKenzie River Hiway) near MP 41, go 4 miles north on FS15 to site, on left.

Loc: West Side of Blue R. Lk		**Road:** Dirt, primitive	
L/L: N44 11 816/W122 15 760		**Access:** Check MVUM	
Cell: Along OR 126 near Blue River Res.		**Tents:** 2	
Nearest H2O: Nearby creeks		**El:** 1425	
Lndmk: Mona Cg., 0.4 M. N		**RV:** MH and TT	

Campers doing it right on the west side of Blue River Lake.

Description: A waterless site on a blunt point some 70 feet above Blue River Lake that offers a breathtaking view up and down the lake. Since the view comes at the expense of privacy from the few vehicles that drive the road on this side of the lake, you will need to employ some kind of POYP system along with a privacy shelter. Despite the sheer drop to the water, fishing is possible from the rocks above. Downsides: This site is not recommended for parties with small children because of the sheer drop-off to the lake. Also, the frequent roar of power boats and the voices of the people in them can be heard pretty much all day long, especially on weekends.

Getting there: *(See map pg. 96)* From OR 20, take FS15 south from a point about 0.6 miles west of the Tombstone Sno-Park and drive 11 miles to FS15/2656 junction, then continue another 11.8 miles on FS15 to the turn-off to Mona Campground, on right. Follow Mona Campground Rd. (Spur 120) 0.8 mile from the bridge .

From OR 126 (the McKenzie River Hiway) near MP 41, go 3.8 miles north on FS15 to Spur 120, on left.

Loc: West side of Blue River Lk	Road: Dirt, primitive
L/L: N44 11 605/W122 15 846	Access: Check MVUM
Cell: Along OR 126 near Blue River Res.	Tents: 1–2
Nearest H2O: Nearby creeks	El: 1425
Lndmk: Mona Cg., 0.6 M. N	RV: MH and TT

Description: Another small campsite above the lake with an excellent view. See Site #23.

Getting there: *(See map pg. 96)* From OR 20, take FS15 south from a point about 0.6 miles west of the Tombstone Sno-Park and drive 11 miles to FS15/2656 junction, then continue another 11.8 miles on FS15 to the turn-off to Mona Campground, on right. Follow Mona Campground Rd. (Spur 120) 1.1 mile from the bridge to site, on left.
From OR 126 (the McKenzie River Hiway) near MP 41, go 3.8 miles north on FS15 to Spur 120, on left.

Loc: West side of Blue River Lk	Road: Dirt, primitive
L/L: N44 11 572/W122 15 893	Access: DTC, UOP
Cell: Along OR 126 near Blue River Res.	Tents: 1–2
Nearest H2O: Nearby creeks	El: 1425
Lndmk: Mona Cg., 0.7 M. N	RV: MH and TT

Description: See site #23.

Getting there: *(See map pg. 96)* From OR 20, take FS15 south from a point about 0.6 miles west of the Tombstone Sno-Park and drive 11 miles to FS15/2656 junction, then continue another 11.8 miles on FS15 to the turn-off to Mona Campground, on right. Follow Mona Campground Rd. (Spur 120) 1.2 mile from the bridge to site, on left.
From OR 126 (the McKenzie River Hiway) near MP 41, go 3.8 miles north on FS15 to Spur 120, on left.

Loc: FS15, 0.2 M. S of bridge over Blue River	Road: Paved, then rough dirt
L/L: N44 13 044/W122 15 775	Access: Check MVUM
Cell: Along OR 126 near Blue River Res.	Tents: 15–20, total
Nearest H2O: Local Creeks	El: 1430
Lndmk: Bridge over Blue R., 0.2 M. N	RV: MH and TT

Description: Here Spur roads 175 and 180 form a loop that gives access to four nice campsites, each sitting well above the river and with plenty of separation from the next. There is almost complete privacy except from those who might be passing by on the dirt track that connects these campsites. There is abundant shade and soft forest duff on which to pitch your tent. The river below is pleasing to listen to without being intrusive. Downsides are that people know about these camps. At least one of them bore evidence of having been the scene of a party when discovered in 2013. Also, one or two of the camps are perched very near a sheer drop to the river, which should be considered a hazard.

Getting there: *(See map pg. 96)* From OR 20, take FS15 south from a point about 0.6 miles west of the

Tombstone Sno-Park and drive 11 miles to FS15/2656 junction, then continue another 11.1 miles on FS15 to site, on right.

From OR 126 (the McKenzie River Hiway) near MP 41, go 4.6 miles north on FS15 (Blue River Rd) to site, about 0.2 mile south of the split with FS1509. Look for one of two primitive dirt roads taking off from the west side of the road. Take care when using the Spur 180 entrance. The drop-off from the roadway is severe enough to cause a passenger vehicle to scrape the pavement if not taken at an angle.

Loc: FS15 near FS15/1509	**Road:** Paved
L/L: N44 13 205/W122 15 855	**Access:** Check MVUM
Cell: Along OR 126 near Blue River Res.	**Tents:** 5–6
Nearest H20: Blue R.	**El:** 1370
Lndmk: Bridge over Blue R. and FS15/1509	**RV:** MH and TT

Description: An excellent large site at a bend in the river surrounded and sheltered by cedar and fir trees. Downside: campsites are visible from the road.

Getting there: *(See map pg. 96)* From OR 20, take FS15 south from a point about 0.6 miles west of the Tombstone Sno-Park and drive 11 miles to FS15/2656 junction, then continue another 10.9 miles on FS15 to site, on left, just after crossing the bridge over the Blue River.

From OR 126 (the McKenzie River Hiway) near MP 41, go 4.7 miles north on FS15 (Blue River Rd) to site, on right, near the bridge over the Blue River. *Drivers should be careful of the high shoulder of the road here.*

Loc: On Blue R., near Spur 500	
L/L: N44 13 557/W122 15 463	**Road:** Gravel
Cell: Along OR 126 near Blue River Res.	**Access:** Check MVUM
Nearest H20: Blue R., upstream or local creeks	**Tents:** 1–2
Lndmk: Spur 500, 0.1 mile SW	**El:** 1520
	RV: On road only

Description: Located in a rugged section of the river canyon, this small, waterless campsite above and well away from the river has more privacy from the road than several others along this stretch of the river. A trail that leads out of the downstream side of camp toward the river only goes far enough to give a tantalizing view of the river carving its way through solid rock.

Getting there: *(See map pg. 96)* From OR 20, take FS15 south from a point about 0.6 miles west of the Tombstone Sno-Park and drive 11 miles to FS15/2656 junction, then continue another 10.3 miles on FS15 to site, on left.

From OR 126 (the McKenzie River Hiway) near MP 41, go 5.3 miles north on FS15 (Blue River Rd) to site, on right, 0.1 mile NE of Spur 500.

Loc: On Blue R. near Spur 500	**Road:** Gravel
L/L: N44 14 010/W122 14 841	**Access:** Park and short carry
Cell: Along OR 126 near Blue River Res.	**Tents:** 1–2
Nearest H20: Blue R.	**El:** 1500
Lndmk: Spur 500, 0.9 M. SW (downstream)	**RV:** On road only

Description: A nice, small site on a shelf about 25 feet above the river that is, again, visible from the road. You will want to spend the entire day exploring the pools in the river near camp.

Getting there: *(See map pg. 96)* From OR 20, take FS15 south from a point about 0.6 miles west of the Tombstone Sno-Park and drive 11 miles to FS15/2656 junction, then continue another 9.6 miles on FS15 to site, on left. If you pass Spur 500 coming in from the west, you have gone too far.

From OR 126 (the McKenzie River Hiway) near MP 41, go 6.1 miles north on FS15 (Blue River Rd) to site, on right. Site is 0.9 mile NE of Spur 500. Camp is visible from the road, but there is no driveway to it. You will have to park near the road and schlep your gear to camp.

Loc: On the Blue R., 1.1 M. NE of Spur 500	**Road:** Gravel
L/L: N44 14 171/W122 14 645	**Access:** Park and short carry
Cell: Along OR 126 near Blue River Res.	**Tents:** 2–3
Nearest H2O: Blue R.	**El:** 1530
Lndmk: Spur 500, 1.1 M. SW (downstream)	**RV:** MH and TT

Description: A site some 20 feet above the river that is visible from the road. A trail leads to the river on the downstream side of camp.

Getting there: *(See map pg. 96)* From OR 20, take FS15 south from a point about 0.6 miles west of the Tombstone Sno-Park and drive 11 miles to FS15/2656 junction, then continue another 9.3 miles on FS15 to site, on left.

From OR 126 (the McKenzie River Hiway) near MP 41, go 6.3 miles north on FS15 (Blue River Rd) to site, on right.

Loc: FS15	**Road:** Gravel
L/L: N44 14 328/W122 14 482	**Access:** Park and short carry
Cell: Along OR 126 near Blue River Res.	**Tents:** 2–3
Nearest H2O: Blue R.	**El:** 1570
Lndmk: Spur 500, 1.4 M. SW (downstream)	**RV:** MH and TT

Description: This campsite, on a bluff about 12 feet above the river, is visible from the road and features a rectangular, sunken fire pit. It was relatively clean in 2013, but.....

Getting there: *(See map pg. 96)* From OR 20, take FS15 south from a point about 0.6 miles west of the Tombstone Sno-Park and drive 11 miles to FS15/2656 junction, then continue another 9 miles on FS15 to site, on left.

From OR 126 (the McKenzie River Hiway) near MP 41, go 6.6 miles north on FS15 (Blue River Rd) to site, on right. Site is about 100 feet off FS15.

Loc: Blue R. near Cook Cr., off FS15	**Road:** Gravel, then dirt
L/L: N44 15 097/W122 13 918	**Access:** Park and short carry
Cell: Along OR 126 near Blue River Res.	**Tents:** 3–5
Nearest H2O: Cook Cr.	**El:** 1720
Lndmk: FS15/520 junction, 100 yds	**RV:** Small MH, N of bridge only

Description: *(a twofer)* Two campsites set among fir and cedar trees on the Blue River on opposite sides of tributary Cook Creek. The site north of Cook Creek has the potential for being a comfortable and private camp notwithstanding the fact that a large puddle of water forms near the entrance in rainy weather. The southern camp has fewer possibilities for tent sites, but the river in front of it has more recreational potential due to the presence of some enticing, deep, clear pools there. The water of the Blue River is swimmable, at least in August. Both sites were in need of cleanup in the summer of 2013.

Getting there: *(See map pg. 96)* From OR 20, take FS15 south from a point about 0.6 miles west of the Tombstone Sno-Park and drive 11 miles to FS15/2656 junction, then continue another 7.9 miles on FS15 to site, on, on left near Spur 520.
From OR 126 (the McKenzie River Hiway) near MP 41, go 7.7 miles north on FS15 (Blue River Rd) to site, or right, at the confluence of Cook Creek and Blue River. Site is about 50 feet from FS15.

Loc: Near Lookout Cr., off FS1506	**Road:** Gravel, mountain
L/L: N44 13 944/W122 11 013	**Access:** Park and carry
Cell: Along OR 126 near Blue River Res.	**Tents:** 6–15
Nearest H2O: Lookout Cr.	**El:** 1996
Lndmk: Classical Basalt Cliff where road turns sharply	**RV:** Use judgment w/Small MH

Description: A meadow camp in a grassy field near lightly-traveled FS1506 sheltered to the northeast by an imposing basalt cliff. You will find shade along the margins of the field. A rough trail takes you through a tunnel of dense alder and big leaf maple to a fast section of Lookout Creek.

Getting there: *(See map pg. 96)* From OR 20, take FS15 south from a point about 0.6 miles west of the Tombstone Sno-Park and drive 11 miles to FS15/2656 junction, then continue another 12.1 miles on FS15. Turn left onto FS1506 and go 5.5 miles to site, on right, where a rough dirt track leads down to an open field.
From OR 126 (the McKenzie River Hiway) near MP 41, go 3.0 miles north on FS15, then right on FS1506.

*Note 1: You can follow FS1506 another 1.4 miles to hike the Lookout Creek Old Growth Trail, which takes off from FS1506 and meanders through the H.J Andrews Experimental Forest. Here you will have the opportunity like no other to learn about how a mature forest works.

The H.J Andrews Forest **"...is the most studied primal forest ecosystem on this continent, and perhaps the planet. That does not mean that scientists here have found every cog and wheel, much less every relationship between them. But here they have discovered a host of species previously unknown to science, and interactions in the forest ecosystem that no one previously imagined. Here, in the shadows of this wood, in its rivulets and streams, under its soil, and high overhead, they have discovered a hidden forest."** from The Hidden Forest by Jon Luoma

*Note 2: Though there are some sections of FS1506 where evasive driving is required, generally speaking, it is above average, as mountain roads go.

Loc: Wolf Meadow, off FS15	Road: Gravel, then dirt track
L/L: N44 18 140/W122 08 517	Access: Check MVUM
Cell: Along OR 126 near Blue River Res.	Tents: 6–10
Nearest H2O: Possibly Wolf Creek near camp	El: 3715
Lndmk: Junction FS15/2656, 0.8 M. W	RV: Use judgment

Description: A comfortable and secluded camp in a large clearing on Wolf Meadow at the end of FS1500-635 that was occupied when discovered. There are plenty of trees around to provide shade and privacy, but water for camp use might not be a given here. Make sure you are traveling with enough to get you through until the next day if you camp here.

Getting there: *(See map pg. 94)* From OR 20, take FS15 south from a point about 0.6 miles west of the Tombstone Sno-Park and drive 11 miles to FS15/2656 junction, then continue another 0.8 miles on FS15 to site, on left, about 0.1 mile from FS15 on a dirt track.
From OR 126 (the McKenzie River Hiway) near MP 41, go 14.9 miles north on FS15 to Spur 635, on right. Site is 0.75 miles west of FS15/2656.

Loc: FS19, 0.1 M. past Augusta Cr. FS1927 Bridge	Road: Paved, then dirt to camp
L/L: N43 59 207/W122 10 557	Access: DTC, UOP
Cell: Along OR 126 near Blue River Res.	Tents: 10–15
Nearest H2O: S.F McKenzie R.	El: 2085
Lndmk: Augusta Creek Bridge, 0.1 M.	RV: Check MVUM

Description: Classic Pacific Northwest camping among soaring conifers on the shore of one of Oregon's most iconic wild rivers. In addition to the three campsites here, each capable of accommodating at least two tents, there are two camper-maintained outhouses. Each campsite offers privacy and easy access to the river. The last and largest offers a dilapidated picnic table and an open, grassy area as well as a small, stony beach overlooking a deeper, slower section of the river.

Getting there: *(See map pg. 98)* Driving east on OR 126 (McKenzie Pass Hiway), turn south on FS19 about a third of a mile past MP 45. Continue south 15.9 miles. At 0.1 mile past the Augusta Creek Bridge (FS1927), turn right into the camping area using either the second or third entries. Avoiding the abrupt shoulder of the first one may save the bottom of your vehicle from contact with the pavement.

Loc: FS1927, on Loon Cr.	Road: Gravel, mountain
L/L: N43 58 470/W122 10 912	Access: Park and carry
Cell: Along OR 126 near Blue River Res.	Tents: 1–2
Nearest H2O: Loon Cr.	El: 2520
Lndmk: Junction FS19/1927, 1 M. N	RV: Small MH

Description: A relatively nice campsite in a thick grove of mixed alder and conifer trees near an attractive and deep pool formed where Loon Creek emerges from a huge culvert under the road.

Getting there: *(See map pg. 99)* Driving east on OR 126 (McKenzie Pass Hiway), turn south on FS19 about a third of a mile past MP 45. Continue south 15.8 miles, where you will cross the South Fork of the McKenzie River on a bridge, then take FS1927 to the right for one mile to Loon Creek. Park and carry gear to camp is at the end of an unmarked 150-foot track leading off to the left almost directly opposite Spur 200.

Loc: On Augusta Creek and FS1927	**Road:** Gravel, mountain
L/L: N43 58 030/W122 10 784	**Access:** Park and carry
Cell: Along OR 126 near Blue River Res.	**Tents:** 2–3
Nearest H2O: Augusta Cr.	**El:** 2390
Lndmk: Junction FS19/1927, 1.6 M. N	**RV:** Small MH

Description: A roomy and pleasant little camp under a towering fir tree and several smaller big leaf maple trees.

Getting there: *(See map pg. 99)* Driving east on OR 126 (McKenzie Pass Hiway), turn south on FS19 about a third of a mile past MP 45. Continue south 15.8 miles, where you will cross the South Fork of the McKenzie River on a bridge, then take FS1927 to the right 1.6 miles to site, on left, where you will see an opening in the trees toward the creek. Park and carry gear to camp.

Loc: S. Fk. McKenzie R., 1.7 miles from FS1927	**Road:** Paved, then dirt
L/L: N43 58 089/W122 09 512	**Access:** Park and carry
Cell: OR 126 around Blue Riv. Res.	**Tents:** 5–10
Nearest H2O: S. Fk. McKenzie R.	**El:** 2300
Lndmk: Homestead Camp	**RV:** No

Description: *(Homestead Campground)* This site, the old decommissioned Homestead Campground would be great for a group. It features plank benches arranged around a fire ring in full view of the river running along energetically just a few feet below. The reward for those willing to carry their gear the extra hundred yards is escape from the internal combustion engine for the duration of their stay.

Getting there: *(See map pg. 99)* From OR 126 (McKenzie Pass Hiway), turn south on FS19 about a third of a mile past MP 45. Continue south 17.5 miles to site, on right, 1.7 miles past the Augusta Creek Bridge (FS1927). Park and carry 100 yards beyond a locked gate.

Loc: S. Fk. McKenzie R., 2,5 miles from FS1927	**Road:** Paved, then forest track
L/L: N43 57 823/W122 08 604	**Access:** DTC, UOP
Cell: OR 126 around Blue Riv. Res.	**Tents:** 3–4
Nearest H2O: S. Fk. McKenzie R.	**El:** 2420
Lndmk: Homestead Cg., 0.8 M. WNW	**RV:** Small MH, Use judgment with TT

Description: Here a huge, overhanging cedar tree leans against its equally imposing neighbor like a drunken sailor to shelter the center of this camp from anything but a steady, day-long downpour. An easy path crosses a shallow branch of the river to the McKenzie, some hundred yards behind camp. Closer to camp, this branch offers convenient access to water for camp use. The huge cedar trees are dwarfed by two humongous fir trees on the edge of camp, one of which looks to be close to eight feet in diameter at chest height. This camp was pleasingly clean when discovered, but there was a definite toilet paper garden about a hundred yards out in the woods that was crying to be cleaned up. Got glompers?

Getting there: *(See map pg. 99)* From OR 126 (McKenzie Pass Hiway), turn south on FS19 about a third of a mile past MP 45. Continue south 18.3 miles to site, on right, 0.8 mile past a decommissioned Homestead Cg. at the end of a wide, dirt track.

40	Loc: FS19, 3.7 miles past the Augusta Cr. Bridge	Road: Paved, then forest track
	L/L: N43 57 865/W122 08 242	Access: DTC, UOP
	Cell: OR 126 around Blue Riv. Res.	Tents: 3–5
	Nearest H2O: S. Fk. McKenzie R.	El: 2430
	Lndmk: Homestead Camp, 1 M. W	RV: Entry road may be too rough

Description: This camp is in a clearing ringed by soaring fir trees growing on a shelf about fifteen feet above a flat, overgrown, ancient flood plain of the McKenzie. There is a small creek feeding into the river directly across from camp. A path drops steeply toward the river for about ten feet, and then levels out to easier walking. The McKenzie narrows and runs very swiftly here, so parties with children should take heed.

Getting there: *(See map pg. 100)* Driving east on OR 126 (McKenzie Pass Hiway), turn south on FS19 about a third of a mile past MP 45. Continue south 18.6 miles to site, on right, 1 mile past Homestead Camp. The dirt road leading to the site is rocky and rutted and needs to be driven with considerable care.

41	Loc: S. Fk. McKenzie R., 4.1 miles from Augusta Cr. Br.	Road: Paved, then forest track
	L/L: N43 57 713/W122 07 891	Access: DTC, UOP
	Cell: Along OR 126 near Blue River Res.	Tents: 1–2
	Nearest H2O: S. Fk. McKenzie R.	El: 2450
	Lndmk: FS1900-435, 0.6 M. E	RV: Use judgment w/small MH

Battened down for rain along the McKenzie

Description: A charming, comfortable, sheltered and picturesque little camp very close to a more moderate section of the McKenzie. Ease of access to the river, privacy, and solitude.

Getting there: *(See map pg. 100)* From OR 126 (McKenzie Pass Hiway), turn south on FS19 about a third of a mile past MP 45. Continue south 19 miles to site, on right, 1.5 miles past Homestead Camp. Take the dirt track to camp. Check MVUM.

Loc: S. Fk. McKenzie R., 0.5 M. W of 1900-435	Road: Paved, then forest track
L/L: N43 57 706/W122 07 840	Access: DTC, UOP
Cell: Along OR 126 near Blue River Res.	Tents: 1
Nearest H2O: S. Fk. McKenzie R.	El: 2470
Lndmk: FS1900-435, 0.5 M. E	RV: Small MH

Description: Another inviting camp in the sheltering conifer trees along the shores of the McKenzie. This site is just a few hundred feet east of Site #41. Camp overlooks a huge log jam, which causes the river to break into rapids. Privacy, solitude, shade, and a view of the river. Camp was clean when discovered.

Getting there: *(See map pg. 100)* Follow directions to Site #41. Entrance is about a hundred yards beyond that camp's entryway. Camp is seventy-five yards off FS19.

Loc: FS1900-436, 4.6 miles from Augusta Cr. Br.	Road: Paved, then forest track
L/L: N43 57 657/W122 07 332	Access: DTC, UOP
Cell: Along OR 126 near Blue River Res.	Tents: 4–6 total
Nearest H2O: S. Fk. McKenzie R.	El: 2520
Lndmk: Spurs 428, 902, 903, across from entrance	RV: MH and TT

Camper maintained outhouse along the McKenzie

Description: *(a twofer)* There are two campsites nestled here under the forest giants so typical of this lush temperate forest. Though both are large in area, choice tents sites are limited to just a few in each site. The river is about a hundred yards away via a path through the brush and trees and is not visible from camp. All sites offer shade, privacy and solitude. There is a camper-maintained outhouse. A stout wooden pedestal with two upright galvanized pipes marks the spot and indicates that this may once have been a pay campground.

Getting there: *(See map pg. 100)* From OR 126 (McKenzie Pass Hiway), turn south on FS19 about a third of a mile past MP 45. Continue south 19.4 miles to site, on right, 1.5 miles past Homestead Camp. Take the dirt track 200 yards to camp. Watch for a wide dirt track leading toward the river from a concrete apron. The first campsite is 50 yards from the road.

Loc: FS19, near Frissell Crossing Cg.	Road: Paved, then forest track
L/L: N43 57 372/W122 05 143	Access: DTC, UOP
Cell: Along OR 126 near Blue River Res.	Tents: 15–20
Nearest H2O: Local creeks	El: 2420
Lndmk: Frissell Crossing Cg, 0.25 mile	RV: MH and TT

Description: A huge clearing perched on a shelf about 25 feet above the South Fork of the McKenzie. There are several campsites here and the location, though conducive to neither privacy nor seclusion, is ideal for a large group. The sheer drop to the river below makes getting water here next to impossible, however. Avoid the temptation to use the facilities in nearby campgrounds.

Getting there: *(See map pg. 100)* From OR 126 (McKenzie Pass Hiway), turn south on FS19 about a third of a mile past MP 45. Continue south 22 miles to intersection with FS1964 (Elk Creek Rd.). Turn right at an acute angle just after crossing bridge.

Loc: Elk Cr. Rd. FS1964, near Frissell Crossing	Road: Gravel, then forest track
L/L: N43 57 476/W122 03 392	Access: Check MVUM
Cell: Along OR 126 near Blue River Res.	Tents: 1 small
Nearest H20: S. Fk. McKenzie R. or local creeks	El: 2820
Lndmk: Frissell Crossing Cg., 1.6 M. W	RV: No

Description: A small and very secluded camp way off the beaten path. The McKenzie can be heard clearly through the trees to the north, but there is no apparent path to it, so water will probably need to be brought in from somewhere else.

Getting there: *(See map pg. 100)* From OR 126 (McKenzie Pass Hiway), turn south on FS19 about a third of a mile past MP 45. Continue south 22 miles to the intersection with FS1964 (Elk Creek Rd.). Turn left and drive 1.6 miles to an unmarked dirt track curving off to the north. Camp is about 200 yards along dirt track.

Loc: FS19, on Roaring R.	Road: Paved, then forest track
L/L: N43 57 176/W122 05 091	Access: Check MVUM
Cell: Along OR 126 near Blue River Res.	Tents: 1–3
Nearest H20: Roaring R.	El: 2430
Lndmk: Roaring R. Cg., 0.2 M. S	RV: Small MH only

Description: This site is in a grove of giant fir trees on the edge of the river with mixed shade and sun, due to the spacing of the trees. There is easy access to the river, which runs swiftly enough to cause concern if there are small children about.

Getting there: *(See map pg. 100)* From OR 126 (McKenzie Pass Hiway), turn south on FS19 about a third of a mile past MP 45. Continue south 22.2 miles. Site is on the right on dirt track, 0.2 miles past the bridge over the South Fork of the McKenzie R. and the same distance north of the official Roaring River Group Campground and 0.1 mile from FS19. Avoid the temptation to use the facilities of Roaring River Cg.

Loc: Near McBee Cr., 05 M.	Road: Paved, gravel, mountain
L/L: N43 54 732/W122 04 707	Access: Check MVUM
Cell: Along OR 126 near Blue River Res.	Tents: 3–4
Nearest H20: Local creeks	El: 3685
Lndmk: Landis Cabin, 0.3 M. S	RV: MH and TT

Abandoned outhouse stands as lonely sentinel near the Landis Cabin

Description: Though effectively waterless, there is something that makes you want to linger at this site. It could be the loneliness of the place or the way the meadow turns gold under the afternoon sunlight near the curving line of wooden fencing at the bottom of the hill. Or maybe it's the little outhouse standing like a sentinel off in the woods, abandoned so long now that there is no trace of the path that hurried feet must have once worn to it. Getting to sluggish McGee Creek, a few hundred yards down a gentle slope is easy enough, but you won't want to take your water from it.

Getting there: *(See map pg. 100)* From OR 126 (McKenzie Pass Hiway), turn south on FS19 about a third of a mile past MP 45. Continue south 25.8 miles. Turn left onto FS1958. At the bottom of the hill near the wooden fencing, go left a few hundred yards toward the trees. Park and camp near the road on the right, where you will see the outhouse.

From SR 58, drive 35 miles to FS1958, 0.3 miles past the Landis Cabin. Turn right and follow directions above.

48

Loc: FS1509, just north of MP 18, near Bear Pass	Road: Gravel
L/L: N44 19 273/W122 15 353	Access: Park and short carry
Cell: Along OR 126 near Blue River Res.	Tents: 3–4
Nearest H2O: Nearby creeks	El: 4095
Lndmk: Junction FS1509/1532, 0.2 M. N	RV: MH and TT

The lake and marshy meadow near Site #48

Description: There is an unforgettable sense of solitude and tranquility to be found just listening to the insects and watching the birds flying over the marshy area surrounding the tiny lake near this old hunters' camp just south of Bear Pass. Stay long enough for the breeze to activate the surrounding trees, and the feeling will become transcendent. Camp is about fifty feet off the road on forest duff under tall conifers, but is nevertheless relatively private by virtue of the fact that FS1509 is one of those seldom-traveled mountain roads. The elevation here should make it a good hot weather choice as well. A grove of large, closely spaced fir and hemlock trees provide shade and shelter. The lake's inlet is not apparent, but its outlet crosses under the road about 0.1 mile north on FS1509 and might be a source of running water for camp at that point if you can get to it through the brush. Otherwise, bring water from elsewhere. And, oh, yeah, there will be mosquitoes...

Getting there: *(See map pg. 94)* From OR 20 near MP 55, go south 10.1 miles on FS2044 (road to House Rock Campground) to its junction with FS1509. Continue 1.9 miles west (right) on FS1509, bearing left at its junction with FS2032, to site, on right.

From OR 126, take FS15 4.8 miles, turning left onto FS1509 and driving 17.4 miles to camp, on left.

Alternatively, it is possible to pick up FS1513 about 8.4 miles north of OR 20, following that 11.3 miles to the junction with FS1509, from which camp is another 0.4 north, on left.

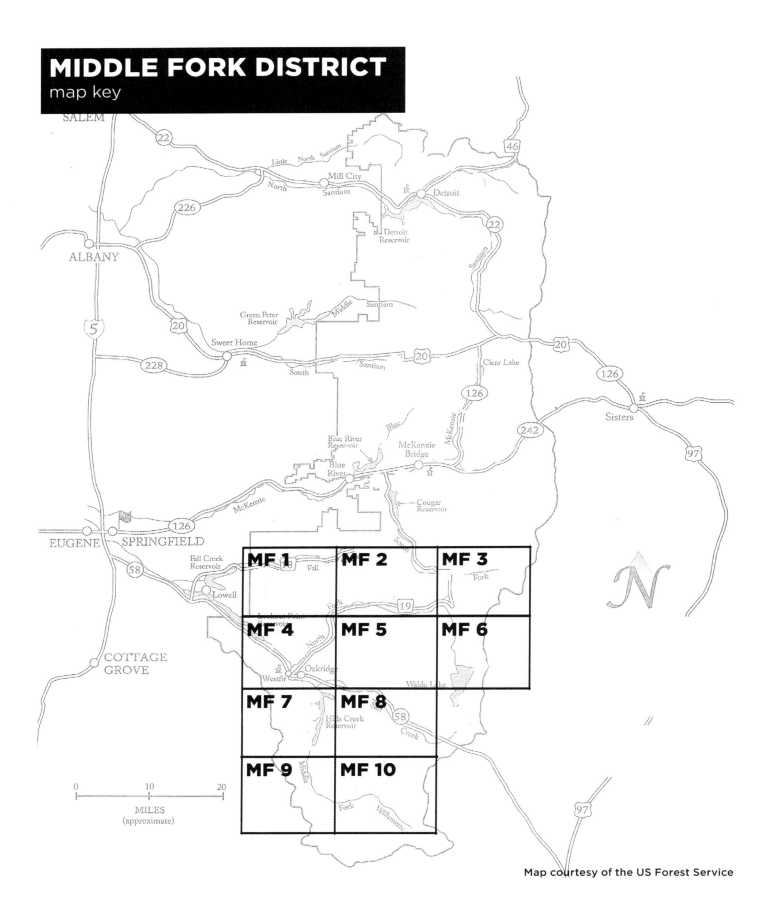

MIDDLE FORK DISTRICT
map key

Map courtesy of the US Forest Service

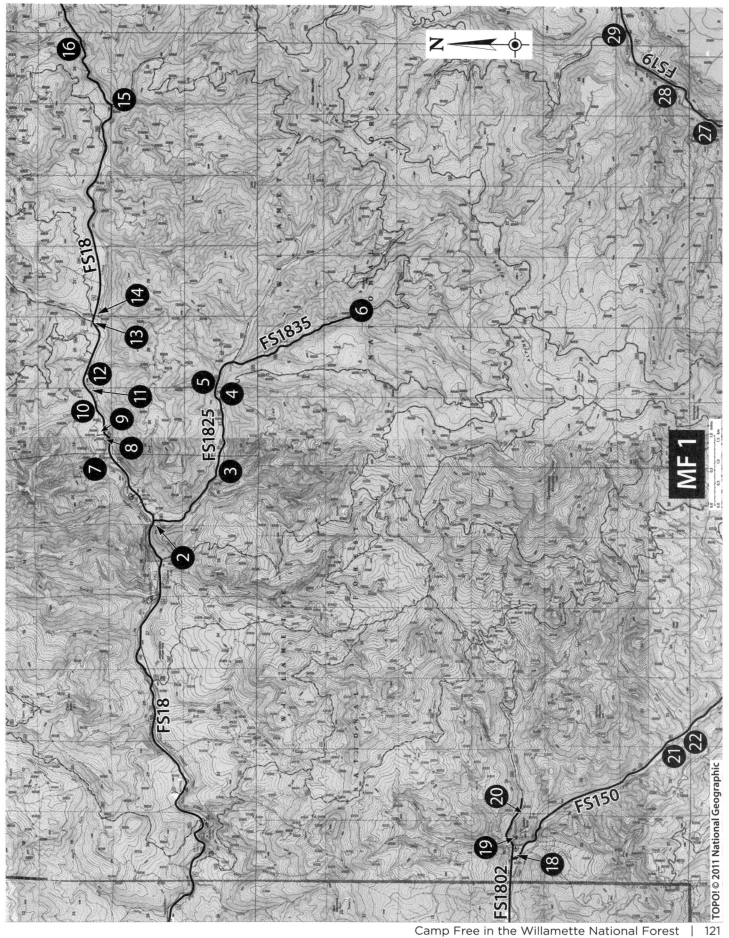

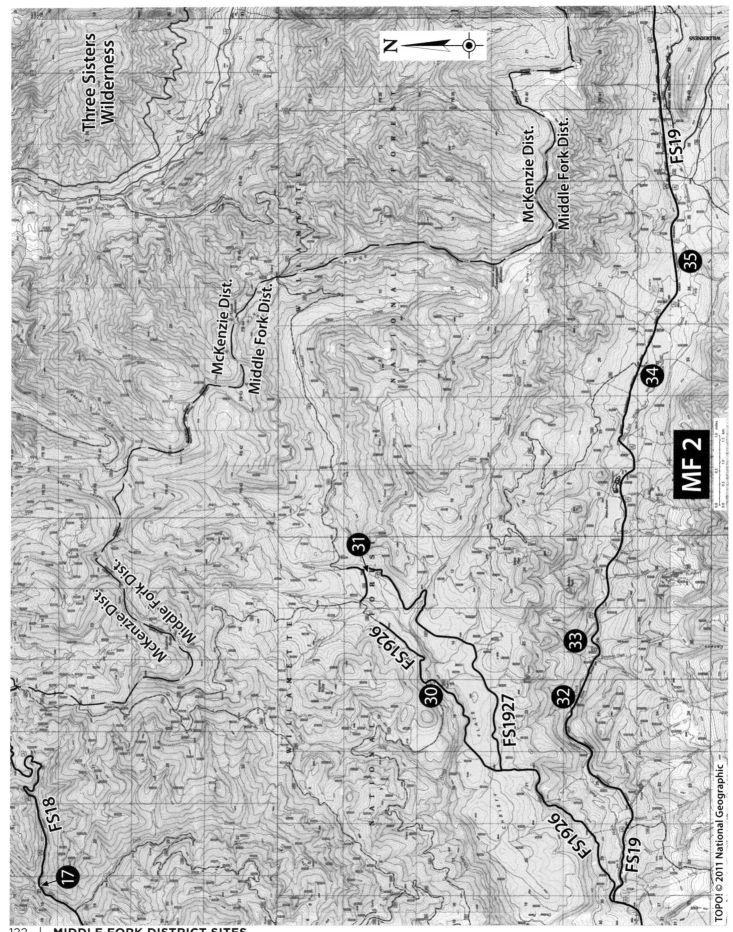

Three Sisters
Wilderness

McKenzie Dist.
Middle Fork Dist.

McKenzie Dist.
Middle Fork Dist.

McKenzie Dist.
Middle Fork Dist.

FS19

35

34

MF 2

FS1926

31

30

33

FS1927

32

FS1926

FS19

FS18

17

N

TOPO! © 2011 National Geographic

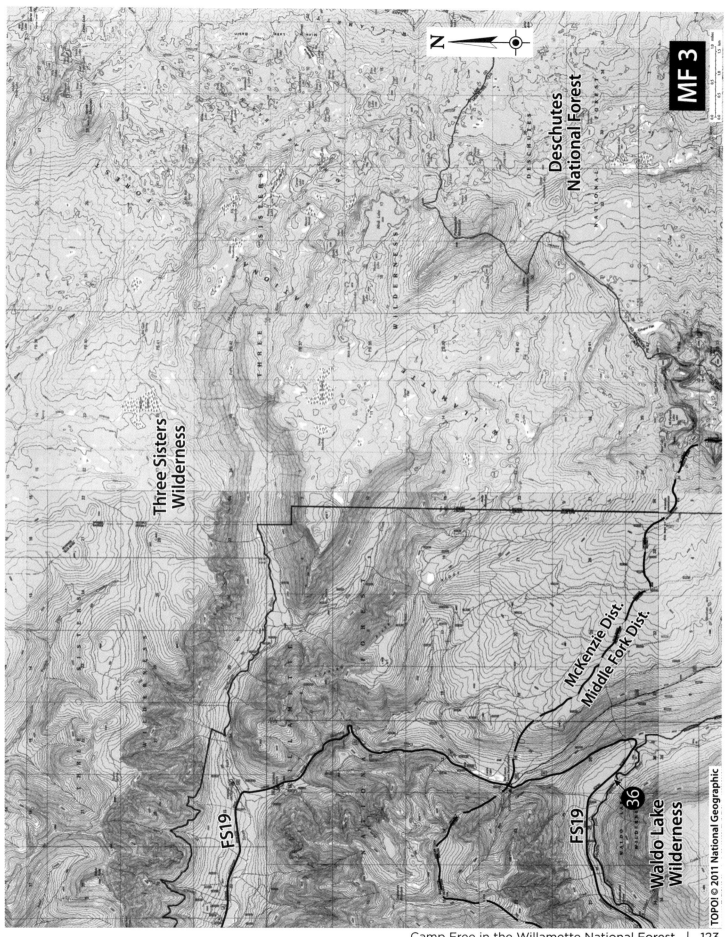

MF 3

N

Three Sisters
Wilderness

Deschutes
National Forest

McKenzie Dist.
Middle Fork Dist.

FS19

FS19

36

Waldo Lake
Wilderness

TOPO! © 2011 National Geographic

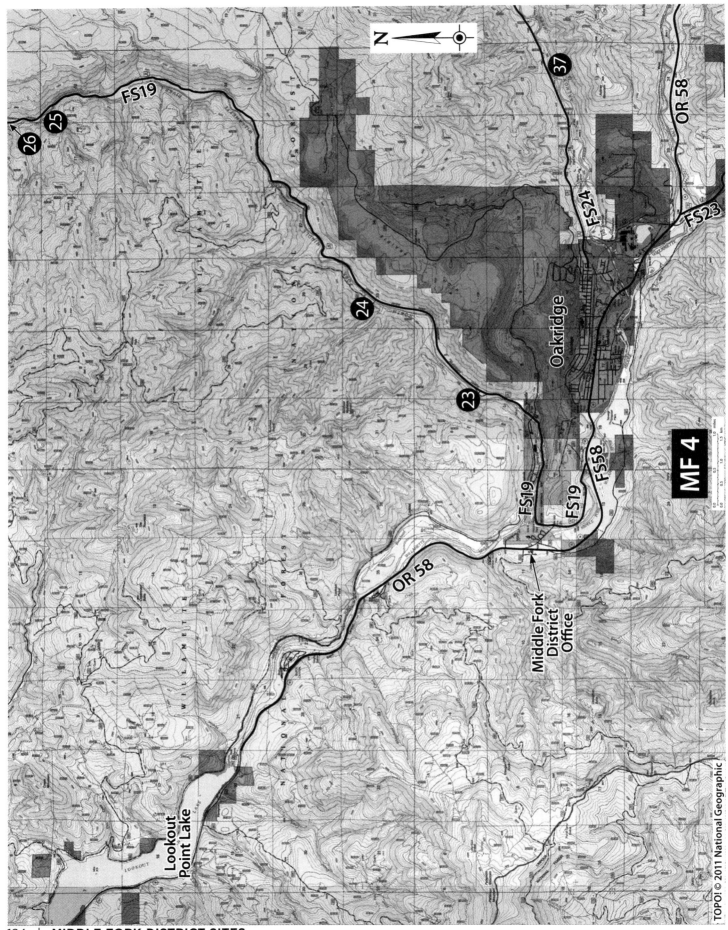

N

FS19

26
25

37

OR 58

FS24

FS23

24

Oakridge

23

MF 4

0.0   0.5   1.0   1.5 km
0.0   0.5   1.0   miles

FS19

FS19

FS58

OR 58

Middle Fork
District
Office

Lookout
Point Lake

TOPO! © 2011 National Geographic

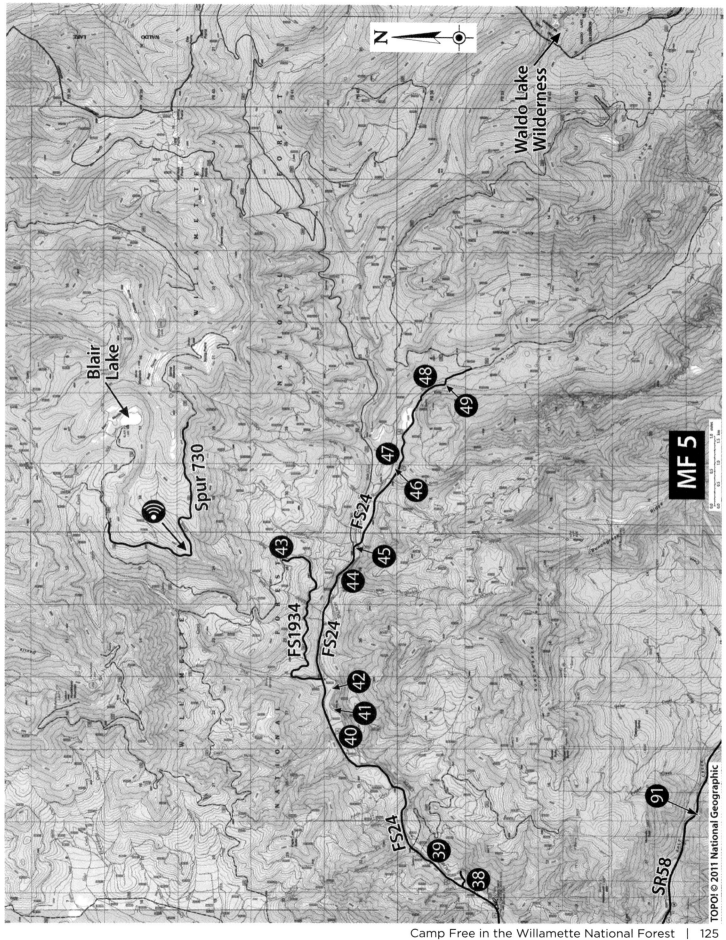

Blair Lake

Spur 730

Waldo Lake Wilderness

N

MF 5

Willamette National Forest

FS24

FS1934

FS24

FS24

FS24

SR58

48
49
47
46
45
44
43
42
41
40
39
38
91

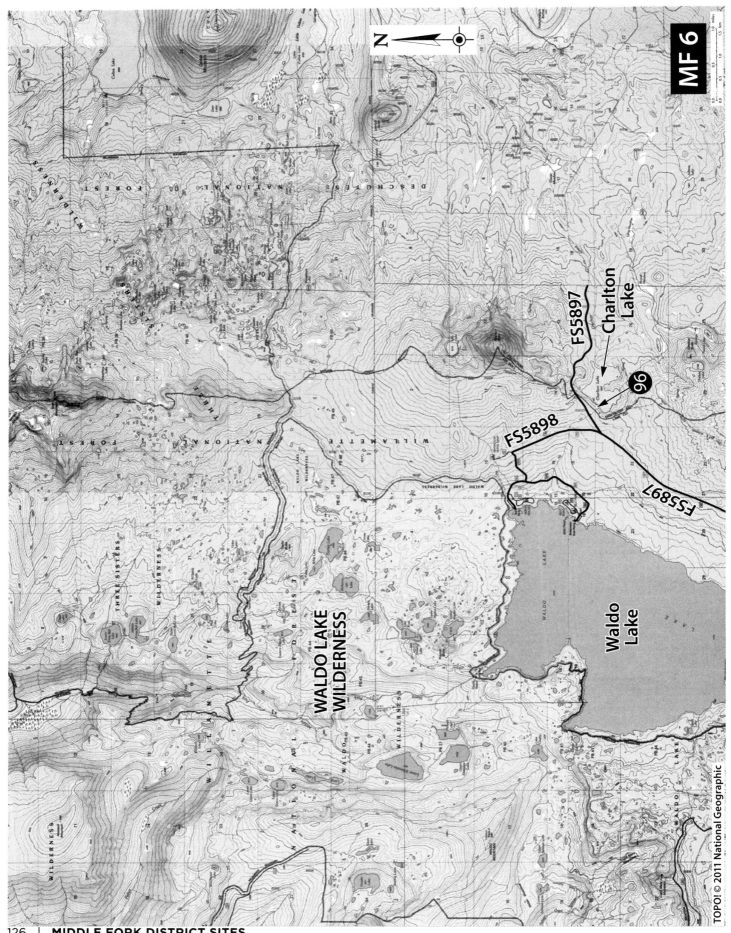

WALDO LAKE
WILDERNESS

Waldo Lake

Charlton Lake

FS5897

FS5898

FS5897

96

N

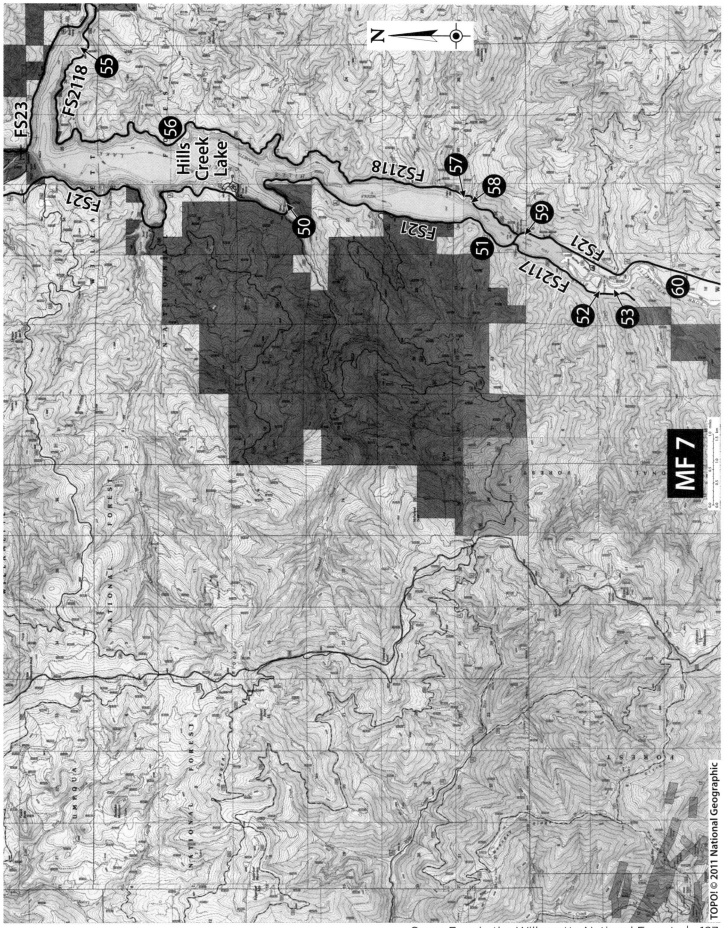

MF 7

TOPO! © 2011 National Geographic

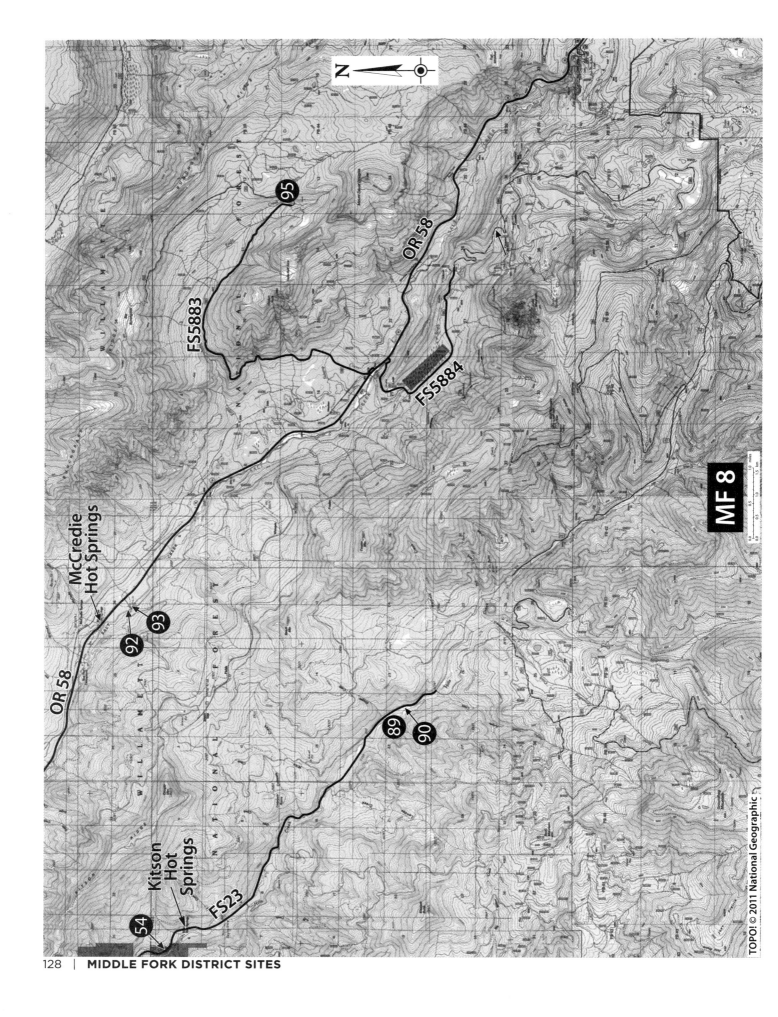

N

OR58

FS5883

95

FS5884

MF 8

1.0 miles
1.5 km

McCredie
Hot Springs

93

92

OR 58

89

90

Kitson
Hot
Springs

FS23

54

TOPO! © 2011 National Geographic

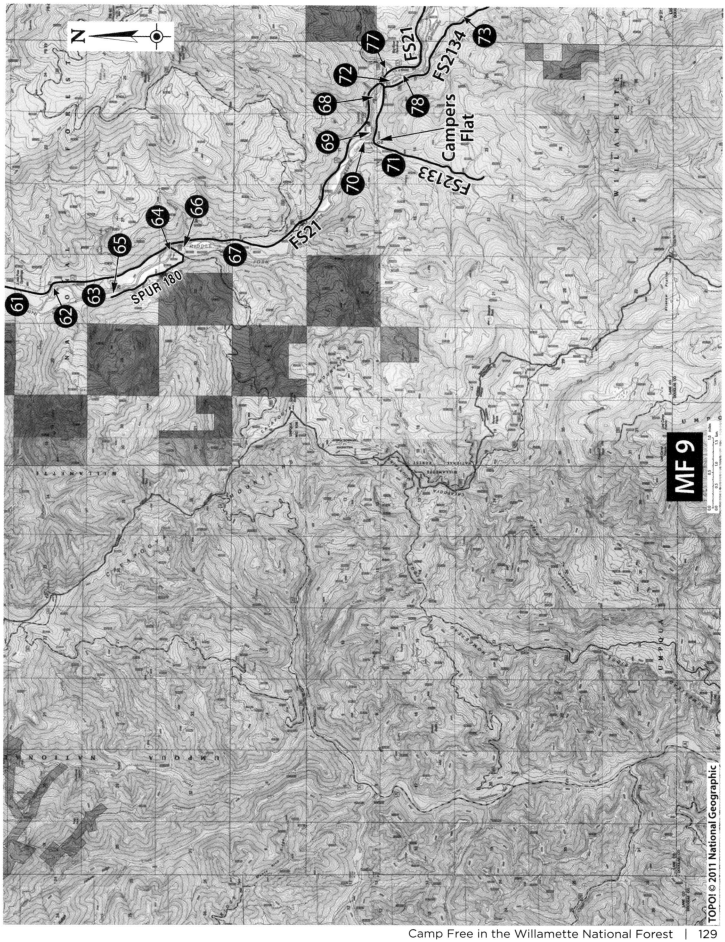

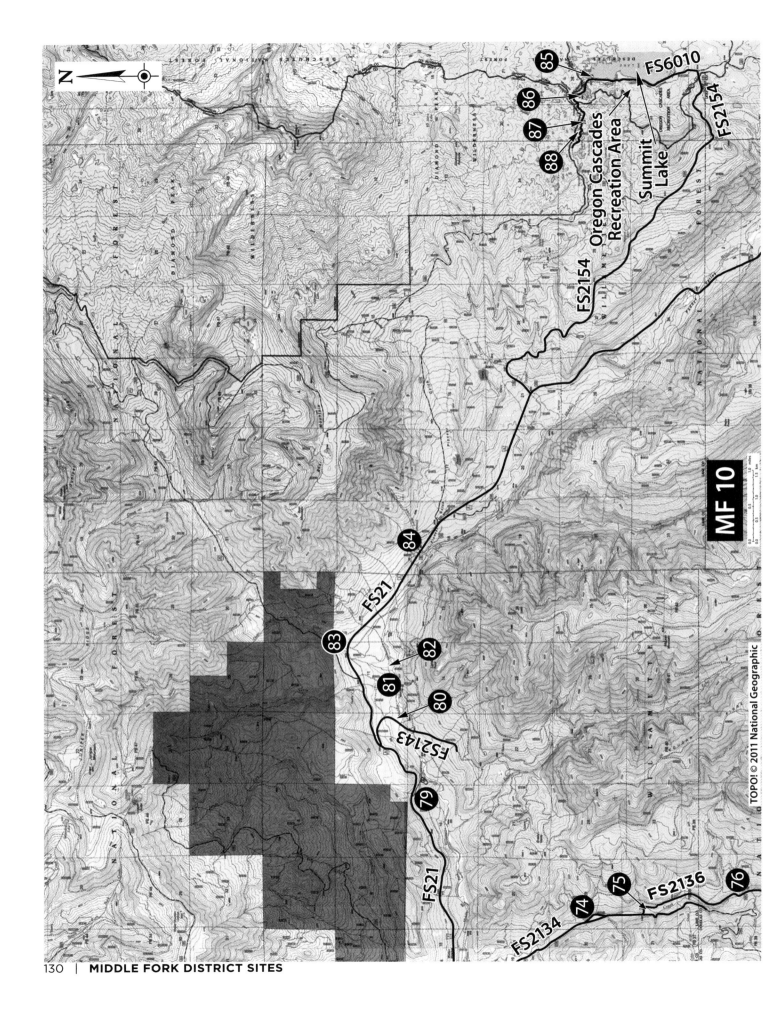

N

FS6010

85

86

87

88

Oregon Cascades
Recreation Area

Summit Lake

FS2154

FS2154

MF 10

84

FS21

83

82

81

80

FS2143

79

FS21

75

FS2136

76

74

FS2134

TOPO! © 2011 National Geographic

MIDDLE FORK DISTRICT SITES

"We are in danger of destroying ourselves by our greed and stupidity. We cannot remain looking inwards at ourselves on a small and increasingly polluted and overcrowded planet."
—Stephen Hawking

Loc: FS1825, near junction with FS18, on Portland Cr.	**Road:** Paved, then gravel
L/L: N43 58 337/W122 31 519	**Access:** DTC, UOP
Cell: From west end of Fall Cr. Reservoir to town of Lowell	**Tents:** 3–5
Nearest H2O: Portland Cr., near Camp	**El:** 1120
Lndmk: Puma and Bedrock Cgs.	**RV:** MH, yes; TT?

Description: Surrounded by maple and alder trees, this camp is in an open, circular area on hard-packed ground, with a border of dense foliage all around. Camp was in need of some clean-up in 2014.

Getting there: *(See map pg. 121)* Starting at the intersection of OR126 and Main Street in Springfield, drive south 2.1 miles to the Jasper-Lowell Road. Turning left (south) travel 15 miles to the unincorporated little town of Unity. *Warning: It is easy to take a wrong turn off of the Jasper-Lowell Road, so pay attention.* From the Unity Covered Bridge, follow the Fall Creek Road east another 0.4 miles, then turn left and take FS18 approximately 15 miles to FS1825. You will turn right onto FS1825 about half a mile past Bedrock Cg., and proceed 0.1 mile to a gravel road on the right leading downhill to camp.
A second, smaller camp is to be found by following the road to the left about a hundred yards past the first camp.

Loc: FS1825 at junction with spur 217, 1.4 miles from FS18	**Road:** Paved, then dirt
L/L: N43 57 618/W122 30 667	**Access:** DTC, UOP
Cell: From west end of Fall Cr. Reservoir to town of Lowell	**Tents:** 1
Nearest H2O: Portland Cr., 100 Ft.	**El:** 1311
Lndmk: Junction FS1825/217	**RV:** Use judgment with MH

Deep pool near Spur 214 Bridge

Description: Though there is only one truly level tent site here, this cool and densely shaded site on Portland Creek is ideal for camping in the heat of summer. The site is surrounded by maple trees and dense underbrush that provide the shade and that feeling of privacy and seclusion that you seek in a campsite. Site may need some cleanup before use.

Getting there: *(See map pg. 121)* Site is on the right, 1.3 miles beyond Site #2.

Loc: FS1825, near the FS1825/1835 junction	Road: Paved to bridge
L/L: N43 57 558/W122 29 350	Access: Park and carry
Cell: From west end of Fall Cr. Reservoir to town of Lowell	Tents: 4-5
Nearest H2O: Portland Cr.	El: 1420
Lndmk: Bridge near FS1825/1835 junction	RV: Use judgment w/small MH

Description: A very private and comfortable camp set in a shaded clearing among straight, tall conifers and a few maple trees. The sound of Portland Creek, which runs moderately fast through a deep channel about a hundred yards from camp, is muted by dense underbrush. Downed logs in camp provide handy benches for relaxing. Water is best obtained about a hundred yards upstream of the bridge, where a short road leads directly to the creek.

Getting there: *(See map pg. 121)* This site is 2.4 miles beyond Site #2. Park in a wide spot in the road just past the bridge over Portland Creek and carry gear a few hundred feet to camp, on right.

Loc: On Portland Cr., near the FS1825/1835 junction	Road: Gravel, then dirt track
L/L: N43 57 627/W122 29 195	Access: DTC, UOP
Cell: From west end of Fall Cr. Reservoir to town of Lowell	Tents: 1-2 (small)
Nearest H2O: Portland Cr.	El: 1360
Lndmk: Bridge near FS1825/1835 junction	RV: Small MH only

Description: This densely shaded site is close to sparsely traveled FS1835 and directly above Portland Creek. A fire ring in the middle of camp limits the number of level tent sites. Portland Creek can be reached from camp, but, using a rope would be a good idea due to the steepness of the bank. Otherwise, water can be obtained more easily near the bridge, about a tenth of a mile west. Upstream of camp, a submerged log forms a shallow dam completely across the creek. There is a moderately deep pool and some promising trout habitat a short distance downstream.

Getting there: *(See map pg. 121)* Follow the directions to site #2, then continue 2.4 miles to FS1825/1835 junction. Fork left on FS1835. Camp is about 0.2 miles beyond the junction, on right.

Loc: FS1835, 2.6 miles from FS1825/1835 junction	Road: Gravel
L/L: N43 55 963/W122 27 954 (road coordinates)	Access: Check MVUM
Cell: From west end of Fall Cr. Reservoir to town of Lowell	Tents: 1 (small)
Nearest H2O: Portland and Nevergo Crs.	El: 1710
Lndmk: Bridge over Portland Cr, 2.6 miles NW	RV: No

Description: A somewhat littered but nevertheless charming site at the end of a rocky track taking off down-hill from FS1835 that is better suited to a small party due to scarcity of level tent sites. Use caution and judgment with the primitive bridge across Nevergo Creek. Because of the ravine and the density of the surrounding foliage, the coolness of the morning seems to linger here on hot days.

Getting there: *(See map pg. 121)* Follow the directions to site #5, but keep left where FS1835 splits off from FS1825. Camp is 2.6 miles from the FS1825/1835 junction. Look for a rock and gravel track taking off to the left toward the creek (which is probably Spur 102).

Loc: 0.3 mile N. of FS18 and 0.5 mile east of Puma Cg.	Road: Dirt and very rutted
L/L: N43 58 818/W122 30 497 (coordinates taken from FS18)	Access: Park and carry (0.3 M)
Cell: Along OR 126 near Blue River Res.	Tents: 5–7
Nearest H2O: Fall Cr.	El: 1160
Lndmk: Puma Cg., 0.5 mile west	RV: No

Description: Here you will find two spacious and comfortable campsites near Fall Creek. Ample shade is available from surrounding trees and vegetation.

Getting there: *(See map pg. 121)* Follow the directions to Site #2 but continue past FS1825 about a mile. About 0.5 mile beyond Puma Cg. you will find Spur 407 taking off toward the Creek. Park and carry gear to camp near Fall Creek, 0.3 mile from FS18). *Warning: This road is currently not shown on the MVUM.*

Loc: FS18, 0.9 mile NE of Puma Cr. Cg.	Road: Paved
L/L: N43 58 905/W122 30 098	Access: DTC, UOP
Cell: From west end of Fall Cr. Reservoir to town of Lowell	Tents: 3–4
Nearest H2O: Fall Cr.	El: 1190
Lndmk: Bridge across Fall Creek near FS1828	RV: MH and TT

Description: Fall Creek here is wide, clear and slow-moving, turning to audible riffles just downstream, where it narrows and begins to pick up speed. This site may require some cleaning before you take possession of it, since it is sandwiched between a well-traveled paved road and a scenic creek. Get out your garbage glompers. *There is a large level site on firm ground near the creek that would be an ideal overnight spot for a self-contained RV.*

Getting there: *(See map pg. 121)* Follow directions to Site #2, but continue on FS18. Camp is 0.9 mile past Puma Cr. Cg., on left, just before the bridge over Fall Creek.

Loc: FS18, 100 yards east of Fall Cr. Bridge	Road: Paved
L/L: N43 58 944/W122 29 973	Access: DTC, UOP
Cell: From west end of Fall Cr. Reservoir to town of Lowell	Tents: 1–2 small
Nearest H2O: Fall Cr.	El: 1200
Lndmk: Fall Cr. Bridge and FS1828	RV: No

Description: *(Overnight/Emergency)* A small but comfortable site exposed to the road.

Getting there: *(See map pg. 121)* Follow instructions to site #2. Continue past FS1825. Look for camp about a mile ENE of Puma Cg., on right and just beyond the bridge.

Loc: FS18, 1.3 miles past Puma Cr. Cg.	**Road:** Paved
L/L: N43 59 049/W122 29 591	**Access:** Park and carry
Cell: From west end of Fall Cr. Reservoir to town of Lowell	**Tents:** 3–4
Nearest H20: Alder or Fall Creeks	**El:** 1130
Lndmk: Bridge across Alder Cr.	**RV:** No

Description: Though I was unable to inspect this site up close, it appeared to be a private and comfortable camp on a bench above the road, near a wide, gravel parking area.

Getting there: *(See map pg. 121)* Follow instructions to site #2, but continue past FS1825. Find site 1.3 miles from Puma Cr. Cg., on left, just before crossing over Alder Cr.

Loc: FS18, 1.6 miles east of Puma Cr. Cg	**Road:** Gravel
L/L: N43 59 103/W122 29 312	**Access:** DTC, UOP
Cell: From west end of Fall Cr. Reservoir to town of Lowell	**Tents:** 3–5
Nearest H20: Fall Cr.	**El:** 1200
Lndmk: FS18/1828 junction, 0.6 mile west	**RV:** MH and TT

Description: A large, sunny, open area amid tall trees a hundred yards off FS18. The surrounding vegetation is mainly alder, maple, and mixed conifers. Fall Creek appears to be about a hundred yards from camp. Author was unable to inspect this camp or discover access to Fall Creek.

Getting there: *(See map pg. 121)* Follow directions to site #2. Continue past the FS18/1825 junction. Site is about 100 yards off FS18 on wide, curving gravel track, 0.6 mile beyond the FS18/1828 junction and about 1.6 miles beyond Puma Cr. Cg.

Loc: FS18, 2.0 miles past Puma Cg., on Fall Cr.	**Road:** Paved, then dirt
L/L: N43 59 178/W122 28 895	**Access:** DTC, UOP
Cell: From west end of Fall Cr. Reservoir to town of Lowell	**Tents:** 3–4
Nearest H20: Fall Cr.	**El:** 1110
Lndmk: FS18/1828 junction, 1 mile west	**RV:** Small MH; TT (?)

Description: A comfortable, shaded camp which is visible from the road.

Getting there: *(See map pg. 121)* Follow directions to site #2. Continuing on FS18, the site is 1 mile past the FS18/1828 junction, on right and about 100 feet from the road.

Loc: FS18 and across road from FS18/1831 junction, on Hehe Cr.	**Road:** Paved, then dirt
L/L: N43 59 091/W122 28 103	**Access:** DTC, UOP
Cell: From west end of Fall Cr. Reservoir to town of Lowell	**Tents:** 2–3
Nearest H20: Hehe Cr.	**El:** 1250
Lndmk: FS18/1831 junction, across road from camp	**RV:** MH and TT

Description: A large, shaded, but open area just downstream from a bridge. For a cooling summertime soak, there is an easily accessible pool just downstream of camp.

Getting there: *(See map pg. 121)* Follow instructions to site #2. Continuing on past FS1825, camp is 2.6 miles beyond Puma Cg., on right. Look for the junction with FS1831, and you're there.

Loc: On Hehe Cr. near its confluence w/Fall Cr.	**Road:** Paved, then dirt
L/L: N43 59 057/W122 28 001	**Access:** DTC, UOP
Cell: From west end of Fall Cr. Reservoir to town of Lowell	**Tents:** 1–3
Nearest H2O: Hehe Cr.	**El:** 1360
Lndmk: FS18/1831 junction, 100 yds.	**RV:** MH

Description: A comfortable and shady site near the confluence of the two creeks.

Getting there: *(See map pg. 121)* Follow directions to site #2. Site is 0.1 mile beyond site #13 and 100 yards off the right side of the road at the end of a dirt track and within a few hundred feet of the FS18/1832 junction.

Loc: At junction of FS18/1835	**Road:** Paved
L/L: N43 58 869/W122 24 413	**Access:** Park and short carry
Cell: From west end of Fall Cr. Reservoir to town of Lowell	**Tents:** 5–6
Nearest H2O: Creek near Camp	**El:** 1450
Lndmk: FS18/1835 junction	**RV:** MH

Description: This site at the junction of Gold and Fall Creeks is a mining claim, so beware of the law and the claim owner's rights when using it. It is set in a good-sized clearing surrounded by maple, cedar and conifer trees. A large fire ring in the center of camp limits the number of level tents sites, but a bench above and behind the clearing offers more tent sites and another fire ring. Access the creek via a steep, short path or from the other side of the bridge.

Getting there: *(See map pg. 121)* Follow directions to site #2. Continuing on FS18, drive approximately another 5.8 miles past Puma Cg. to the junction with FS1835 and you're home.

Loc: FS18, 7.2 miles from Puma Cg.	**Road:** Paved
L/L: N43 59 220/W122 23 398	**Access:** Park and carry
Cell: From west end of Fall Cr. Reservoir to town of Lowell	**Tents:** 3–5
Nearest H2O: Fall Cr.	**El:** 1425
Lndmk: FS18/1835 junction, one mile west	**RV:** No

Description: A large camp below the road on Fall Creek that was occupied at the time of discovery and which the author was unable to inspect.

Getting there: *(See map pg. 121)* Follow directions to site #2. Continuing on FS18, go another 7.2 miles beyond Puma Cg. Site is on Fall Creek, one mile past the FS18/1835 junction.

Loc: FS18, 0.6 mile past FS18/1839 junction	Road: Gravel, then dirt
L/L: N43 59 956/W122 22 145	Access: DTC, UOP
Cell: From west end of Fall Cr. Reservoir to town of Lowell	Tents: 2–4
Nearest H2O: Fall Cr.	El: 1975
Lndmk: FS18/1839 junction, 0.6 mile SW	RV: MH

Description: If you're looking for a comfortable, creekside camp in the shade, this site on Fall Creek near its confluence with Saturn Creek, is home.

Getting there: *(See map pg. 122)* Follow directions to site #2. Continue another 8 miles on FS18 to site, on right, 0.6 mile past FS18/1839 junction.

Loc: On the N. Fk. of Winberry Cr., just south of FS1802	Road: Paved, then dirt
L/L: N43 54 063/W122 37 154	Access: DTC, UOP
Cell: From west end of Fall Cr. Reservoir to town of Lowell	Tents: 3–4
Nearest H2O: Winberry Cr.	El: 1200
Lndmk: Junction FS1802/150/160	RV: MH and TT

Description: A large, circular camp with lots of room to spread out. Shaded by soaring conifers and surprisingly breezy despite the thick underbrush around camp, this would be a better choice than Winberry Campground for those who come to the woods in search of solitude. There is easy access to the North Fork of Winberry Creek.

Getting there: *(See map pg. 121)* Starting at the intersection of OR126 and Main Street in Springfield, drive south 2.1 miles to the Jasper-Lowell Road. Turning left (south) travel 15 miles to the unincorporated little town of Unity. *Warning: It is easy to take a wrong turn off of the Jasper-Lowell Road, so pay attention.* From the Unity Covered Bridge, follow the Fall Creek Road east another 0.4 miles, keeping right on the Winberry Cr. Road where it splits off from the North Shore Road (FS18). Follow the Winberry Creek Road, which turns into FS1802, 8.9 miles to its junction with Spurs 150 and 160. Turn right off of FS1802 just after the junction with FS150. Camp is about 100 yards from road, on dirt track.

Loc: FS1802 (Winberry Cr. Rd.), 9 miles from Unity	Road: Paved, then dirt
L/L: N43 54 090/W122 37 007	Access: DTC, UOP
Cell: From west end of Fall Cr. Reservoir to town of Lowell	Tents: 5–15
Nearest H2O: N. Fork, Winberry Cr.	El: 1195
Lndmk: Winberry Cr. Cg.	RV: MH and TT

Description: Decommissioned Winberry Creek Campground offers five nice campsites with good, solid picnic tables, fire pits with grates and a pit toilet that is camper maintained. The dense foliage around each site provides shade and a good deal of privacy. The sound of Winberry Creek gurgling by below camp is as calming as meditation. *There is a beautiful swimming hole about 1.8 miles west of Winberry Cg on FS1802, just downstream from the bridge over Winberry Creek.*

Getting there: *(See map pg. 121)* Follow directions to Site #18. Site is on right, 0.1 mile past Spurs 150 and 160.

Loc: FS1802, 0.8 miles from junction with spurs 150/160		**Road:** Gravel	
L/L: N43 54 024/W122 36 363		**Access:** DTC, UOP	
Cell: From west end of Fall Cr. Reservoir to town of Lowell		**Tents:** 2–3	
Nearest H2O: N. Fk., Winberry Cr.		**El:** 1420	
Lndmk: Junction FS1802/164, w/in 100 yds.		**RV:** MH and Small TT	

Description: A charming campsite in tall trees by the North Fork of Winberry Creek.

Getting there: *(See map pg. 121)* Follow the directions to site #18. Keep straight 0.8 mile past the FS1802/150/160 junction to site, on right, very near junction with Spur 164.

Loc: Spur 150, 2.9 miles from FS1802, on S. Fk. Winberry Cr.		**Road:** Paved to dirt track	
L/L: N43 52 345/W122 35 345 (road coordinates)		**Access:** Park and short carry	
Cell: From west end of Fall Cr. Reservoir to town of Lowell		**Tents:** 4–5	
Nearest H2O: South Fk. Winberry Cr.		**El:** 1565	
Lndmk: Junction FS1802/150/160, 2.9 miles NW		**RV:** MH and TT	

Waterfall and pool behind Site #21

Description: A spacious, secluded, shady, and comfortable campsite all by itself, but the beautiful waterfall on the South Fork of Winberry Creek, just a short distance from camp elevates it to a status all its own. There is also a deep, clear pool for swimming.

Getting there: *(See map pg. 121)* Follow directions to site #18 but turn right onto Spur 150. Drive 2.9 miles on a one-lane paved road to site, on right.

Loc: Spur 150, on S. Fk. Winberry Cr., near Monterica Cr.		**Road:** Paved to dirt track	
L/L: N43 52 059/W122 35 080		**Access:** DTC, UOP	
Cell: From west end of Fall Cr. Reservoir to town of Lowell		**Tents:** At least one	
Nearest H2O: S. Fk. Winberry Cr.		**El:** 1610	
Lndmk: FS1802/150/160 Junction, 3.2 miles NW		**RV:** Use judgment	

Description: Unable to inspect this site, but it appears to be a pleasant and comfortable site on the South Fork of Winberry Creek.

Getting there: *(See map pg. 121)* Follow directions to site #18, but turn onto Spur 150 and drive 3.2 miles on a one-lane paved road to site, on right.

Loc: FS19, near MP 1	Road: Paved
L/L: N43 46 155/W122 29 261	Access: DTC, UOP
Cell: Town of Oakridge and maybe Westfir	Tents: 1–2
Nearest H2O: N. Middle Fk. Willamette R.	El: 921
Lndmk: MP 1, 200 yards south of loop	RV: MH and TT

Description: This campsite is well shaded by trees and about ten feet above a clear, wide, slow section of the Willamette. You'll find privacy, solitude and access to the river, not to mention a cheeseburger in nearby Westfir or Oakridge.

Getting there: *(See map pg. 124)* From OR 126 (McKenzie Pass Byway), turn south on FS19 about a third of a mile past MP 45. Continue south 56.8 miles on FS19. Campsite is along a paved side road on the west side of FS19 that loops back onto same about 0.7 mile south, near MP 1.
From SR 58, drive 6 miles on FS19, and then follow directions above to site.

Loc: Near the FS19/1910 junction	Road: Gravel
L/L: N43 47 379/W122 27 767	Access: Park and carry
Cell: Towns of Oakridge or Westfir	Tents: 1–2
Nearest H2O: N. Middle Fk. Willamette R.	El: 1150
Lndmk: FS1910 bridge over the Willamette	RV: On road only

Description: This site, at the other end of the FS1910 bridge across the North Middle Fork of the Willamette, sits about twenty-five feet above the river. There is a steep trail from camp to the river, but walking it with a bucket of water might be tricky. A well-worn fishermen's trail that would make good single track for a mountain bike leads past camp and along the river in both directions. Shade and solitude are givens here, but the necessity of obtaining water somewhere else and the fact that the traffic across the river can be plainly heard are two apparent downsides.

Getting there: *(See map pg. 124)* From OR 126 (McKenzie Pass Byway), turn south on FS19 about a third of a mile past MP 45. Continue south 54.7 miles on FS19, crossing the bridge at its junction with FS1910. Campsite is 0.1 mile from FS19, on right. Park on road and carry gear a short distance.
From SR 58, drive 8 miles on FS19, and then follow directions above.

Loc: FS19, 0.5 M. S of MP 10	Road: Paved, then dirt track
L/L: N43 51 201/W122 24 543	Access: Park and carry
Cell: Towns of Oakridge and Westfir	Tents: 2–4 total
Nearest H2O: N. Middle Fk. Willamette R.	El: 1430
Lndmk: FS1920 bridge, 0.2 M. S	RV: MH and TT

Description: *(a twofer)* These two sites are a bit too close to the road and lacking in privacy to be considered anything more than **overnighting sites**. The smaller of the two is directly above a section of the river that runs clear and wide. Unfortunately, the only apparent tent site here is too close to the fire ring. Both sites are along a road that loops away from FS19, though one of the entrances is too abrupt and steep for practical use.

Getting there: *(See map pg. 124)* From OR 126 (McKenzie Pass Highway), turn south on FS19 about a third of a mile past MP 45. Continue south 48.2 miles on FS19. Look for a broad paved apron leading toward the river about 0.5 mile south of MP 10 and 0.2 mile north of the FS1920 bridge.

From SR 58, drive 12.5 miles on FS19, and then follow directions in the paragraph above.

Loc: FS19, opposite MP 10	**Road:** Paved and gravel
L/L: N43 51 601/W122 24 742	**Access:** DTC, UOP
Cell: Towns of Oakridge and Westfir	**Tents:** 10–20 total
Nearest H20: N. Middle Fk. Willamette R.	**El:** 1460
Lndmk: MP 10, across road	**RV:** MH and TT

Description: *(a "threefer")* Three good-sized campsites are to be found here. All provide easy access to a clear, wide section of the Willamette, shade, and privacy from any traffic passing by on FS19, though not necessarily from other campers.

Getting there: *(See map pg. 124)* From OR 126 (McKenzie Pass Highway), turn south on FS19 about a third of a mile past MP 45. Continue south about 48 miles on FS19. Near MP 10 take a wide, gravel and dirt turn-out toward the river. Campsites are spread out along the side road, which parallels the river for 0.2 miles before rejoining FS19 .

From SR 58, drive 13 miles on FS19, and then follow directions above.

Loc: FS1920, 0.9 M. from FS19	**Road:** Gravel, then dirt track
L/L: N43 51 719/W122 24 741	**Access:** DTC, UOP, or P&C
Cell: Towns of Oakridge and Westfir	**Tents:** 5–6
Nearest H20: N. Middle Fk. Willamette R.	**El:** 1380
Lndmk: FS1920 bridge, 0.9 M. S	**RV:** Road too rough

Description: Except for the difficulty of access, this is an excellent site, offering two campsites and a bit of beach on a wild section of the river, not to mention shade, seclusion and privacy. The second and larger campsite is hidden back in the trees behind the first and most obvious one.

Getting there: *(See map pg. 121)* From OR 126 (McKenzie Pass Hiway), turn south on FS19 about a third of a mile past MP 45. Continue south approximately 47 miles on FS19. Between MP 9 and 10, cross the river on the FS1920 bridge and drive 0.9 miles. Take a short, rough, steep, and rocky road a hundred yards down to more moderate terrain, where it makes an abrupt change of direction back toward the grove of trees above the river where the campsites are located. Be warned, after a rain you may encounter a dauntingly large puddle at the bottom of the initial steep stretch. Walk this road before you attempt to drive it, especially if you are traveling in a low-clearance vehicle.

From SR 58, drive 12.4 miles on FS19, and then follow directions in the paragraph above.

Loc: Off FS19, near MP 11	Road: Paved
L/L: N43 52 192/W122 24 006	Access: Park and carry, 100 yds.
Cell: Towns of Oakridge and Westfir	Tents: 3–4
Nearest H2O: N. Middle Fk., Willamette R.	El: 1600
Lndmk: MP 11, 100 yards, FS1920 1.7 M. south	RV: No

Description: Several welcoming and shady campsites that provide both privacy and seclusion along a path through the trees to the river.

Getting there: *(See map pg. 121)* Driving east out of Eugene or west from Oakridge on SR 58, turn north onto FS19 between MP 33 and 34. Camp is on left, about a hundred yards SW of MP 11. Park on a wide apron beside the road and carry gear a hundred yards or so on a trail that drops steeply for the first ten feet, then levels out and winds through the trees to the river.

Loc: FS1925-639, on the N. Middle Fk. Willamette R.	Road: Gravel, then forest track
L/L: N43 52 832/W122 23 137	Access: DTC, UOP, Check MVUM
Cell: Towns of Oakridge and Westfir	Tents: 3–4
Nearest H2O: N. Middle Fk. Willamette R.	El: 1690
Lndmk: MP 12, 0.2 mile	RV: Use judgment, small MH

Description: A private and shady camp with easy access to the river.

Getting there: *(See map pg. 121)* From OR 126 (McKenzie Pass Byway), turn south on FS19 about a third of a mile past MP 45. Continue south 45.6 miles on FS19. Turn right on FS1925 (Christy Creek Road) near MP 12 and cross the bridge. Campsite is on left after you cross the bridge, 0.1 mile from FS1925, at the end of Spur 639. From SR 58, drive 15.1 miles on FS19 to FS1925, and then follow directions in the paragraph above.

Loc: Off FS1926, above Christy Cr.	Road: Gravel to dirt
L/L: N43 55 448/W122 18 551	Access: Park and carry
Cell: Town of Oakridge	Tents: 2–6
Nearest H2O: Christy Cr.	El: 2880
Lndmk: Junction FS1926/1925, 0.1 M north	RV: On road only

Description: This well-shaded camp in a stand of mixed conifer and alder trees is located on a ledge above Christy Creek, which runs pleasantly by about 20 feet below camp. A clearing near camp would allow for several more tents beyond the two sites under the trees.

Getting there: *(See map pg. 122)* Heading east out of Eugene on SR 58, turn left (north) onto FS19 between MP 33 and 34. Go left onto FS1926 at around MP 13. Camp is at the end of a short, steep dirt track at 4.6 to 4.8 miles from FS19 and a few hundred yards south of the junction with FS1925.
Note: There might be a decent campsite at the end of a short spur that drops down from FS1925 to Christy Creek about 0.4 mile WSW of the FS1925/1926 Junction.

Loc: FS1927, 4.5 M from FS1926	Road: Paved to dirt track
L/L: N43 56 061/W122 16 821	Access: Park and carry
Cell: Towns of Oakridge and Westfir	Tents: 2–3
Nearest H2O: Christy Cr.	El: 3100
Lndmk: FS1927/576 junction, 0.1 M north	RV: MH and TT, near bridge only

Description: *(overnight/emergency)* There are at least three possibilities here: You can camp in the clearing near the bridge on the west side of FS1927, near a large fallen tree. Or you can carry your gear along a primitive dirt track bending south 0.1 mile to a second and much more isolated campsite beside Christy Creek The third possibility is a few hundred yards off the east side of FS1927 at the end of a faint track.

Getting there: *(See map pg. 122)* Heading east out of Eugene on SR 58, turn left (north) onto FS19 between MP 33 and 34. Go left onto FS1926 at around MP 13. Take FS1926 for three miles, then turn right onto paved FS1927 and follow it 4.5 miles to sites, on left and right, just beyond the bridge over Lowell or Christy Creek.

Loc: On river, off FS19, 0.3 M. E of MP 16	Road: Footpath
L/L: N43 53 590/W122 18 998	Access: Park and carry, 100 yards
Cell: Towns of Oakridge and Westfir	Tents: 1–2
Nearest H2O: N. Middle Fk. Willamette R.	El: 2175
Lndmk: MP 16, 0.3 mile east	RV: On road only

Description: When it comes down to just needing a place to camp for the night, you will appreciate this place. Its location on a gentle, wide section of the river under a big leaf maple tree should be shady and cool during hot weather.

Getting there: *(See map pg. 122)* From OR 126 (McKenzie Pass Byway), turn south on FS19 about a third of a mile past MP 45. Continue south 41.3 miles or somewhere in the vicinity of MP 16. Mileage markers are not dependable along this highway, but the campsite is 3.7 miles west of MP 20 and about a third of a mile east of MP 16. Look for a pull-out along a straight stretch where the road runs close to the river. Park on the road. Depending on foliage and time of year, your car should be visible from camp.
From SR 58, drive 19.4 miles on FS19. Around 3.5 miles from the FS19/1926 junction, or around MP 16, slow down and start looking, and then follow directions in the paragraph above. If you pass MP 20, you have gone 3.7 miles too far.

Loc: On river, off FS19, 1.0 mile W of FS1934	Road: Paved, then forest track
L/L: N43 53 498/W122 18 022	Access: Check MVUM
Cell: Towns of Oakridge and Westfir	Tents: 5–6
Nearest H2O: N. Middle Fk. Willamette R.	El: 2220
Lndmk: FS19/1934 junction, 0.6 mile east	RV: Road too difficult

Description: Another unexpected gem campsite located right on the river at the end of a spur road. The North Fork of the Middle Fork of the Willamette is unusually wide and shallow here and easy to get to from camp. There is a wide, rocky beach directly in front of camp for those who can figure out how to take advantage of it.

Just downstream, the river splits around a rocky island. The many cedar trees almost keep the sun from touching the ground and will keep you dry for days in a driving rain.

Getting there: *(See map pg. 122)* From OR 126 (McKenzie Pass Hiway), turn south on FS19 about a third of a mile past MP 45. Continue south 40.3 miles or somewhere between where MP 17 and 18 should be. Here an unmarked and rocky track that may be Spur 062 drops off steeply to the right. Park and walk the road to the campsite (0.1 mile) before attempting to drive it. The road levels out shortly after its initial steep drop from FS19, but during wet weather you may encounter a rutted section with standing water as you near camp.

From SR 58, drive 20.4 miles on FS19. Look for turn-off a few hundred yards east of MP 17, and then follow directions in the

Like many sites along this stretch of road, Site #33 seems to have been lightly used

paragraph above. If you pass FS1934, you have gone about a mile too far.

34

Loc: Near FS19/1940 junction	**Road:** Paved, then forest track
L/L: N43 52 694/W122 13 705	**Access:** Check MVUM
Cell: Towns of Oakridge and Westfir	**Tents:** 3–4
Nearest H2O: N. Middle Fk. Willamette R.	**El:** 2320
Lndmk: Junction FS19/1940, 0.7 mile NNE	**RV:** Road probably too overgrown

Upstream view of the river from site #34

Description: *(two separate sites)* these two sites will give you practically everything you dream of getting from your camping experience. The clearing that defines this riverside campsite is ringed closely with four trees so colossal that they call to mind the legs of elephants as seen from the perspective of a mouse. In clear weather, you can put your tent on the grass next to the river. Come foul weather, you can move it back under the sheltering branches of one of the four forest giants.

Lacking the rock star sex appeal of the campsite by the river, the campsite closer to FS19 is still a nice place for an overnight stay or even an extended one if you happen to need a base camp for exploring the area. Though waterless, it is set comfortably back in a grove of trees near a park-like clearing. Its coordinates are N43 52 815/W122 13 544.

Getting there: *(See map pg. 122)* From OR 126 (McKenzie Pass Byway), turn south on FS19 about a third of a mile past MP 45. Continue south 35.9 miles, turn south on an unmarked dirt track (Spur 755) near the junction with FS1940. Follow Spur 755 a few hundred yards to the waterless camp. The camp by the river is another 0.3 mile further.

From SR 58, drive 24.8 miles on FS19 to FS1940, and then follow directions in the paragraph above.

Loc: Off FS19, on the N. Middle Fk. Willamette R	**Road:** Forest track, 0.5 mile
L/L: N43 52 335/W122 11 602	**Access:** Check MVUM
Cell: Towns of Oakridge and Westfir	**Tents:** 1–2
Nearest H2O: N. Middle Fk. Willamette R.	**El:** 2365
Lndmk: MP 23 on FS19	**RV:** Road too overgrown

35

Campsite on the North Middle Fork of the Willamette

Description: *(a twofer)* There are two campsites here at the end of two branches of an unmarked dirt track (probably Spur 060) that lead to the North Middle Fork of the Willamette River. The first and least impressive is on an abrupt shelf about eight feet above the river. Getting to the river for water here might be problematic, due to the steepness of the bank. Also, the fire ring was badly in need of cleaning and rebuilding in 2013.

The second campsite is the gem along this section of river. Overlooking a beautiful stretch of the river, it offers a view, privacy, solitude, and easy access to the river.

Getting there: *(See map pg. 122)* From OR 126 (McKenzie Pass Hiway), turn south on FS19 about a third of a mile past MP 45. Continue south 34.7 miles, turn south on an unmarked dirt track near MP 23. Follow the fork in the road to the right 0.5 mile to the less desirable camp and the river. Follow the road to the left about a third of a mile to the second and more desirable camp.

From SR 58, drive 26 miles on FS19 to MP 23, then follow directions above.

Loc: Off FS19, on the N. Middle Fk. Willamette R.	**Road:** Paved, then forest track
L/L: N43 53 008/W122 04 816	**Access:** Check MVUM
Cell: Towns of Oakridge and Westfir	**Tents:** 4–6
Nearest H2O: N. Middle Fk. Willamette R.	**El:** 2890
Lndmk: MP 29, 0.4 W	**RV:** Check MVUM

36

Description: A prime site directly on the North Middle Fork of the Willamette in a tree-ringed clearing just outside the Waldo Lake Wilderness that features convenient access to a pristine section of the river. In 2013, the site was unusually clean and well-maintained for a site so close to a paved road. A fisherman's trail leads downstream along the river. Cool and shaded, with a view of a wild river. What more could you ask for?

Getting there: *(See map pg. 123)* From OR 126 (McKenzie Pass Hiway), turn south on FS19 about a third of a mile past MP 45. Continue south 28.3 miles. Site is a hundred feet south of the road, on left, between MP 29 and 30, at the bottom of a huge curve to the east in FS19, which here is called Aufderheide Drive Memorial Scenic Byway.

From SR 58, drive 32.4 miles on FS19 to MP 29, then watch for turn-off to camp, on right.

CAMPING ALONG SALMON CREEK:

Campsites directly along Salmon Creek are often at the end of dirt tracks that are muddy and so deeply rutted from the passage of four-wheel-drive vehicles with large traction tires that many of them are now virtually impassible to anyone without one. The good news is that many of the sites are cleaner than the average Willamette National Forest dispersed campsite.

Even though Salmon Creek looks and behaves more like a river for most of its length, there are not many campsites along it with access to deep pools for swimming or a summertime soak.

While you're here, hike or mountain bike along Salmon Creek on Trail #4365 or hike into the hot springs off FS1934 on the way to Blair Lake.

Loc: FS24, 2.5 miles east of Oakridge	**Road:** Paved to dirt track
L/L: N43 45 318/W122 23 859	**Access:** DTC, UOP
Cell: Town of Oakridge	**Tents:** 10–15
Nearest H2O: Salmon Cr.	**El:** 1420
Lndmk: Spur 207 Bridge across Salmon Cr., 0.6 M. west	**RV:** MH and TT

Description: Several campsites spread out along a rocky track that parallels Salmon Creek's exceptional riparian environment for a mile or more. The downstream end of the dirt track gives way to an inviting trail along the creek.

Getting there: *(See map pg. 124)* Take Highway 58 out of Eugene about 40 miles to the town of Oakridge. Turn left onto Crestview Street, cross the bridge over the railroad tracks, then go right on E 1st St. and drive 1.2 miles to the Fish Hatchery Road. Site is 2.5 miles ahead, on FS24. Look for a short road leading down to the rough and rocky dirt track.

Loc: FS24, on Salmon Cr.,0.3 M past Salmon Cr. Falls Cg.	**Road:** Paved to dirt track
L/L: N43 45 979/W122 22 272	**Access:** DTC, UOP
Cell: Town of Oakridge	**Tents:** 2–3
Nearest H2O: Salmon Cr.	**El:** 1635
Lndmk: Salmon Cr. Cg., 0.3 M	**RV:** Use judgment

Description: A secluded and shady camp in a grove of tall, straight conifer trees with easy access to a moderately swift section of the creek.

Getting there: *(See map pg. 125)* Follow directions for site #37 as far as Fish Hatchery Road. From there, site is 4.8 miles ahead on FS24, on right. Look for a dirt track that curves to the right toward Salmon Creek, (about 0.1 mile).

Loc: On Salmon Cr., 1 mile north of Salmon Cr. Falls Cg.	**Road:** Paved, then very bad dirt
L/L: N43 46 487/W122 21 769	**Access:** DTC, UOP or P&C
Cell: Town of Oakridge	**Tents:** 2–3
Nearest H2O: Salmon Creek	**El:** 1600
Lndmk: Salmon Cr. Falls Cg., one mile SW	**RV:** No

Description: A secluded and comfortable camp on a creek that behaves more like a wild river.

Getting there: *(See map pg. 125)* Follow directions for site #37 as far as Fish Hatchery Road, then drive another 5.5 miles on FS24 to where a rutted dirt track takes off toward the creek about 200 yards to camp. *Unfortunately, this road was so rutted and ruined from the wheels of four-wheel drive vehicles in July of 2014 that it is now very difficult to get to the campsite without one. Walk it before attempting to drive it!*

Loc: FS24, on Salmon Cr., 3.5 M NE of Salmon Cr. Falls Cg.		**Road:** Paved, then very bad dirt
L/L: N43 47 610/W122 19 761		**Access:** Park and carry
Cell: Town of Oakridge		**Tents:** 2–3
Nearest H2O: Salmon Creek		**El:** 1790
Lndmk: FS1934, 0.9 miles east		**RV:** No

Description: Although usable, this camp has two strikes against it. The first is the very poor road leading into camp. The second is that the camp itself is in a stony patch of ground that does not provide a view of the creek. Still, it's a port in a storm.

Getting there: *(See map pg. 125)* Follow directions for site #37 as far as Fish Hatchery Road, then drive another 7.2 miles on FS24 to a short, dirt track taking off downhill from a steep, paved apron. There is a severe drop of about ten inches at the end of the apron, so use good judgment if you intend to drive this road. You will probably run into muddy spots about a hundred yards in, and the road crosses a small creek at about 200 yards.

Loc: FS24, 3.8 M past Salmon Creek Falls Cg.		**Road:** Paved, then dirt
L/L: N43 47 721/W122 19 439		**Access:** DTC, UOP or P&C
Cell: Town of Oakridge		**Tents:** 1–2
Nearest H2O: Salmon Creek		**El:** 1855
Lndmk: FS1934, 0.7 M east		**RV:** No

Description: *(Overnight/Emergency)* A rocky, open camp shaded from the sun in the morning, but open to it at midday. It is located almost directly above the water on an outside curve of the creek.

Getting there: *(See map pg. 125)* Follow directions for site #37 as far as Fish Hatchery Road, then drive another 7.6 miles to a dirt track that might be too muddy to drive until late summer. Walk it before you try to drive it.

Loc: FS24, a little over 0.1 M west of FS1934		**Road:** Paved, then dirt
L/L: N43 47 766/W122 18 857		**Access:** DTC, UOP
Cell: Town of Oakridge		**Tents:** 3–5
Nearest H2O: Salmon Creek		**El:** 1845
Lndmk: FS1934, 0.1 mile east		**RV:** Use judgment with MH

Description: A nicely shaded camp on a wide, shallow section of the creek. It also features a bright, green picnic table. This camp was remarkably clean when discovered.

Getting there: *(See map pg. 125)* Follow directions for site #37 as far as Fish Hatchery Road, then continue another 8 miles. If you pass FS1934, turn around and go back a tenth of a mile. Turn south onto a dirt track that curves a little over 0.1 mile down to a wide, shallow section of the creek. This is home.

Loc: FS1935, 0.1 M from FS1934, near Moss Cr.	Road: Gravel, then dirt
L/L: N43 48 247/W122 16 663	Access: Check MVUM
Cell: Town of Oakridge	Tents: 3–4
Nearest H2O: Moss Cr., 50 yards	El: 2570
Lndmk: Junction FS1934/1935	RV: MH and TT

Description: Huge grey-barked conifers soar above this spacious and comfortable camp, which is just far enough away from Moss Creek so that its rambunctious gurgling is muted to a pleasant whisper. A short trail leading out of camp leads to Moss Creek and a made-to-order rock that provides a convenient platform for dipping your water out of the stream. FS1935 is so lightly trafficked that your solitude is unlikely to be disturbed, even on a busy weekend.

Getting there: *(See map pg. 125)* Follow directions to site #37 as far as Fish Hatchery Rd. Continue 10.1 miles on FS24 to junction with FS1934. Go left (north) 2.6 miles to junction with FS1935. Drive 0.1 mile to camp, on right, just past gate.

Loc: FS24 and spur 290, 1.7 M east of FS24/1934 and 0.3 M west of FS24/2417 junction	Road: Paved, then gravel
	Access: Park and carry
L/L: N43 47 510/W122 16 928	Tents: 3–4
Cell: Town of Oakridge	El: 1860
Nearest H2O: Salmon Cr.	RV: On road only
Lndmk: Spur 290 Bridge, FS1934, 1.7 mile west	

Description: A large, comfortable and shaded spot capable of accommodating several tents.

Getting there: *(See map pg. 125)* Follow directions for site #37 to Fish Hatchery Road, then continue another 9.8 miles to bridge where Spur 290 crosses Salmon Creek (Bridge may be unmarked on map). Cross bridge and park about 100 yards from FS24.

Loc: Between FS24/2417 junction and FS24 bridge over Creek	Road: Paved, then dirt track
L/L: N43 47 420/W122 16 498	Access: Check MVUM
Cell: Town of Oakridge	Tents: 4–6
Nearest H2O: Salmon Cr.	El: 1965
Lndmk: FS24/2417 and bridge over FS24	RV: No

Description: A large, secluded, comfortable campsite near Salmon Creek.

Getting there: *(See map pg. 125)* Follow directions for site #37 to Fish Hatchery Road, then continue on. At 10.5 miles and about 100 yards beyond the FS24/2417 split, you will see a dirt track that curves 0.1 mile down toward the creek. This is a road that is best driven in a high-clearance vehicle. Watch out for two deep, muddy pockets as you approach this campsite, even in mid-summer.

Loc: FS24, 1.2 M from FS24/2417 split	**Road:** Paved, then dirt track
L/L: N43 46 921/W122 15 217	**Access:** Check MVUM
Cell: Town of Oakridge	**Tents:** 10–15
Nearest H2O: Salmon Cr.	**El:** 2170
Lndmk: FS2418, 0.2 mile NW	**RV:** Use judgment

Description: This large site in an open, grassy clearing near the creek with one fire ring under a single towering fir tree is ideal for a gathering of the tribe. A trail leads 200 yards to a shallow stretch of the creek. Alternatively, you can always haul water by car from the bridge, 1.2 miles back toward town.

Getting there: *(See map pg. 125)* Follow directions for site #37 as far as Fish Hatchery Road, then continue on. At 11.2 miles, look for the junction with FS2418, on right. Two-tenths of a mile beyond, you will come to a dirt track on the left leading about 100 yards to the creek.
There is also another emergency/overnight campsite close nearby and about 50 yards off the road, with a small rill that should be a dependable source of water for camp use.

Loc: At end of spur 260, 1.8 miles from FS224	**Road:** Dirt track
L/L: N43 47 005/W122 14 954	**Access:** Check MVUM
Cell: Town of Oakridge	**Tents:** 3–4
Nearest H2O: Black Creek, 200 yards	**El:** 2115
Lndmk: FS24 bridge across Black Creek	**RV:** No

Description: A secluded, private, quiet camp in a large clearing at the end of Spur 260. A rough path out of camp leads 200 yards downhill through the woods to a fast-moving and relatively shallow section of Black Creek, but it may be easier to get water by driving back to FS24 and the bridge.

Getting there: *(See map pg. 125)* Follow directions to site #37 as far as Fish Hatchery Rd. Continue on FS24 another 13 miles to bridge over Black Creek and FS24/2420 junction. Cross bridge and go left 1.6 miles to camp, at the end of Spur 260. This road doesn't get driven much. Watch for rocks hidden in the tall grass ahead of you.

Loc: On Black Cr., 0.2 mile N of FS24/2420 split and bridge	**Road:** Paved, then dirt
L/L: N43 46 495/W122 13 781	**Access:** DTC, UOP
Cell: Town of Oakridge	**Tents:** 3–4
Nearest H2O: Black Cr.	**El:** 2300
Lndmk: Bridge across Black Cr, 0.2 M south	**RV:** Small MH

Description: A modest but pleasant little camp on a relatively straight section of Black Creek. Watch out for an exposed section of logging cable in the ground near the creek.

Getting there: *(See map pg. 125)* Follow directions to site #37 as far as Fish Hatchery Road. Continue on FS24 another 12.7 miles to a short, dirt road on the left. Take this (about 150') to camp and Black Cr.

Loc: Black Cr. at the FS24/2420 Junction	Road: Paved to dirt track
L/L: N43 46 345/W122 13 740	Access: DTC, UOP
Cell: Town of Oakridge	Tents: 2-3
Nearest H2O: Black Cr.	El: 2380
Lndmk: Bridge at FS24/2420 Junction	RV: Small MH

Description: A serviceable but uninspiring site near the bridge where the creek runs fast and shallow.

Getting there: *(See map pg. 125)* Follow directions to site #37 as far as Fish Hatchery Road. Continue on FS24 another 13 miles to its junction with FS2420. Keep straight onto the grassy lane where road splits sharply to left to cross Black Creek. Follow a short road leading to the creek.

Loc: FS21, 0.2 M from Packard Cr. Rd	Road: Paved
L/L: N43 39 555/W122 26 173	Access: DTC, UOP
Cell: Oakridge and near Hills Cr. Lake Dam	Tents: 2-3
Nearest H2O: Hills Cr. Lake or pack you own	El: 1560
Lndmk: Packard Cr. Rd., 0.1 mile	RV: MH and TT

Description: There are two and possibly three campsites at this location on a point over the lake. One is graveled camping area just off the road and about 30' above the lake with just enough flat space for a few tents or a small RV. This site is open to the sun from about noon until late mid-afternoon in the summertime. The second site is a large, flat area about a hundred yards beyond the first, with room for two to three RV's or four to five large tents. The third campsite is to be found by following the short track that drops steeply to the lake between the two above mentioned sites, where there is room for maybe one tent.

Getting there: *(See map pg. 127)* Heading east out of the town of Oakridge, go right onto FS23-21. Drive 0.5 mile and turn right onto FS21. Drive 6.2 miles to camp, about 0.2 mile beyond the junction withFS2110. Camp is on left, just after you cross Packard Cr.

Loc: FS21, near MP 10, on Hills Cr. Lk.	Road: Paved to gravel
L/L: N43 37 199/W122 26 652	Access: DTC, UOP
Cell: Oakridge and near Hills Cr. Lake Dam	Tents: 3-4
Nearest H2O: Lake or nearby creeks	El: 1565
Lndmk: Bingham Boat Ramp, about 0.5 mile S	RV: Use judgment w/small MH

Description: A large, flat campsite with room for at least two families, though the author was unable to inspect thoroughly at the time of discovery.

Getting there: *(See map pg. 127)* Heading east out of the town of Oakridge, turn right onto FS23-21 and go 0.5 mile. Go south on FS21 for 10.3 miles. Look for a short, steep drive descending toward the lake on the left. *Use caution when accessing this site, since FS21 is relatively narrow and can carry a lot of traffic at times.*

Loc: FS2117 (Gold Cr. Rd.), 1.3 M south of FS21	Road: Paved, then dirt
L/L: N43 35 904/W122 27 643	Access: P&C, Check MVUM
Cell: Oakridge and near Hills Cr. Lake Dam	Tents: 2–3
Nearest H2O: Windfall Cr. (in camp)	El: 1635
Lndmk: FS21/2117, 1.3 M north	RV: Small MH only

Description: This camp on Windfall Creek rates an easy 8 out of 10. It offers shade, privacy, seclusion and a pool deep enough for a cooling soak on a hot day. There is no apparent trail to the Middle Fork of the Willamette River, which is only a couple of hundred yards through the trees to the east.

Getting there: *(See map pg. 127)* Heading east out of the town of Oakridge, turn right onto FS23-21. Drive 0.5 mile and turn right onto FS21. Drive 10.5 miles and turn south at the junction with 2117. Drive 1.3 miles to camp, on left, just past Windfall Creek. *Caution for those with low-clearance vehicles: the drop off from the shoulder of paved 2117 is abrupt.*

Loc: FS2117, 1.4 M from FS21	Road: Paved, then rough, rocky track
L/L: N43 35 874/W122 27 653	Access: P&C, Check MVUM
Cell: Oakridge and near Hills Cr. Lake Dam	Tents: 1–3
Nearest H2O: Middle Fk., Willamette R.	El: 1640
Lndmk: FS21/2117 junction, 1.4 M	RV: No

The Middle Fork of the Willamette near Site 53.

Description: A marginal campsite in a densely shaded small clearing near an outside bend of the North Fork of the Willamette that may require you to carry your gear further than you'd like. Mid to late summer, look for a fairly productive patch of blackberries ripening in the sun where the trail from camp debouches onto a strikingly scenic stretch of the river.

Getting there: *(See map pg. 127)* Follow directions to site #52. Just beyond that, look for rough and rocky track that winds 0.1 mile through the trees to within about a hundred and fifty feet of the site. Park and carry gear.

Loc: Hills Cr. Lake near FS2118/2302 junction	Road: Paved
L/L: N43 41 794/W122 22 884	Access: Park and carry, 100 yds
Cell: Oakridge and near Hills Cr. Lake Dam	Tents: 10–15
Nearest H2O: Lake and nearby creeks	El: 1575
Lndmk: Junction FS23/2118	RV: No

Description: A football field-sized clearing below the bridge where FS2118 crosses over the point where Hills Creek enters the lake. The entire area is exposed to the sun a good part of the day. This camp may require clean-up.

Getting there: *(See map pg. 128)* Heading east out of the town of Oakridge, turn right onto FS23 and drive 4.3 miles. Turn right on FS2118 and cross the bridge. The trail to camp is on the other side of the bridge, on left. Park near the junction of 2118 and 2302 and carry gear downhill about a hundred yards to this huge camp.

Loc: FS2118, 0.8 mile from FS23	**Road:** Paved	
L/L: N43 41 902/W122 23 648	**Access:** Park and carry	
Cell: Oakridge and near Hills Cr. Lake Dam	**Tents:** 4–5	
Nearest H2O: Lake or nearby creeks	**El:** 1575	
Lndmk: FS23, 0.8 mile	**RV:** No	

Description: A shady camp on a north-facing shore of the lake that offers some of the feel of a backcountry campsite on Hills Creek Lake. This site is well-suited to a larger group or family. Campers can expect to be exposed to the afternoon sun.

Getting there: *(See map pg. 127)* Follow directions to site #54, then continue on 0.8 mile. Site is on right, near a break in the trees. Park and carry gear 0.1 mile down a rough dirt track that descends gradually to campsites in the trees about a hundred yards from the lake.

Loc: FS2118, 4.6 miles from the FS23/2118 junction	**Road:** Paved	
L/L: N43 40 824/ W122 25 090 (road coordinates)	**Access:** Park and carry, 0.2 M	
Cell: Oakridge and near Hills Cr. Lake Dam	**Tents:** 6–10	
Nearest H2O: Lake or nearby creeks	**El:** 1575	
Lndmk: Junction FS23/2118, 4.6 M north	**RV:** No	

Description: A shaded track that gives access to a large beach. Swim, boat, fish, and play in the sun.

Getting there: *(See map pg. 127)* Follow directions to site #54, then continue another 4.6 miles to site, on right. Park on road and carry gear down a wide, gradual path about 0.2 mile to campsites.

Loc: East shore of Hills Cr. Lk., near Coffeepot Creek	**Road:** Paved	
L/L: N43 37 475/W122 26 030	**Access:** DTC, UOP	
Cell: Oakridge and near Hills Cr. Lake Dam	**Tents:** 2–3	
Nearest H2O: Coffeepot Cr.	**El:** 1575	
Lndmk: Junction FS2118/479, 0.1 mile south	**RV:** MH and TT	

Description: Set back in the trees and overlooking the lake this small site is breezy and shady, but will not accommodate a large party.

Getting there: *(See map pg. 127)* Follow directions to site #54, then continue 9.6 miles south along the lake to site, on right, just before crossing the bridge over Coffeepot Creek. Alternatively, coming from FS21, follow the instructions to site #58 and continue north 0.1 mile on FS2118 to site, on left.

Loc: FS2118, 0.8 mile north of FS21	Road: Paved
L/L: N43 37 395/W122 26 092	Access: Park and carry, 100 yds.
Cell: Oakridge and near Hills Cr. Lake Dam	Tents: 5-10
Nearest H2O: Coffeepot Cr. up spur 479	El: 1540
Lndmk: Bingham Boat Ramp, 0.8 M south	RV: Parking area only

Description: A large, breezy, shaded area overlooking popular Hills Creek Lake.

Getting there: *(See map pg. 127)* Follow directions to site #52 as far as the junction with FS2117, cross FS21 bridge to the Bingham Boat Ramp, then turn left (north) and drive another 0.8 mile to site, on left, just south of Spur 479.

Loc: FS21, 0.1 M from Bingham Boat Ramp	Road: Paved to dirt track
L/L: N43 36 752/W122 26 652	Access: DTC, UOP
Cell: Oakridge and near Hills Cr. Lake Dam	Tents: 4-10
Nearest H2O: Coffeepot Cr. up spur 479	El: 1490
Lndmk: Bingham Boat Ramp, 0.1 M north	RV: Use judgement

Description: *(a twofer)* Two good sites at opposite ends of a dirt track that goes downhill to the north and south from FS21 to rocky beaches by the lake. The northern site will accommodate maybe 4-5 tents. The site at the end of the lane to the south offers more shade and a wide turnaround at the bottom which would easily handle several more tents or a few RVs. This site is frequently used. Do it right. Set up a privacy shelter and toilet, then POYP.

Getting there: *(See map pg. 127)* Heading east out of the town of Oakridge, turn right onto FS23-21. Drive 0.5 mile and turn right onto FS21. Drive 10.8 miles. Site is on right, just past the Bingham Boat Ramp.

Loc: FS21/150 1.5 miles S of Sand Prairie Cg.	Road: Paved to dirt track
L/L: N43 34 895/W122 27 337	Access: Check MVUM
Cell: Oakridge and near Hills Cr. Lake Dam	Tents: 5-10
Nearest H2O: Middle Fk., Willamette R.	El: 1645
Lndmk: Sand Prairie Cg., 1.5 M north	RV: MH and TT

Description: Located in a flat meadow about a hundred yards off FS21, this camp is secluded and private. The main attraction here is Trail #3609, which provides 25 miles of riverside hiking and single track bliss for mountain bike riders. It is rated as a moderately difficult mountain bike ride.

Getting there: *(See map pg. 127)* Heading east out of the town of Oakridge, turn right onto FS23-21. Drive 0.5 mile and turn right onto FS21. Drive 13.2 miles, then take Spur 150 to right about a hundred yards to camp.

Loc: On the M. Fk., Willamette R., 2.5 M from Sand Pr. Cg.	Road: Paved, then gravel to camp
L/L: N43 34 128/W122 27 603	Access: Check MVUM
Cell: Oakridge and near Hills Cr. Lake Dam	Tents: 6–10
Nearest H2O: Middle Fk., Willamette R.	El: 1755
Lndmk: Sand Prairie Cg, 2.5 miles N	RV: MH and TT

Description: *(a twofer)* Two sites near the river about 0.2 mile from FS21. The first is in a large clearing a few hundred yards from the river that is open to the sun. The second, at the end of the left fork in the road, is more shaded and is also closer to an especially fast-moving chunk of the river. There are few swimming holes in evidence. The river here has an unforgettably timeless and wild aspect about it.

Getting there: *(See map pg. 129)* Heading east out of the town of Oakridge, turn right onto FS23-21. Drive 0.5 mile and turn right onto FS21. Drive 14.1 miles to site, on right, at the end of Spur 156.

Loc: FS21, 2.9 M from Sand Prairie Cg.	Road: Paved to gravel to dirt
L/L: N43 33 749/W122 27 502	Access: DTC, UOP
Cell: Oakridge and near Hills Cr. Lake Dam	Tents: 7–10
Nearest H2O: Middle Fk., Willamette R., Estep Cr.	El: 1720
Lndmk: MP 15, about 0.3 M south	RV: Use judgment w/small MH

Description: Camp in a shady clearing about 100 yards from FS21. Estep Creek, a pleasant, shallow creek is just a stone's throw over the bluff from this fenced area, but getting to it is difficult.

Getting there: *(See map pg. 129)* Heading east out of the town of Oakridge, turn right onto FS23-21. Drive 0.5 mile and turn right onto FS21. Drive 14.6 miles (2.9 M past Sand Prairie Cg.) to site, on right, at the end of a difficult dirt track and just north of MP15). The approach is easier via the left fork of the track, which is circular. Walk before driving.

Loc: Middle Fk., Willamette, end of Spur 022	Road: Paved, then gravel
L/L: N43 33 159/W122 27 419 (road coordinates)	Access: Park and carry
Cell: Oakridge and near Hills Cr. Lake Dam	Tents: 2–4
Nearest H2O: Middle Fk., Willamette R.	El: 1850
Lndmk: MP 15, about half-mile north	RV: Small MH, maybe

Description: A delightful and secluded site close to the river at the end of a rough, dirt track.

Getting there: *(See map pg. 129)* Heading east out of the town of Oakridge, turn right onto FS23-21. Drive 0.5 mile and turn right onto FS21. Drive south on FS21 some 15.5 miles. Take Spur 022 two-tenths mile to the right toward the river. Drive with care.
There is also another nice riverside site at the end of Spur 165, which takes off from the FS21 a couple of hundred yards to the south of Spur 022.

Loc: FS2127, 0.1 mile from FS21	**Road:** Paved, then gravel
L/L: N43 32 300/W122 26 936	**Access:** Check MVUM
Cell: Oakridge and near Hills Cr. Lake Dam	**Tents:** 3–10
Nearest H2O: Middle Fk., Willamette R.	**El:** 1820
Lndmk: Junction FS21/2127, 0.1 M.	**RV:** MH and TT, near road only

Description: *(A "threefer")* Three campsites that will accommodate three to ten tents.

Getting there: *(See map pg. 129)* Heading east out of the town of Oakridge, turn right onto FS23-21 and drive 0.5 mile. Go south on FS21 about 16.3 miles. Take FS2127 one-tenth mile to the right somewhere about halfway between MP15 and 16. Look for the first site on right just where Spur 028 takes off to the river. The second site is at the end of a rough, dirt track leading down toward the river. The third is at the end of another rough, dirt track that splits off and descends to the river from near the first site. The tracks leading to the two sites closest to the river are too steep to be driven.

Loc: FS2127-188, 1.1 miles from FS2127-2125	**Road:** 1.1 mile of rough, dirt track
L/L: N43 33 017/W122 27 648	**Access:** Park and carry, 100 yards
Cell: Oakridge and near Hills Cr. Lake Dam	**Tents:** 1–2
Nearest H2O: M.F., Willamette R.	**El:** 1765
Lndmk: FS21/2127	**RV:** No

Description: This site on the west bank of the Middle Fork of the Willamette is as secluded as it is hard to reach. It is somewhat open to the morning sun but shady in the afternoon. One downside about this camp is that the one really decent level tent site is a bit too close to the fire ring. The river here is relatively broad and shallow as it glides smoothly past camp in a northerly direction from the rapids upstream, which can be heard from camp. The water in a shallow pool just below camp was pleasantly cool in mid-July.
The unnumbered campsite mentioned at the end of Spur 165 is visible across the river and a bit downstream from this camp.

Getting there: *(See map pg. 129)* Heading east out of the town of Oakridge, turn right onto FS23-21 and go 0.5 mile. Go south on FS21 about 16.3 miles. Take FS2127 0.3 miles to Spur 180, which follows the river north roughly 0.6 mile before forking off as Spur 188. Follow Spur 188 along the river roughly 0.4 mile to site, on right. The entire section of road from FS2127/2125 should be driven with great care. Site is about 100 yards from Spur 188. There is a deeply rutted spot that will prevent any but the highest clearance vehicles from driving all the way to camp.
Caution: signage in this area can be confusing.

Loc: M.F., Willamette R., off spur 029, near FS2125/2127	**Road:** Dirt track
L/L: N43 32 202/W122 26 865	**Access:** Check MVUM
Cell: Oakridge and near Hills Cr. Lake Dam	**Tents:** 3–5
Nearest H2O: M.F., Willamette R.	**El:** 1700
Lndmk: FS 21/2127 junction	**RV:** Use judgment with MH, TT

Description: There is room for several tents in this grove of mixed alder, maple and conifer trees. The Middle Fork of the Willamette Trail runs along between camp and the river. Getting to the river for water is a bit difficult from this site. You'll probably want to haul water for camp use from near the bridge where FS2127 crosses the river.

Getting there: *(See map pg. 129)* Heading east out of the town of Oakridge, turn right onto FS23-21 and go 0.5 mile. Go south on FS21 about 16.3 miles. Take FS2127 roughly 0.3 mile to a Spur 029, which takes off to the left about a hundred yards before the FS2125 splits off to the left. Site is at the end of Spur 029, which is rocky in places.

Loc: On M.F., Willamette R., 0.2 M from FS21	**Road:** Very rough dirt track
L/L: N43 31 670/W122 26 895	**Access:** Check MVUM, P&C
Cell: Oakridge and near Hills Cr. Lake Dam	**Tents:** 5–10
Nearest H2O: M.F., Willamette R.	**El:** 1880
Lndmk: FS 21/2127 junction, 0.3 M	**RV:** No

Downstream view of timeless Willamette

Description: *(a twofer)* A sandy, rocky clearing in an inviting and pristine setting along a fast-moving section of the river midway between two sets of rapids. Cool and breezy, even on a hot day. Definitely a place where you will want to linger and explore May need some cleanup. In 2014, the fire pit was piled high with debris and unusable.

Getting there: *(See map pg. 129)* Heading east out of the town of Oakridge, turn right onto FS23-21 and go 0.5 mile. Go south on FS21 about 17.3 miles and take Spur 023, which angles off toward the river, about 0.8 mile past FS2127. Caution: Shoulder drop-off from FS21 is severe. Camp is about 0.2 mile from FS21. *A second smaller but shadier camp with one good tent site is to be found 0.2 mile south of this location at the end of a fork that splits off to the left from Spur 023.*

Loc: Near FS2133/2134 junction	**Road:** Rough dirt track
L/L: N43 29 991/W122 24 327	**Access:** DTC, UOP
Cell: Oakridge and near Hills Cr. Lake Dam	**Tents:** 2–3
Nearest H2O: M.F., Willamette R.	**El:** 2070
Lndmk: FS2133 bridge over M.F., Willamette R.	**RV:** No

Description: *(another twofer)* You will find one site just a few hundred feet from FS2133, but will probably want to continue on to the second site, another 0.2 mile further on, which a cooler, much more private, and has easier access to the river.

Getting there: *(See map pg. 129)* Heading east out of the town of Oakridge, turn right onto FS23-21 and go 0.5 mile. Go south on FS21 about 20.6 miles, then go right 0.1 mile across the bridge on FS2133, staying on FS2133 where it splits off from FS2134. Take the dirt track from FS2133 near its junction with FS2134 a hundred yards to the first site, on left, and 0.2 mile to the second site at the end. Be prepared to straddle the deep ruts.

Loc: M.F., Willamette R., off FS2133, 06 M from FS2134	Road: Gravel
L/L: N43 29 986/W122 24 950 (road coordinates)	Access: DTC, UOP
Cell: Oakridge and near Hills Cr. Lake Dam	Tents: 1–3
Nearest H2O: M.F., Willamette	El: 2000
Lndmk: FS2133/2134 junction, 0.6 M east	RV: MH and TT

Description: An open and easily accessed site close to the river.

Getting there: *(See map pg. 129)* Heading east out of the town of Oakridge, turn right onto FS23-21 and go 0.5 mile. Go south on FS21 about 20.6 miles, then go right across the bridge on FS2133 one-tenth of a mile, staying on FS2133 where it splits off from FS2134. Drive 0.6 mile west on FS2133 to site, on right, just a few hundred yards before FS2133 curves to the left.

Loc: 0.2 M from FS 2133 on unmarked dirt track	Road: Rough dirt track
L/L: N43 30 067/W122 25 102	Access: Check MVUM
Cell: Oakridge and near Hills Cr. Lake Dam	Tents: 7–10
Nearest H2O: M.F., Willamette R.	El: 2025
Lndmk: FS2133/2134 junction, 0.8 M east	RV: Use judgment with small MH

Description: A spacious and shady, grassy clearing at the end of a rough, dirt track near a log jam on an outside bend of the river. The water runs very fast here, so parties with children need to use judgment.

Getting there: *(See map pg. 129)* Heading east out of the town of Oakridge, turn right onto FS23-21 and go 0.5 mile. Go south on FS21 about 20.6 miles, then go right across the bridge on FS2133 one-tenth of a mile, staying on FS2133 where it splits off from FS2134. Take FS2133 eight-tenths of a mile to where it starts to curve off to the south. Camp is near the river, at the end of a rough, dirt track which will need to be driven strategically.

Loc: On Coal Cr., 0.1 M from FS2133 and 1.1 M from FS2134	Road: Gravel to dirt track
L/L: N43 29 709/W122 25 338	Access: Check MVUM
Cell: Oakridge and near Hills Cr. Lake Dam	Tents: 6–8
Nearest H2O: Coal Cr., 150'	El: 2050
Lndmk: FS2133/2134 junction	RV: Use judgment w/MH

Description: *(a twofer)* The first site, located at coordinates N43 29 761/W122 25 248 is surrounded by large trees that provide ample shade but lacks apparent access to water. The second site, in a breezy, secluded little clearing surrounded by maple and tall, straight conifer trees at coordinates N43 29 709/W122 25 338, is within earshot of pleasantly burbling little Coal Creek. Follow a faint path to the creek.

Getting there: *(See map pg. 129)* Heading east out of the town of Oakridge, turn right onto FS23-21 and go 0.5 mile. Go south on FS21 about 20.6 miles, then go right across the bridge on FS2133 one-tenth of a mile, staying on FS2133 where it splits off from FS2134. Drive 1.1 mile. Sites are along a dirt track to the right, about 0.2 mile N of Spur 200 or 201. Watch for deep ruts in dirt track.

Loc: FS2134, 0.3 M south of FS2133/2134 junction	Road: Gravel to rough dirt track
L/L: N43 29 792/W122 24 073	Access: DTC, UOP
Cell: Oakridge and near Hills Cr. Lake Dam	Tents: 7–10
Nearest H2O: M.F., Willamette R.	El: 2110
Lndmk: FS2133/2134 junction, 0.3 M north	RV: Road too rough

View from campsite along the Middle Fork of the Willamette off FS21

Description: A pleasant and breezy site directly on the river which is well shaded, flat and suitable for a large group. Camp was clean in 2014. Find a handy shelf table left by some previous camper. The rapids in front of camp make this site a questionable choice for those traveling with children.

Getting there: *(See map pg. 129)* Heading east out of the town of Oakridge, turn right onto FS23-21 and go 0.5 mile. Go south on FS21 about 20.6 miles, then go right across the bridge on FS2133 one-tenth of a mile to its junction with FS2134. Go left 0.3 mile on FS2134 and take a dirt track that curves back north parallel to the river for a quarter of a mile to camp. This track is alternately rocky and forest duff, with a few wet spots and oil pan-piercing rocks to negotiate along the way.

Loc: FS2134, on Staley Cr., 1.6 M from FS2133	Road: Gravel, very steep & short
L/L: N43 28 959/W122 23 013	Access: Park and carry, 100 yds.
Cell: Oakridge and near Hills Cr. Lake Dam	Tents: 2
Nearest H2O: Staley Cr.	El: 2190
Lndmk: FS2133, 1.6 mile N	RV: On road only

Description: *(a marginal site)* A small site just off FS2134 on Staley Creek. The site is secluded from the road. It is open to the sun in the morning, but there is good shade in the evening. Because of the steepness of the access road, this site requires parking on the road and carrying gear down to camp.

Getting there: *(See map pg. 129)* Heading east out of the town of Oakridge, turn right onto FS23-21 and go 0.5 mile. Go south on FS21 about 20.6 miles, then go right across the bridge on FS2133 one-tenth of a mile to its junction with FS2134. Go left 1.6 miles on FS2134 to site, on left. Park and carry gear to camp.

Loc: On Staley Cr. off FS2134, 3.3 M from FS2133	Road: Rough dirt track
L/L: N43 27 594/W122 22 040	Access: Check MVUM
Cell: Oakridge and near Hills Cr. Lake Dam	Tents: 2–3
Nearest H2O: Staley Cr.	El: 2985
Lndmk: FS2133/2134 Junction, 3.3 miles N	RV: No

Description: This camp on a wide spot in Spur 239 overlooks a unique section of Staley Creek, where fast-moving water has carved out a noteworthy series of pools in the bedrock below. Be aware that during fire season fire crews might occasionally want to use this spot to take on water or just relax a bit.

Getting there: *(See map pg. 130)* Heading east out of the town of Oakridge, turn right onto FS23-21 and go 0.5 mile. Go south on FS21 about 20.6 miles, then go right across the bridge on FS2133 one-tenth of a mile to its junction with FS2134. Go left 3.3 miles to Spur 239, on left. Park and carry gear north 0.2 mile along Staley Creek to site, in a wide spot in the road.

Loc: Off FS2136 near its junction with FS2134	Road: Gravel to dirt track
L/L: N43 27 145/W122 21 990 (road coordinates)	Access: Check MVUM
Cell: Oakridge and near Hills Cr. Lake Dam	Tents: 5–7
Nearest H2O: Staley Cr.	El: 2460
Lndmk: Bridge across Staley Cr., near FS2135/2136 junction	RV: MH and TT

Description: A large, comfortable camp almost hidden in the trees in a bend in Staley Creek.

Getting there: *(See map pg. 130)* Heading east out of the town of Oakridge, turn right onto FS23-21 and go 0.5 mile. Go south on FS21 about 20.6 miles, then go right across the bridge on FS2133 one-tenth of a mile to its junction with FS2134. Go left 3.9 miles on FS2134, then take FS2136 left a few hundred yards to a dirt track on the right, near the bridge across Staley Creek. Camp is just beyond a circular dirt track, about 0.1 mile from FS2136 and the bridge.

Loc: Near Bridge, where FS2136 crosses Staley Cr.	Road: Gravel, then short, rocky
L/L: N43 26 019/W122 21 674	Access: Check MVUM
Cell: Oakridge and near Hills Cr. Lake Dam	Tents: 1
Nearest H2O: Staley Cr.	El: 2640
Lndmk: Staley Cr. Bridge, 1.5 M from FS2134/2136	RV: Small MH

Description: There is a marvelous natural pool in the bedrock of Staley Creek just below this camp at the end of a short spur off of FS2136. In mid-July, its clear water registered an amazingly warm 60 degrees when the author visited the place. A series of three cascading waterfalls create a mild roar just upstream of the pool. Unfortunately, there is only one truly level tent site here, and the site is visible from the road.

Getting there: *(See map pg. 130)* Heading east out of the town of Oakridge, turn right onto FS23-21 and go 0.5 mile. Go south on FS21 about 20.6 miles, then turn right across the bridge on FS2133 one-tenth of a mile to its junction with FS2134. Go left 3.9 miles on FS2134, turning left at its junction with FS2136. Follow FS2136 across the bridge and up the hill for 1.5 miles to a short, rocky road descending down to camp on the left, a few feet from the second bridge across Staley Creek. Camp is about 150 yards from FS2136.

Loc: On Simpson Cr., 0.1 M from FS21	Road: Gravel
L/L: N43 29 867/W122 23 827	Access: Check MVUM
Cell: Oakridge and near Hills Cr. Lake Dam	Tents: 1
Nearest H2O: Simpson Cr.	El: 2150
Lndmk: FS21/2133, 0.2 M north	RV: MH, TT?

Description: Medium-sized Simpson Creek is deeply shaded by tall trees and underbrush but is easily accessible from this campsite, which is cool and breezy and a handy stopover because of its proximity to FS21.

Getting there: *(See map pg. 129)* Heading east out of the town of Oakridge, turn right onto FS23-21 and go 0.5 mile. Go south on FS21 about 20.8 miles and turn left onto FS2135 about 0.2 mile past the junction with FS2133. Camp is in the trees to the right, about 0.1 mile from FS21.

Loc: Off FS21, 0.1 S of FS2135	Road: Paved to dirt track
L/L: N43 29 672/W122 23 935	Access: P&C, Check MVUM
Cell: Oakridge and near Hills Cr. Lake Dam	Tents: 10–20
Nearest H2O: M.F., Willamette R.	El: 2070
Lndmk: FS21/2135 junction, 0.3 M north	RV: Use judgment w/Small MH

Description: A large site that is sunny, level and sandy. There is a pleasant but small grassy area on the river downstream of camp.

Getting there: *(See map pg. 129)* Heading east out of the town of Oakridge, turn right onto FS23-21 and go 0.5 mile. Go south on FS21 about 20.9 miles. Watch for Spur 029, which will be on the right and may be unmarked, 0.3 mile south of FS2133, and leads 0.2 mile down to the site, near the river.

Loc: Near Sacandaga Cg and about 0.4 M from FS21	Road: Dirt track
L/L: N43 29 811/W122 20 055	Access: DTC, UOP
Cell: Oakridge and near Hills Cr. Lake Dam	Tents: 15–20
Nearest H2O: Waterless	El: 2490
Lndmk: Sacandaga Cg., 0.3 M east	RV: MH and TT

Description: *(two sites)* Experience the sublime solitude of camping in a scenic mountain meadow in one of these spacious sites along Spur 276. The only drawback is the lack of a handy nearby mountain stream for water. The first site is shadier and features a concrete pad that might have been a foundation for an old cabin. Both sites feature picnic tables. Don't use the facilities of nearby for-profit campgrounds if you're not paying for them.

Getting there: *(See map pg. 130)* Heading east out of the town of Oakridge, turn right onto FS23-21 and go 0.5 mile. Go south on FS21 about 24.7 miles to the turnoff to Sacandaga Cg. Go right down the hill about 0.2 mile, then right again on Spur 276 (or 279) near the entrance to the campground. Find the first campsite near a picnic table about 0.1 mile from this junction. The second site is another tenth of a mile further on. Hike or bike Trail #3609 along the river.

Loc: FS2143, 0.6 M from FS21	Road: Gravel to dirt track
L/L: N43 30 089/W122 18 788 (road coordinates)	Access: Check MVUM
Cell: Oakridge and near Hills Cr. Lake Dam	Tents: 2–3
Nearest H2O: M.Fk., Willamette R.	El: 2490
Lndmk: FS2143 bridge over the M.F., Willamette R.	RV: MH and TT

Description: (a twofer) A hunters' camp in the trees, about 200 yards from the river. A small rill that might be a good source of water for camp use bubbles along a couple of hundred feet from camp.

Getting there: *(See map pg. 130)* Heading east out of the town of Oakridge, turn right onto FS23-21 and go 0.5 mile. Go south on FS21 about 25.8 miles, then right onto FS2143. At about 0.6 mile, turn right near the sign announcing the bridge. It is about a hundred yards to the first site, on the right.

A second site is to be found about a hundred yards from the east side of FS2143 in a small clearing under tall trees near a fast section of the river.

Loc: Spur 382, about 100 yards from the FS21/23 junction	**Road:** Paved to primitive D.T.
L/L: N43 30 151/W122 18 182	**Access:** DTC, UOP
Cell: Oakridge and near Hills Cr. Lake Dam	**Tents:** 6-8
Nearest H2O: M.F., Willamette R.	**El:** 2580
Lndmk: Junction FS21/23, 0.5 M north	**RV:** Use judgment with road

Willamette River from Site #81

Description: Scenery, seclusion, solitude and privacy: This site immediately overlooking a wide, braided section of the river make it one of the most desirable summertime campsites for miles around. While the river brings a cooling breeze through camp on hot afternoons, the surrounding tall trees provide dense shade from the sun. A large cable spool from some previous logging operation serves as a convenient and welcome work space for preparing meals.

Getting there: *(See map pg. 130)* Heading east out of the town of Oakridge, turn right onto FS23-21 and go 0.5 mile. Go south on FS21 about 26.8 miles to Spur 382, about a hundred yards from the FS21/23 junction. Follow Spur 382 for about half a mile to camp. The quality of the road deteriorates considerably shortly after passing through an area of old logging debris.

Loc: 0.7 M off FS21 on Spur 393	**Road:** Rough and rocky track
L/L: N43 30 143/W122 17 874	**Access:** Check MVUM
Cell: Oakridge and near Hills Cr. Lake Dam	**Tents:** 3-4
Nearest H2O: M.F., Willamette R.	**El:** 3000
Lndmk: FS21/23 junction, 0.5 M west	**RV:** Use judgment

Description: Camp on forest duff near a wide and braided section of a wild river. This site, shaded by tall and widely spaced trees feels wild, isolated and secluded enough to leave the camper with a sense of timelessness that he or she won't soon forget. Find a path to the river near the upstream side of camp.

Getting there: *(See map pg. 130)* Follow the directions to Site #81. Look for Spur 393, which may not be marked, on right, about a hundred yards or so past Spur 391 (Site #83). Follow Spur 393 for 0.7 mile as it gradually descends to camp and the river. It is rough and there are a few large rocks that you will need to avoid along the way. Those with low clearance vehicles or RV's should walk it before attempting to drive any part of it.

83

Loc: Spur 391, 0.5 M east of the FS21/23 junction	Road: Gravel, rough
L/L: N43 30 729/W122 17 542	Access: P&C, Check MVUM
Cell: Oakridge and near Hills Cr. Lake Dam	Tents: 3-4
Nearest H2O: Swift Cr.	El: 2685
Lndmk: FS 21/23 junction, 0.5 M west	RV: Use judgment w/MH

Description: An inviting little camp under the shade of tall conifer trees. Swift Creek lives up to its name and is a good source of water for camp use but offers little else to the camper.

Getting there: *(See map pg. 130)* Heading east out of the town of Oakridge, turn right onto FS23-21 and go 0.5 mile. Go south on FS21 about 27.3 miles to Spur 391, 0.5 mile past the FS21/23 junction. Follow Spur 391 for 0.1 mile to site, set back in the trees, on the right.

84

Loc: Indigo Springs Cg. on FS21 by MP 30	Road: Paved
L/L: N43 29 830/W122 15 917	Access: DTC, UOP
Cell: Oakridge and near Hills Cr. Lake Dam	Tents: 5-6
Nearest H2O: Indigo Cr.	El: 2800
Lndmk: FS21/2149 junction, 0.4 mile SE	RV: Small MH only

Description: The three campsites in this decommissioned campground offer everything a campground is supposed to, including sturdy picnic tables, fire pits, and a vault toilet. Indigo Creek flows vigorously through camp to join the Middle Fork of the Willamette less than a quarter of a mile away. Cross the little bridge over Indigo Creek and enjoy a short interpretive trail. Show your appreciation for the use of this beautiful little campground by paying something forward.

Getting there: *(See map pg. 130)* Heading east out of the town of Oakridge, turn right onto FS23-21 and go 0.5 mile. Go south on FS21 about 29.3 miles to campground, on left.

85

Loc: Summit Lake on FS6010	Road: Dirt, awful
L/L: N43 27 768/W122 08 036	Access: DTC, UOP
Cell: Oakridge and near Hills Cr. Lake dam or Summit Lk.	Tents: 5-10
Nearest H2O: Summit Lk.	El: 5500
Lndmk: Junction FS2154/6010	RV: Road too rough

Description: This prime site on the northwest shore of Summit Lake in the Deschutes National Forest is decommissioned Summit Lake Campground. Because it is much easier to reach from FS21 in the Willamette National Forest, it is the one of two sites in this book that are not in the Willamette National Forest. Here you will not only find all the amenities of a standard campground, but also many recreational opportunities. By midsummer the water of the lake near camp warms up to a temperature that is quite tolerable for swimming. The lake is large enough to explore by boat, and those with kayaks or canoes can load their gear and strike out for an even more remote campsite if they so choose. Mosquitoes can be a problem around the lake, making late summer a good time for a visit since their numbers tend to dwindle by then. When the author visited the place, a few campers reported being able to get enough bars on their cell phones near the campground to make calls out.

Summit Lake on a summer day

Smoke rises from a campfire on Summit Lake

Another group of campers along the north shore of the lake reported finding some decent single track for their mountain bikes off rutted and rocky FS6010, which continues in a roller-coaster path several miles to Crescent Lake.

Getting there: *(See map pg. 130)* Heading east out of the town of Oakridge, turn right onto FS23-21 and go 0.5 mile. Go south on FS21 to where it splits into FS2153 and 2154 at about 32.1 miles. Go left 6.6 miles on FS2154, then turn left again onto FS6010, a road that requires evasive driving and will discourage most people. Find decommissioned Summit Lake Campground a mile and a half past the junction with FS2154. There is another smaller campsite with room for a single tent about 200 yards past the campground where FS6010 curves to the northeast. Yet another is to be found on the north shore of the lake a mile and a half past the campground.

Loc: Unnamed Lake, 0.2 M from Summit Lk.	Road: Dirt, primitive
L/L: N43 27 850/W122 08 267	Access: DTC, UOP
Cell: Oakridge and near Hills Cr. Lake dam or Summit Lk.	Tents: 5–6
Nearest H2O: Lake	El: 5680
Lndmk: Summit Lk, 0.2 M east	RV: No

Description: Another unnamed little gem of a mountain lake for those who dare to brave the puddles and rocks of Spur 380. Mosquitoes!

Getting there: *(See map pg. 130)* Follow the directions to site #85. Continue on Spur 380 0.2 mile to campsite, on left and visible from the road.

Loc: On Sunrise Lk. Off FS2154-380, 0.8 M from Summit Lk.	Road: Dirt and deeply rutted
L/L: N43 27 874/W122 08 725	Access: 4WD only
Cell: Oakridge and near Hills Cr. Lake dam or Summit Lk.	Tents: 2–3
Nearest H2O: Sunrise Lk.	El: 5560
Lndmk: Summit Lk., 0.8 M east	RV: No

Description: One of several small lakes along Spur 380 which, if you can reach it with your gear, you will most likely have all to yourself, since driving primitive Spur 380 involves negotiating several sections with deep, water-filled ruts. The best time to try for this site would be late summer, when the ruts should be dryer and the mosquito population thinned out considerably.

Getting there: *(See map pg. 130)* Follow the directions to Summit Lake Campground. Pick up Spur 380 at the junction near the vault toilet on the northwest shore of the lake and follow it 0.8 mile to Sunrise Lake, on right. Use judgment driving this road. And don't push your luck!

Loc: Unnamed Lk. off Spur 380, 0.9 M from Summit Lk.	**Road:** Practically impassible
L/L: N43 27 950/W122 08 888	**Access:** Park and carry
Cell: Oakridge and near Hills Cr. Lake dam or Summit Lk.	**Tents:** 5–6
Nearest H2O: Lake or Lake outlet	**El:** 5565
Lndmk: Summit Lk, 0.9 M east	**RV:** No

View from one of the several difficult-to-reach lake campsites along Spur 380, just west of Summit Lake

Description: There is no denying the reward at the end of the trail here: the magic of enjoying a beautiful mountain lake in complete solitude. Still, only the most adventurous campers with high clearance four-wheel drive vehicles should even think about trying to make the trip. From Summit Lake, Spur 380 deteriorates rapidly into a series of deeply rutted and muddy sections containing standing water. The wiser and more stress-free choice would be to find a comfortable camp near Summit Lake and visit the place by hiking or mountain biking Spur 380, which, with its roller-coaster profile, is a fun trip. Bring lunch, water, and plenty of mosquito repellent.

Getting there: *(See map pg. 130)* Follow the directions to site # 87. Site is another 0.1 mile past Sunrise Lake, just to the north of Spur 380. If you do manage to get a vehicle near the lake, park on the ledge where the road dips severely down to the lake's outlet. Carry gear a hundred and fifty yards to camp, on the other side of the outlet.

Loc: FS23-018 (Hills Cr. Rd.) on Hills Cr., near MP 6	**Road:** Paved to dirt
L/L: N43 38 924/W122 18 778	**Access:** DTC, UOP
Cell: Oakridge and near Hills Cr. Lake Dam	**Tents:** 1–2
Nearest H2O: Hills Cr.	**El:** 2235
Lndmk: MP 6 on FS23	**RV:** Road too difficult

Description: Not the most inspiring site in the Forest, but a wonderfully private one with a gorgeous upstream view of Hills Creek, which flows by moderately fast here. Tent sites are on a rocky ledge a few feet above the creek, so you might want to use a tarp or ground cloth to protect your tent. Privacy is guaranteed by the narrow, tree-shrouded access road.

Getting there: *(See map pg. 128)* Follow SR 58 east out of Oakridge to its junction with FS23, just outside of town. Take FS23 to Spur 018, on right and near MP 6, about 0.7 mile beyond FS5875. Spur 018 is steep but short. You might want to consider parking and carrying your gear.

Waking up to Hills Creek on a misty July morning

Loc: FS23-019 on Hills Cr, just past MP 6	**Road:** Paved to dirt
L/L: N43 38 744/W122 18 637	**Access:** DTC, UOP
Cell: Oakridge and near Hills Cr. Lake Dam	**Tents:** 3–4
Nearest H20: Hills Cr.	**El:** 2190
Lndmk: MP 6, 0.1 mile west	**RV:** MH and TT

90

Description: This site is more spacious and comfortable than site # 89, but has less privacy from the paved Hills Creek Road, though most cars going by at speed would only have time to note that someone was using the spot. Maple and alder trees line the perimeter around camp, which has probably been used as a hunters' camp in the past. There is easy, shaded access to Hills Creek, which carries as much water as a small mountain river.

Getting there: *(See map pg. 128)* Follow the instructions for site #89. Look for Spur 019 on the right, about a tenth of a mile past MP 6. Those driving an RV should use the entrance beyond Spur 019, which gives more gradual access to the area.

Loc: On Salt Cr., just past MP 42 on SR 58	**Road:** Paved to short dirt track
L/L: N43 43 364/W122 20 852	**Access:** P&C, Check MVUM
Cell: Town of Oakridge	**Tents:** 3–4
Nearest H20: Salt Cr.	**El:** 1655
Lndmk: MP 42	**RV:** Access road too difficult

91

Description: *(overnight/emergency)* A beguiling little spot on a slow, deep section of Salt Creek despite several drawbacks for those seeking the solitude of a wilderness experience. With busy SR 58 on one side of the creek and a train track on the other, this site will probably not be everyone's cup of cappuccino, but it will work as a one night stand for someone who happens to be travelling through and needs a convenient place to stay. And, if you find this site in the dark or when it is raining, there are several restaurants in nearby Oakridge that will welcome your business.

Getting there: *(See map pg. 125)* Driving east out of the town of Oakridge on SR 58, look for MP 42, about five miles out of town. Just past MP 42, look for an opening in the trees to the left. Site is less than a hundred yards from SR 58. Park and carry.

Loc: FS5875, 0.1 M from SR 58, downstream of bridge	Road: Paved, gravel
L/L: N43 42 042/W122 16 964	Access: Check MVUM
Cell: Oakridge and 0.8 mile from bridge on FS5876	Tents: 2–3
Nearest H2O: Salt Cr.	El: 1965
Lndmk: McCredie Hot Springs, 0.6 mile NW, on SR 58	RV: MH and TT

Description: *(overnight/emergency)* A usable but otherwise unremarkable hunters' camp on the edge of a good-sized clearing in the surrounding alder trees next to Salt Creek. Nevertheless, it could be mean salvation if you find yourself caught by darkness or bad weather on your way out of nearby Oakridge. There is convenient water in the creek, which also offers a pool that would be fine for a summertime cold water soak. Follow the primitive dirt track that tunnels through the trees downstream to a second, smaller and much more private site offering only enough level space for a single, small tent.

Getting there: *(See map pg. 128)* Driving east out of Oakridge, turn right onto FS5875 between MP 45 and 46 and about 0.6 mile past the McCredie Hot Springs parking lot. Site is about 0.1 mile from SR 58, on right, just before the bridge.

Loc: FS5875, on Salt Cr., between MP 45 and 46	Road: Paved to gravel
L/L: M43 42 028/W122 16 906	Access: Check MVUM
Cell: Oakridge and 0.8 mile from bridge on FS5876	Tents: 2–3
Nearest H2O: Salt Cr.	El: 1965
Lndmk: McCredie Hot Springs, 0.6 mile NW, on SR 58	RV: MH and TT

Description: *(overnight/emergency)* Another less than prime site, but one that also offers easy access to the amenities of Oakridge, which can be especially important if you are traveling or the weather is bad. Forget the cooking. Just get the tent up and drive the ten miles back to town for a hot dinner and a drink. Fill up with gas, stop for groceries, and then return to camp to relax in your tent and fall asleep to the background noise of Salt Creek, which flows along noisily just below camp.

Getting there: *(See map pg. 128)* Follow directions to Site #92. Site is on left, just before the bridge.

Loc: Off FS5883, 5.5 miles from SR 58	Road: Gravel to dirt track
L/L: N43 40 217/W122 10 156	Access: Check MVUM
Cell: Along FS5883 from SR 58 to 0.6 miles, Oakridge	Tents: 1–2
Nearest H2O: Eagle Creek, about 0.1 M from camp	El: 4585
Lndmk: Bridge over Eagle Cr., 0.2 mile S	RV: Use judgment w/road

Description: A campsite near seldom-traveled FS5883 that is remote and quiet enough to make you believe that on a calm day you could, if you listened hard enough, hear individual air molecules colliding with one another. Pitch your tent on yielding forest duff with tall conifer trees close around. Eagle Creek whispers along soothingly in a brushy ravine about forty feet below camp, but it is difficult to reach.

Getting there: *(See map pg. 128)* Headed east out of Oakridge, turn left onto FS5883 just short of MP 51. Continue another 5.5 miles, gaining altitude as you go, to campsite, on left, several hundred yards from TH 3686 to Hell's Half Acre and about a tenth of a mile before the road makes a sharp bend to the left to cross over the headwaters of Eagle Creek.
Find another potential campsite with easier access to Eagle Creek on Spur 375, which takes off to the left about 4 miles from OR 58. Follow Spur 375 about three-tenths of a mile to where a short track leads down to Eagle Creek and a small meadow with room for one or two tents.

Loc: Charlton Lake, off FS5897	Road: Paved and gravel
L/L: N43 44 657/121 58 627	Access: Park and carry, 0.1 M
Cell: Check for receptivity near Lake	Tents: 15–20
Nearest H2O: Lake	El: 5740
Lndmk: Charlton Lake	RV: No

Description: This is the second of two sites in this book that are actually under the jurisdiction of the Deschutes National Forest but are easily reached from the Willamette N.F. as well. Find high altitude camping in several beautiful, sup-alpine lakeside campsites here, each capable of accommodating multiple tents and featuring an inspiring view of the lake. The trail from the parking area to the lake is wide and easy to follow. The lake warms up enough around the edges by at least August to allow for swimming just when the mosquito population should be starting to taper off. One caveat: With no public toilets or garbage pickup, this site is strictly pack it in/pack it out. And not only is there no fee for camping here, but a Northwest Forest Pass is not required, according to Amy Tinderholt of the Deschutes National Forest. Be observant, however, as Forest Service rules and policies can change rapidly. Expect company here.

Getting there: *(See map pg. 126)* Head east out of Oakridge on SR 58 about 20 miles to MP 59. Turn left onto F5897 and drive 10.8 miles on paved road. Turn right onto wide, gravel FS5898 and drive 0.3 mile to the parking area, on right. Park and carry gear one-tenth of a mile on a wide forest path to the lake.

"There is a theory which states that if ever anybody discovers exactly what the Universe is for and why it is here, it will instantly disappear and be replaced by something even more bizarre and inexplicable. There is another theory which states that this has already happened."
— Douglas Adams

NOTES

NOTES

NOTES